Miracles to
Yesterday

Miracles to Yesterday
Science and Faith Come Back Together

David Brinkman

Published by HistorySoft, LLC

Printed on acid-free paper.

Notice: The information in this book is correct and complete to the best of our knowledge. It is provided without a guarantee by the author or HistorySoft. The author and HistorySoft disclaim all liability in connection with the use of this book.

HistorySoft, LLC
Cayce, SC 29033
www.historysoft.com
2018

First Edition

All Figures in this book (photos and illustrations) are by the David Brinkman family unless otherwise noted.

Copyedit by:

Joey Holleman
Greg Porr
DC Locke

Dedicated to my mother and father and all the departed history lovers who helped on these projects including Jack Boggs, Larry Burton, Pat Coogler, Wayne Grooms, Jim Merrill, and many crewmen and wives of the USS Lowndes and USS Bayfield.

A special thanks to the history leaders that stuck their necks out and supported me:

Mike Dawson, CEO of The River Alliance

Tom Elmore, Historian and Author

John Hodge, Past Chairman of Greater Piedmont Chapter of the Explorers Club

Joey Holleman, Reporter and Editor, The State newspaper

Dean Hunt, Lexington County Historian and History Teacher

Dr. Jonathan Leader, South Carolina State Archaeologist

DC Locke, Archaeologist and Historical Interpreter

Dr. Warner Montgomery, Historian and President at Columbia Star

Elise Partin, Mayor of Cayce, SC

Natalie Adams Pope, Executive Vice President, New South Associates

Leo Redmond, Former Director of the Cayce Historical Museum

Allen Roberson, Director of SC Confederate Relic Room & Military Museum

David Robichaud, Consultant and father of young Explorers

Robin Waites, Executive Director of Historic Columbia

All Granby and Fort Congaree II diggers (See Appendix E)

Last, and most importantly, those who helped me believe through my historic transition:

My wife Odess and son Jeremy, DC Locke, Canute Magalhaes, The St. Peter's Church Parish (Father Leigh A. Lehocky, Father Gary Linsky, Father Bernard Kyara, Father Andrew Fryml), and Good Shepherd Church (Father William Ladkau, Father Timothy Gahan).

Table of Contents

Introduction

The chapters to follow cover a wide range of historical discoveries from near and far. Forgotten people, places, and things now found, understood, and remembered; mysteries now solved and history corrected.

The first three and last three chapters cover the vital theme of science and faith. My mother helped instill in me a strong love for science and technology. As a young believer, I struggled, however, with the theory of evolution as it seemed to conflict with my faith. Charles Darwin had the same problem, and he sat on his theory of evolution for 22 years before having it published. In the end, Darwin abandoned his faith. The outcome for me was very different. Over the last 22 years, I have come to realize that science and faith have a common goal and I have embraced them together.[1]

All the other chapters in this book cover the historical discoveries. Intertwined with these findings is a common thread that ties them together, a thread of miracles.

Miracle: a surprising and welcome event that is not explicable by natural or scientific laws and is therefore considered to be the work of a divine agency.[2]

---

[1] 1996: Pope John Paul II and the Catholic Church officially accept the theory of evolution: https://www.usatoday.com/story/news/world/2014/10/28/pope-francis-evolution-big-bang/18053509/
[2] The English Oxford Dictionaries

Chapter 1 – Science

In 2008, I was invited to attend a meeting of the Greater Piedmont Chapter of the Explorers Club. In their own words: "The Explorers Club is an international multidisciplinary professional society dedicated to the advancement of field research and the ideal that it is vital to preserve the instinct to explore. Since its inception in 1904, the Club has served as a meeting point and unifying force for explorers and scientists worldwide."[3]

Members of the Club include the first to the North Pole, first to the South Pole, first to the summit of Mount Everest, first to the deepest point in the ocean, and first to the surface of the moon. In fact, Neil Armstrong was a member of the Greater Piedmont Chapter, which is based in Columbia, South Carolina. In more recent times, the Club's membership has grown dramatically in the professional scientific fields. I was immediately impressed with the members, many of whom were distinguished scientists with the University of South Carolina. I applied for membership and was accepted based on my recent historical discoveries.

Over the years, I met some fascinating and brilliant people in the Club. I was soon selected and served as the two-time chairman of the chapter. It was then that a reality check set in. After the death of a member's spouse, I sent an email to the members and friends of the chapter asking them to keep the family of this member in their thoughts and prayers. One esteemed Ph.D. friend of the chapter (not an official club member) responded and told me that he was very disappointed in me. He said, "Do you really believe in that crap? Prayers and god? I expected more of you."

It was at this point that I realized I might have wrongly placed some of these academic people on a pedestal, and I began to take a closer look at the real value these people had given to our society. I even asked the same questions of myself. Fortunately, our members, and most friends of the club, rose above this unhappy individual, but in general I could see the members and friends were dominated by an unambiguous scientific mindset. Brilliant in their own scientific fields, they had difficulty accepting anything that science could not prove. Well, there are many things in the world and the universe that science cannot explain.

---

[3] The Explorers Club: https://explorers.org/

The experience reminded me of the last year of the great American scientist Carl Sagan. Sagan, who did not believe in God, had been diagnosed with terminal cancer. Reaching for a hope that science could not give him, he attempted to find proof of God. Of course, in the end Sagan could not find it. He documented that he had dedicated his life to the scientific method and would not give up on that.[4]

Ten years before his death, Sagan wrote the novel "Contact," which was turned into a movie shortly after his death in 1996. The movie's main character is Ellie (played in the movie by Jodie Foster). Ellie's father died while she was young, but he managed to inspire her to become a scientist. Years later, while preparing for an experiment that might allow Ellie to remotely communicate with a more advanced alien life-form, she meets her old boyfriend Palmer (played by Matthew McConaughey), who has become an evangelist. When she challenges him with a question similar to "do you really believe in that faith crap," Palmer's response was another question: "Did you love your father?" She responds with, "Of course I loved him." Palmer then asks her to prove it. Of course, Ellie's science could not prove that.

The alien worm-hole experiment was a success, and Ellie met with an alien higher intelligence that manifested itself, through the use of her memories, in the image of her father. Ironically, the many minutes of her encounter were instantaneous to the scientists observing the experiment on Earth. Without any recorded data, Ellie had no way to prove her encounter, and the project was ruled a failure in the scientific community and in the courtroom. Ellie's passion for science would continue, but she would never be able to prove her extraterrestrial experience. It would be a truth and faith that only she could hold.

Before his death in October 1996, Sagan said, "I am not an atheist. An atheist is someone who has compelling evidence that there is no God. I am not that wise, but neither do I consider there to be anything approaching adequate evidence for such a god. Why are you in such a hurry to make up your mind? Why not simply wait until there is compelling evidence?"[5]

---

[4] https://en.wikiquote.org/wiki/Carl_Sagan
[5] Washington Post, July 10, 2014: "Carl Sagan denied being an atheist. So what did he believe?" by Joel Achenbach.

Physicist Stephen Hawking seemed to subscribe to a different science than Sagan. Despite no evidence against the existence of God, Hawking was an outspoken atheist. He firmly believed God does not exist.

But let us look at who the multitudes believe are the five smartest physicists ever to live:[6]

1. Galileo Galilei: Devout Christian. "God is known by nature in his works, and by doctrine in his revealed word."
2. Isaac Newton: Devout Christian. Newton spent more time on religion than on science, writing over 1.3 million words on topics of the Bible. He especially had an interest in miracles. "He who thinks half-heartedly will not believe in God; but he who really thinks has to believe in God."
3. Albert Einstein: Believed in the pantheistic God of Baruch Spinoza but sometimes described himself as agnostic. Einstein often used "God" in describing how his theories worked.
4. James Clerk Maxwell: Devout Christian. "Man's chief end is to glorify God and to enjoy him forever."
5. Michael Faraday: Devout Christian. "Nature is our kindest friend and best critic in experimental science if we only allow her intimations to fall unbiased on our minds."

As you can see, there are no modern-day physicists in this list, but there are scientists today who believe science may be on a path to finding God. The American theoretical physicist Michio Kaku is a founding pioneer of String Field Theory. He theorizes that mathematics and String Theory show that there are dimensions yet to be discovered, and he describes them as the domain of God. "The mind of God we believe is cosmic music, the music of strings resonating through 11-dimensional hyperspace," Kaku said. "That is the mind of God."[7]

If so, God would not be confined to our time and space and could be able to see and know everything happening. God could be interactive with every living thing in the universe at the same time. This creation could be an ongoing work of art where God's paintbrush strokes change through what we see as miracles.

---

[6] https://www.theguardian.com/culture/gallery/2013/may/12/the-10-best-physicists
[7] https://en.wikiquote.org/wiki/Michio_Kaku

So, a miracle or not? We can't ultimately depend on science to answer this question today, but fortunately the question can be answered by basic common sense if we have an open mind.

I remember many years ago, after watching a television program about UFOs, my father posed the following situation: A flying saucer lands in the backyard, and you observe little green men moving about. They leave after a few minutes, and no evidence is left behind. No one else saw what you saw. Would you tell the authorities or go to the news media? Would you risk being labeled a nut? I thought about it but could not, then nor now, really answer the question. But this flying saucer sighting is far different from the miracle glue that ties this book together. The many amazing things I call miracles all came together in a way that led to highly unlikely scientific discoveries.

Depending on your ability to see things beyond simple scientific tests, you may see the miracles or maybe you won't. Quite frankly, I'm no longer young, and documenting the experience and the resulting evidence is far more important than the risk of being called a nut.

Chapter 2 – Faith

It is essential in this chapter that I show the foundation and development of my belief and point out early health challenges that profoundly affected my faith. I think it is scientifically important that these are presented and understood.

Like most kids in the 1960s, I was forced to go to church wearing an uncomfortable tie and jacket. I don't think my early church days left much of an impression on me, but my parents were people who always set good examples. They never forced religion on me, other than making me accompany them to church.

Originally, my mother was Baptist and my father, Methodist. When they married, they chose to become Presbyterian. I believe one early turn-off for me with the Christian denominations was the hard line that salvation can only be reached through accepting Jesus Christ as your "personal savior." That was fine for people who live in the bubble of Christianity, but I found it very disturbing as one of my early friends was Jewish. He was a good kid, and his parents were people of very high moral standards. Adding to this was my mother who frequently credited a Jewish family with going out of their way to mentor her in her first job. I suspect her naming me David had something to do with this Jewish family.

Judaism and Christianity share the Ten Commandments. Honoring your father and mother will most likely require you to stick with the religion you were born into. We all know that good and evil are as clear as day and night. Being born into a religion, however, requires much more of you than just the common-sense "right versus wrong." As I heard a Catholic priest recently say: "An African Pigmy, who has never heard of Jesus, has a better chance at entering the Kingdom of God than an American Christian. The Pigmy's basic common sense and awareness of good is his simple path. Americans, however, are blessed with so much more and given a specific way to Heaven. Much more, therefore, is expected of them."

For whatever reasons, the desire to believe in God was in me as far back as I can remember. I was extremely shy, and it took years for me to make a good friend. It was difficult moving to a new school every time my dad took a bigger job, and he ended up doing that about every three years. So, most of the time I had no close friends. Instead of creating imaginary friends or talking to myself, I would talk to God. I remember once challenging God to move an object to show me he was there. The object did not move, but that would not stop me from believing.

> John 20:24-29: Blessed are those who have not seen and yet have believed.

About that time, I started having headaches each day. At the age of 12, I overheard a doctor telling my mother that he thought it was my imagination. It was a terrible feeling to suffer and have no one understand or believe you. I guess I stopped complaining and just accepted that I would have to live with it.

By the time I got to high school[8], my dad had settled into his final job and I had started developing friends. I stopped talking to God until a frightening experience I had at the age of 14. I had just gotten into bed one evening and was wondering how I would get to sleep with my parents still up and about. A creaking sound came from the opposite corner of my room. The house was known to make strange noises, but this turned into something different. I began to hear what I was sure were footsteps coming closer to my bed. Lots of things were going through my head trying to figure out what it could be. Was it my imagination? The footsteps stopped at the point where it reached my bedside. I was beginning to get scared. There was then a "swish," and cold air blew onto my face. It was like something had been thrown through the air just inches from my head. A huge crash occurred on the opposite wall in the direction of this movement. I was frozen with fear for maybe one or two minutes. I then jumped up and turned on the lights. There was nothing there. Expecting to find damage on the wall, there was none there. There was nothing around the wall that could have accounted for the crash. I was shaking with fear. For the next two hours, I would not be able to come up with an explanation. I reluctantly got back into bed but not until I talked with God. Those talks would continue every night until the fear of the incident faded away. The experience became my standard tale I would tell friends when we discussed possible supernatural or paranormal events in our lives. I would associate it with an evil type of force. It would remain a commonly recalled memory for forty years before the true source would be revealed (see Chapter 13: A King's Match in America).

---

[8] Irmo High school, Columbia, SC.

As I turned 15-years-old, new things were coming into my life (girls, cars, and motorcycles). I no longer had time to talk to God until one fateful morning. I woke up with a blurred spot in my right eye. Looking in the mirror, I couldn't see anything in the eye. It just didn't make any sense. I continued to school.

While I was waiting for the first class to begin, an incredibly sharp pain hit me on the left side of my head. It felt like a knife was being driven into my temple. Almost immediately, I completely lost vision in my right eye, and there was the sensation of a loud ringing in my right ear. I became nauseous as I rushed toward the nurse's office, which was about 500 feet across the campus. I was terrified, as I knew something terrible had happened in my brain. In need, and in fear, I asked God to help me as I fought back the tears.

By the time I got to the nurse, paralysis had set in on my right side and I was dragging my right leg. In 1975, severe strokes were unheard of in young people. Today, we know it's not that rare in teenage boys who possess a high level of a blood-clotting chemical which nature provides during these accident-prone years.[9] Back then, the doctors could not explain it, but they knocked me out for 24 hours. I could barely function for the next week and would feel like a zombie for many months. I did, quickly, regain my sight and hearing.

It was a frightening experience that left me feeling vulnerable and fragile. I was supposed to be strong and at the beginning of my life, and yet I felt so close to death. Fortunately for me, at 15 years old, the brain is in its maximum wiring mode and can recover from something like this. I immediately noticed significant difficulty with mathematics, and I had to learn it all over again. Encouraged by my mother, I took guitar lessons, and for the first time in my life I started to build discipline. Having no rhythm and being tone deaf, it was a real challenge. Shamefully, as I recovered I stopped talking to God again.

Maybe because of the headaches, the stroke, or perhaps just out of boredom, I was not much of a student. My report cards showed that. I seemed to take pride in the fact that I made it through high school without ever once taking a book home, doing a homework assignment, or studying for a test.

---

[9] https://www.webmd.com/stroke/news/20110901/strokes-in-chldren-and-young-adults-on-the-rise#1

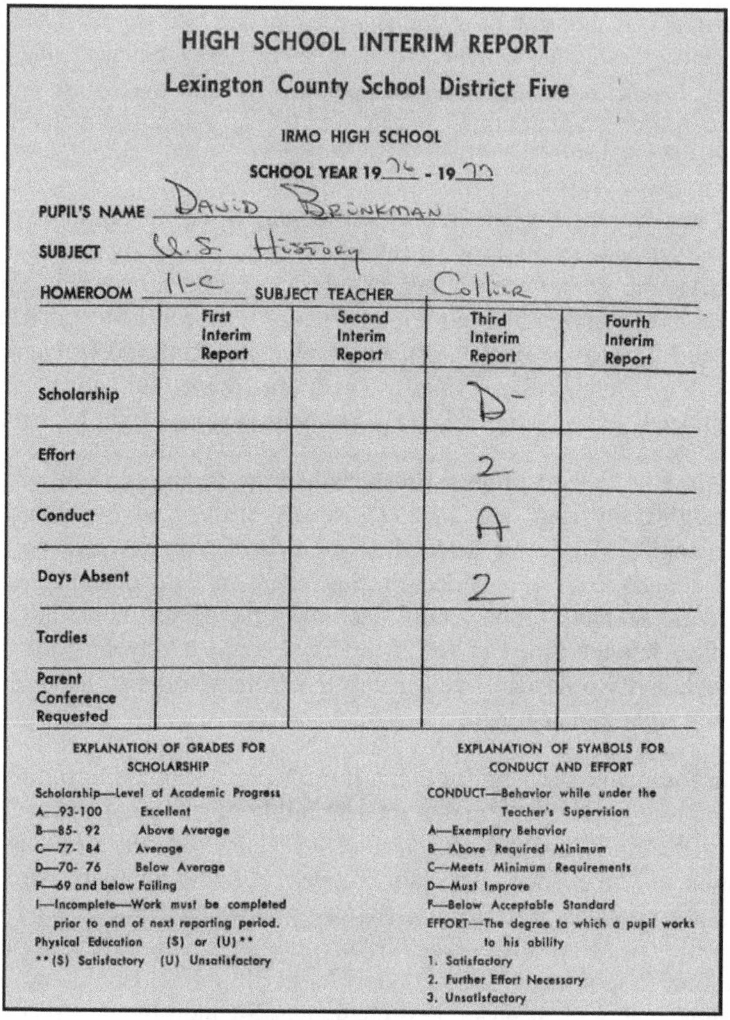

HIGH SCHOOL INTERIM REPORT

Lexington County School District Five

IRMO HIGH SCHOOL

SCHOOL YEAR 19 _7⊾_ - 19 _77_

PUPIL'S NAME _David Brinkman_

SUBJECT _U.S. History_

HOMEROOM _11-C_ SUBJECT TEACHER _Collier_

	First Interim Report	Second Interim Report	Third Interim Report	Fourth Interim Report
Scholarship			D-	
Effort			2	
Conduct			A	
Days Absent			2	
Tardies				
Parent Conference Requested				

EXPLANATION OF GRADES FOR SCHOLARSHIP

Scholarship—Level of Academic Progress
A—93-100   Excellent
B—85- 92   Above Average
C—77- 84   Average
D—70- 76   Below Average
F—69 and below Failing
I—Incomplete—Work must be completed
    prior to end of next reporting period.
Physical Education   (S) or (U)**
**(S) Satisfactory (U) Unsatisfactory

EXPLANATION OF SYMBOLS FOR CONDUCT AND EFFORT

CONDUCT—Behavior while under the
    Teacher's Supervision
A—Exemplary Behavior
B—Above Required Minimum
C—Meets Minimum Requirements
D—Must Improve
F—Below Acceptable Standard
EFFORT—The degree to which a pupil works
    to his ability
1. Satisfactory
2. Further Effort Necessary
3. Unsatisfactory

Figure 1: My typical High School report card

One of the best things I did was to avoid going to college after high school. I would have fallen on my face and flunked out, but the real reason for not going was that I was sick and tired of school. I wanted to get out into the real world. My guitar-practicing regiment of seven hours a day, seven days a week got me to the point where I thought I could make it as a musician, but that wasn't going to pay the bills.

The real world for me would be unloading trucks, stocking store shelves, sweeping parking lots, cleaning public toilets, and working other lousy minimum-wage jobs. In the middle of it all, I was faced with another medical challenge. Those headaches that had plagued me for over ten years turned into something much worse. Apparently, a case of food poisoning changed things. One second, I would feel fine, then the next, for no logical reason, I would be in deep depression. There were moments of amnesia, including one where I was playing the guitar in my room and suddenly did not know where I was.

The depression was the worst part, and today I have so much sympathy for those that live with this type of suffering. There were times when I just wanted to die. To make matters worse, all the effort I had put into my music and building a band fell apart. I was unemployed and unable to find a job. My weight had dropped below 100 pounds. I had hit rock bottom.

After a night of drinking with a friend, I came home about 2 a.m. Back then, even on cable TV, there was not much of anything on that late. As I went through the channels, I found the lone on-air station. It was a new religious show called "The 700 Club." The man talking, Pat Robertson, connected with me, and his message gave me new hope on life. I borrowed money from my mom and joined the 700 Club, and I started to talk to God again.

My suffering continued, but my new hope kept me going. Knocked down and humbled, I accepted my worst job yet. For minimum wage, I was sweeping the parking lot and cleaning the stopped-up and vomit-filled toilets of a sleazy night-club. The only good thing about it was that my father went out of his way to tell me how proud he was of me for doing that.

Within a few months, news came that my sister, Terri Stevens, had been diagnosed with hypoglycemia. Most people associate this with a person with diabetes who has taken an overdose of insulin. Well, some people's bodies produce too much insulin. Terri soon sent us information on the disorder. After reading the literature, I realized I had hypoglycemia. I had had it all my life. I was angry, in a way, that all those doctors my mother took me to had not recognized it. Those headaches always occurred late in the morning and late in the afternoon. It was nothing but low blood sugar. I was relieved to see that it was manageable by just changes in my diet.

Within days of adjusting my diet, the headaches I had had most of my life, the depression, and the amnesia were gone. I had to stay on the strict diet of six low-sugar/low-carb meals a day for more than ten years. Even though I recovered and moved on to the regular ups and downs of life, this time I would continue talking to God.

In 1980, at the age of 20, I was still having trouble finding a good job. With $2,000 saved in the bank, I decided to go where the jobs were, the Disney World area of central Florida. I loved the warm Orlando weather. My job as a motel desk clerk and night auditor was challenging and satisfying at first but still not paying much more than minimum wage.

I did get to work with mostly young ladies my own age, so that was a fringe benefit although one I never took advantage of. I was slow with the girls and uncertain. The hypoglycemia kept my weight low. With no fat in my body, the ability to build muscles was very limited. In other words, I was a 120-pound weakling and women were just not interested in that.

This brings me to the first major personal miracle in my life. I will change her name because it's not a pretty story. Let's just say she was Mindy. Mindy was a 19-year-old desk clerk and the most beautiful girl I had ever known. Guys from all over the Orlando area came to the motel to see Mindy. She was so kind and sweet at work but, outside, I begin to see signs of trouble in her when she was under the influence of alcohol. Mindy took a real liking to me because, as she put it, I was the only guy that did not hit on her. For that reason, I kept my distance from her even though I was probably too scared to do anything in the first place. She would occasionally ask me to go to dinner, a nightclub, or a concert. The looks that I would get from guys when walking into a room with Mindy were classic. Their jaws would drop at the first site of Mindy, and it would change to a complete shocked look as they noticed the pathetic little dude she was with. I loved it. It was hilarious.

On a fateful night for another innocent man, Mindy asked me to come with her to see an Orlando band play at a nightclub. This band was excellent, and people were expecting them to make it big one day. At the heart of the group was their tall, long blond haired, good-looking lead guitarist. We worked our way to the front of the stage where I was very impressed with the guitar playing of this young man. He was only about 18, but he was in a league above me as far as playing the guitar. Mindy seemed utterly

12

infatuated with him. She motioned for him, in the middle of a song, to come over to her. I didn't hear her words, but he was shocked and pulled the piece of gum from his mouth and gave it Mindy. It went straight into her mouth. Without a word, Mindy soon disappeared. I would have to get a ride home from her sister that night.

I had almost forgotten about the chewing gum incident until a month, or so, later when I went over to Mindy's house to pick her up for dinner. As I looked into her bedroom, there on the dresser was the dried piece of chewing gum from that night. There was nothing between Mindy and me, so I held back the questions I had about what happened to her that night. There were other times, though, that I did ask questions and it seems she never remembered anything from the evenings when she was under the influence of alcohol. It was also about this time that it was brought to my attention that Mindy was doing cocaine.

The story now moves to a moment in my life that I will never forget. I was working the 3 p.m. to 11 p.m. desk clerk shift and got a call from co-workers at a nearby lounge. They were having a good time and wanted me to know that Mindy would like me to stop by after work. When I arrived, Mindy was very much intoxicated, and the group of all girls arranged for me to sit next to her. I was stunned as Mindy's hands were soon all over me. The girls were really getting a kick out of it. It seems like this was all planned. They all, at once, got up and asked me to take Mindy home. So many things were running through my head including the fact that I would probably never have an opportunity like this again. As I drove home, Mindy asked to stop the car in a park. She started kissing me but then, suddenly, she violently pushed me back. She grabbed at my 700 Club pin, which I always wore on my shirt, and she cursed God over and over again. I was shocked and said nothing. It was one of the strangest things I had ever seen, but I blamed it on the alcohol. I started the car and headed to her apartment. By the time we got there, Mindy had passed-out. She lived on the second floor of the apartment building. It must have been a site to see this 120-pound weakling carry that 115 pounds of dead weight up the stairs. The apartment door was unlocked but, as I opened it, I lost my balance and fell with Mindy landing on top of me. It knocked the breath out of me and Mindy came-to and ran to the bathroom where she started vomiting. I should have left then, but I wanted to make sure she was alright. I waited a few minutes and then knocked on the bathroom door, and it swung open.

There was Mindy completely naked. She would have put to shame many playmate centerfolds. Within an instant, she was all over me and pulling my clothes off as she pulled me into her bedroom. I made the decision what I would do, even knowing it was wrong. Not even Mindy's vomit breath was going to stop me.

And then it happened. My entire senses were overcome with the image of Jesus on the cross. It was like being locked in Virtual Reality with an image that spans 360 degrees and you can't get away from it. Probably only a few seconds passed but I was soaking wet in sweat, and I pushed Mindy away. As I stumbled toward the door, still blinded by the image, Mindy must have stood up on the bed and jumped through the air to tackle me. My body was slammed against the door. As my senses returned, Mindy was on top of me, punching me, and cursing both God and me. I had to struggle to get her off me. Dazed and bruised, I ran to my car. I was in such a state of shock. All my life I had wanted God to give me sign that he was there, and he now punches me in the face with one. And what did I do? I, shamefully, told God that this was not fair and asked him why he stopped me. When I got back to my apartment, I was still shaking. I tried to tell my roommate the story but, somehow, bypassing the Jesus vision because my roommate was not a religious person. He ended up rolling on the floor in laughter. It was then that I decided this experience could not be revealed to anyone else.

Psychologists would probably have an explanation for what happened to me. They would maybe say it was psychosomatic. Maybe the vision of Jesus on the cross was created in my mind because of guilt for doing something I knew was morally wrong. Well, that's what I begin to wonder, but there's much more to this story.

The next day, one of those girls at the lounge called me to ask how things went the night before. "Did you get lucky?" I told her nothing happened. She seemed surprised and informed me that Mindy did not remember anything and that they had already told her that we slept together. She then said it might be best that I did not get involved with Mindy because she had been going out every night drinking and picking up a stranger and sleeping with him. Mindy never remembered anything, but her friends observed her doing this. I couldn't believe it and asked what had happened to her? The friend then revealed Mindy's dark past. She had been adopted as a baby and had a good life until her mother died of cancer when she was a young teenager. Not long after that, she was brutally gang-raped. I was overwhelmed, and I didn't know how to deal with it.

I did not see or talk to Mindy again until we worked together a few days later. When the front desk area cleared, she walked over to me and cuddled up to me. She really did think that we had slept together that night and had no idea what took place. I was not mature enough to handle this, and I did nothing and said nothing. For reasons unknown to me, Mindy would soon be terminated from her job at the motel.

After almost two months from that night with Mindy, I was surprised to find her at my front door in her new work uniform. She said she had left work sick and that she had been nauseous the last few mornings. I shivered. Mindy was pregnant, and she thought I was the father. She was even happy about it. I was still unable to deal with it and I quickly changed the subject and told her I was late for an appointment. I called that lounge girlfriend of Mindy and told her the joke was over, and they needed to tell Mindy that we did not sleep together that night. I now realized what stopped me that night was a saving miracle. Had I slept with her, her friend would not have revealed Mindy's recent promiscuous activity and her dark past. I would have accepted responsibility for the child, and I would have asked Mindy to marry me. It would have been a disaster for me.

But the story is still not over. Months later, I was in a local music store, and a couple of customers were talking about that band that Mindy and I saw together. I broke into the conversation and asked why that band was not playing in the area anymore. They informed me that the group had broken up because their lead guitarist got "messed up" by some girl. The guitarist had dropped out of the band and out of site. I asked if this girl was named Mindy and their response was positive, and they gave me a physical description which matched Mindy. I then asked what they meant by "messed up." They described the young guitarist as the nicest guy in the world who lost his virginity to Mindy, and the only thing he got in return was a horrible case of gonorrhea. How many more revelations were there? How many more ways could this miracle be shown to me?

Before the other miracles in the book happened to me, this was the miracle that I lived on. Whenever I doubted my belief, all I had to do was relive this experience which was etched into my memory.

While these reinforcements of the miracle were coming in, I changed jobs to another motel in the Orlando area. It was there that I met Jenny, a struggling divorced single mother. Jenny was eight years older than me but very young at heart, bubbly, and cheerful. We quickly became friends, and I helped her by driving her home each night after we worked together.

It was on one of these drives that Jenny entrusted me with a secret. She had recently been raped and was pregnant and was struggling with the choice of abortion or adoption. My hero and the new President was Ronald Reagan. Following him, I did everything I could to support the choice of life and an adoption. Jenny would make her choice, and a loving Christian family was soon found to take the child after birth.

Over the next six or seven months, I supported Jenny as her shoulder to cry on and her cheerleader. Somehow, I fell in love with her. Early on, she had told me that she was afraid of men after the rape. Once again, I kept my distance. It was a true unconditional love I had for Jenny, and I was focused on getting her through the pregnancy. What I didn't realize was that Jenny was keeping the pregnancy a secret from her family. I was an outsider unknown to her family and the perfect choice to help her through this. That's all I was. I was temporary. I didn't know this until Jenny went into labor. I rushed to the hospital only to find that she had not listed me as a person who could visit her. I had no idea what was going on, and I was worried sick. Meanwhile, unseen by me, the adoption of her newborn baby boy was completed.

I rushed to Jenny's apartment as soon as I heard she had been released from the hospital. To my surprise, her door was opened by a maintenance worker at the apartment complex. He was in boxer shorts with no shirt. I didn't even know that Jenny knew this guy and here he was living with her just one day after she left the hospital. Jenny came to the door, and I asked to speak to her in private. I said, "what the hell is going on?" She responded with, "Well, what's your problem?" to which I responded: "My problem? My problem is that I am in love with you." Jenny burst out laughing. I guess when she saw the tears welled up in my eyes, she knew this was serious, and her maturity and experience kicked in. She grabbed me by the shoulders and said: "No! No! This can't be. Look at you. You have your entire life ahead of you. You can do anything. Look at me. I'm a mess. My life is a mess. No! This can't be." Just like that, Jenny removed me from her life. I was heartbroken and lost.

I asked God what the purpose of meeting Jenny was? No response. My motel manager, who had encouraged me to pursue Jenny, and against my opposition, fired her for a bogus reason. I never saw Jenny again, but the question remained. What was the purpose of Jenny and me? The answer would not come until 25 years later in a church sermon. The priest was pointing out how all us can be angels, and he used the example of unconditional love. My mind flashed back, and I thought of Jenny. It was not until then that I realized everything I had done for Jenny helped bring a new life into the world. A life that would now be a 25-year-old man who was maybe starting his own family. Jenny's motherly love and sacrifice made her an angel. But, it was also an angel moment for me, and my purpose 25 years ago.

You learn a lot about yourself as you write your life's story. As I wrote the previous paragraph, I begin to see something that was lost in my selfishness. It was the aborted baby of Mindy. My immaturity with Mindy was tragic. I always changed the subject or ran away from her. Other than get into a doomed relationship with her, was there something else I could have done to help her? Maybe the Mindy experience was a step toward maturity which I would have to make to help save Jenny's baby.

Mindy and I would remain friends until she came by the motel one day with a green-haired girl. She was saying goodbye as they would be moving to Tampa to live with a punk rock band. I still think about Mindy and wonder what happened to her. I've said many prayers asking for her demons to be taken away.

After two years in Florida, my job was not going well. I had worked hard to get a chance at being the night manager at the motel. When the job became available, I was next in line, but the general manager decided they didn't need that position anymore. I was given the responsibilities but not the title, which is what I really wanted.

As night-auditor in a 300-room motel running 100 percent occupancy every night, I was posting all customer charges, balancing the city and guest ledgers, checking in as many as 40 rooms a night, transferring every phone call into the motel, unstopping toilets, dealing with obnoxious customers, and doing it all by myself. I developed a stomach ulcer from the stress.

The accounting part of my job seemed like half of the accounting work done in the motel. I had to work three extra hours a night, off the clock, to get the job done. Because of that, I was making much less than minimum wage. Meanwhile, the motel comptroller was doing the other half of the accounting work and making four times as much money as me. Helping her was an accountant making three times as much as me. Then they hired another accountant with no work experience but with a two-year degree in accounting. She was making twice as much as me. I realized I would never get anywhere in life without that piece of paper from a college.

Never giving up on me was my dad, in the background, encouraging me to go to college. He thought I would make a good engineer. Having managed hundreds of people over his life, he did have good insight. I finally took him up on his offer to pay for college, and I left Florida and moved back home at the age of 22. Sounds like the prodigal son, except I had spent my own savings, not an inheritance, and there were no prostitutes or other immoral activities like that.

Having watched many of my friends stumble in college after doing so much better than me in high school, I feared I would not fare well. That fear of failure and going back to working horrible jobs gave me an unusual motivation. I made a deal with God and pledged to stay away from women and parties if he would help me get through this.

Having graduated at the bottom of my class in high school, and not being able to spell or write, I would not have been accepted at the University of South Carolina. Instead, I went for an Associate Degree in Electronics Engineering Technology at Midlands Technical College, which is a community college. Midlands Tech was designed to handle deficient students like me.

Every day, I got up at 6 a.m. and was at the library by 7 a.m. I studied between every class. When I got home, I studied until my mother had dinner ready. After eating, I studied until it was time to go to bed. The weekends were not a break, as I continued the pace. After the first quarter, I had all A's, more of them than I had probably had in my entire prior education. I thought it was a fluke and did not let up in the second quarter. In two years, I graduated as the top Engineering Technology Student with a perfect 4.0 GPR.

While earning that first degree, I heard lots of talk about computers being designed and manufactured in nearby West Columbia by the NCR Corporation. My dream was to return to Florida and work in the space program, but NCR was very tempting. In 1984, after getting my degree, there was a glut of job candidates in the electronics and space industries. There were no jobs in Columbia or in Florida. My dad stepped in once again. He encouraged me to take the SAT and apply to the College of Engineering at the University of South Carolina. I was able to get in, but the College of Engineering did not accept any of my credits for transfer. My father talked me into doing it anyway, and I started over. Four more years of school.

My streak of straight A's came to a quick end in the second summer school class that I took, English 102 (Literature). I will never forget Dr. Byrd. On the first day, he walked in with a huge copy of the Old Testament. He proudly announced that he was an atheist but that this was the greatest piece of literature ever written. The book quickly disappeared and was never mentioned again. Everything we read and studied had the theme of tragedy, with an older man having a relationship with a younger woman. Pure garbage, but I managed to make an A on every assignment and test.

The final exam ended up being ridiculous and impossible to complete, but I still made a C+ on it, which was enough to hold a final A average. Or so I thought. My final grade was a B+. When I took the numbers to Dr. Byrd, he didn't care. He said I could not get an A because I did not show achievement between the beginning and end of the course. I even calculated the case where, if I had failed the first test instead of making an A on it, my final grade average would still have been an A. Of course, you can't convince someone like this with numbers. I will always remember him as Dr. Byrd-brain.

Despite the rough start, I would bounce back and make straight A's again. My time at the University of South Carolina would prove to be a tumultuous period in the school's history thanks to College President Dr.

James B. Holderman. Today, Holderman is remembered for extravagant expenses and gifts. Trouble with the law would eventually land him in prison. As bad as that sounds, Holderman brought unprecedented accomplishments and recognition to the University of South Carolina. He put USC on the map just as he had promised to do.

Referred to as a politician with a Ph.D., Holderman had an endless stream of dignitaries coming to the campus. Among them: Presidents Ronald Reagan and George H.W. Bush, former President Gerald R. Ford, Secretary of State Henry Kissinger, U.S. Senator Joe Biden, Pearl Bailey, Jim Brady, William F. Buckley, Bill Cosby, Walter Cronkite, Michael Eisner, Dr. Billy Graham, Alex Haley, Helen Hayes, Danny Kaye, Mister Rodgers, and my graduation speaker Jimmy Stewart. Most impressively, despite South Carolina having the lowest percentage of Catholics of any state (only a total of 70,000 in the entire state), Holderman managed to bring Pope John Paul II to the campus where he made trips around the University's famous Horseshoe in the "Popemobile."[10]

Holderman promoted the school as "The USC" as a clear reminder that the University of South Carolina was an institution long before California was even a state. Holderman's approach to sports was no different. He hired NFL player Joe Morrison to be the school's new football coach. In his first season, the Gamecocks stunned "the other USC" crushing the Trojans in Columbia. Morrison was an instant hit. In my freshman year, the football team was a perfect 9-0 and ranked #2. They were looking at the top spot after the top-ranked team lost. All they had to do was beat one of the weaker teams on their schedule (Navy). They failed to do that but, over the next few years, Morrison would establish himself as the winningest coach in the school's history. Not all was well as reports, and drug tests, would uncover that as many as 50% of the players were using steroids. Nevertheless, Morrison was still popular, and expectations were high after the 1988 season. Early 1989 would, however, bring heartbreak to the Gamecock nation as the 51-year-old chain-smoking Joe Morrison suffered a fatal heart attack. The bad habits of Dr. Holderman were now making headlines, and Holderman would resign a year later.

Holderman did, however, make a significant positive contribution to my future. Although his spending was extreme, he had a way of coming up

---

[10] Our Lucky Horseshoe by James B. Holderman.

with money when it was needed. As I finished my sophomore year, he managed to get 16 million dollars in Federal funds to complete a stunning new Engineering School building. It was there that I completed my engineering courses and graduated, two years later, at the top of my Electrical and Computer Engineering program in the spring of 1988.

The Challenger disaster of 1986 ended my dream of working in the United States space program as space projects were placed on indefinite hold. By my junior year, I did get a cool job with the NCR Corporation as an intern writing and supporting software for the automated manufacturing machines which built the circuit boards for NCR computers.

After graduation, I took a job at NCR and worked my way up the engineering ladder. On the side, I continued music in a creative way, writing and recording songs and parodies. Several of my multitrack recorded originals did get airtime on local radio stations, but my attempt to sell songs or get a recording deal fell short. The Grammy award-winning band, Hootie and the Blowfish had formed on campus while I was attending the University of South Carolina. After their graduation and music success, the group began a search of local talent that might be signed to their record label. I submitted a demo CD but never expected to hear anything back. The band, however, was a professional and class act and I received a very gracious rejection letter.

My starting salary as an Engineer was four times that of any job I had before college. I quickly bought a house, and dog, and was expecting my luck with women to change now that I had a good education and job.

I had kept my deal with God and never even looked at a woman in the six years I was in college. All these years later, it seemed like nothing had changed. I was still being rejected by all the women I pursued.

Around 1992, I finally decided to try a dating service. After I answered about 400 questions, the manager of the service interviewed me. She said there must be a mistake on my height and weight. I looked at the numbers, 125 pounds and 5-foot-7, and confirmed them. She suggested that we add 30 or 40 pounds to the weight and a few inches to the height. Imagining the first impression that would give, I said no. She paused and then said: "I don't mean to hurt your feelings, but I've been in this business for ten years and I have a Ph.D. in psychology. The first thing women look at is the height and weight of a man. For you, that's going to also be the last thing they look at. They won't bother to look down at your education, profession, or even your photograph. You need to get your foot in the door by exaggerating the truth."

I wasn't surprised to hear this. I had already figured this out, but it was good to hear it from someone in her position. I still said no and that we would see if she was right. All those answers to the questions went into their database of hundreds of women, and a computer ranked the matches. Within the top 50, I selected a few women, which caused a message to be sent to them showing my interest. There was no reply. I tried a few more times but never received an acceptance.

I did, however, get one reply. The woman was not interested, but she recommended I forget about the service and go to church to find the right person. That also did not surprise me. Even though I had a strong faith, going to church never clicked with me.

Apparently, my failed attempt with the service did lead to something good. The dating service must have sold a list of user addresses to other related services. In my mailbox one day was a publication called "Cherry Blossoms," and on the cover was a beautiful young Filipino woman. As I turned the pages, there were hundreds of them. In the second half of the publication were pictures of hundreds of women from the breakaway republics of the Soviet Union. It was billed as a pen-pal service. Some people called it a mail-order-bride service. I selected one woman and paid $15 to get her address. I wrote to her but received no reply.

The service documentation said you get the best results if you publish your information in a publication of men. I paid $100 for that and sat back and waited. Within a month, the letters started coming in -- over 200 of them. Right along with what that dating service psychologist said, only one Caucasian -- from Russia where women have an average height of 5-foot-6 -- wrote to me. All the rest were Filipino women, who have an average height of only 5 feet. I had "guitar" and "computer programming" as my interests. There was only one woman that met those qualifications, Modesta (Odess) Maingpes from Baguio City, Philippines.

At the time, Odess was working in Hong Kong, and her roommate was the one that received the "Cherry Blossoms" publication with me in it. Her roommate noticed the common guitar and computer programming interests and told Odess she should write me. In her letters, Odess also stood out for more important reasons. She was religious and a devout Catholic. She had a large close family and provided me with all kinds of information on the family members. She also asked me many questions along the same lines. None of the other women did that in those first letters. I didn't write to any of the other women.

Odess was the one, but I had not convinced her of that yet. Challenging my song-writing claims, Odess asked me to write a song about us. Later, she wrote the lyrics for another song about us and asked me to put it to original music. In both cases, I had it done and recorded in a week. That second song would later win an award in the Annual Billboard Amateur Song-Writing Contest.[11] The custom songs made the difference with Odess.

All those thousands of hours I spent playing guitar and singing had not earned me a cent, but it was now priceless. After six months of writing letters and $600-a-month phone bills, Odess and I met in the Philippines. My parents, who had supported me in everything I had done in life, made the trip with me to meet Odess and her family. I would soon become a Catholic and Odess and I married in January of 1994.

Going to church was now a requirement, and it gradually grew on me. I loved the history of the Catholic Church, the openness to science, and its ability to change and grow. Thirty-three years and a miracle search to the other side of the world was a worthwhile wait.

---

[11] 1994 Billboard's 6th Annual Song Contest award winner: "You're All That Matters To Me" by David and Modesta Brinkman: https://youtu.be/iNapOUcJILs

Figure 2: The 1994 wedding of Odess and David
Brinkman in La Trinidad, Philippines.

Chapter 3 – A Father to Many

One person clearly has had the most significant positive influence in my life. Throughout this book, you will see him mentioned. Often noted as the father of tourism in South Carolina, my father, Fred Brinkman, was an institution. U.S. Senator Ernest Hollings remembers my dad when he first came to South Carolina in the 1950s. Managing the Myrtle Beach Chamber of Commerce, my humble and soft-spoken father somehow managed to get every business in Myrtle Beach to join the chamber. That chamber, several times under my father, was recognized as the top chamber in the United States. When my father began his South Carolina tourism career in Myrtle Beach, South Carolina had the 3rd lowest tourism revenue in the United States.

Figure 3: United States Senator Strom Thurman (left) and Fred Brinkman (right.)

Senator Hollings remembered my dad originally telling everyone that Myrtle Beach would soon be the top tourist destination in South Carolina. Hollings said everyone in Charleston thought he was crazy. Today, despite being voted as the most desired destination in the world, Charleston gets less than one-third the visitors of Myrtle Beach. In fact, Myrtle Beach is the top beach destination on the East coast of the United States, with more visitors than even Miami.

By 2016, South Carolina's tourism revenue had grown by a factor of almost 400 (50 million in 1954[12] to 19.1 billion in 2016[13]). Besides impressive Myrtle Beach and state tourism numbers, my dad's 18-year tenure as Director of the South Carolina Department of Parks, Recreation, and Tourism also led to the creation of 18 new state parks. During those 18 years, the little state of South Carolina received more federal money for parks than any other state in the country.[14]

Over the last 20 years, however, I've realized the most important impact my father had was how he touched so many individual lives. Even though he passed away 20 years ago, those who knew him still make a point of how he positively affected their lives. After I gave a history presentation to the Columbia Rotary Club, a long line of about 40 people waited to mostly tell me what a great leader and friend my dad was to them. Most of them said they loved him.

One man who, many years before, had wrongly accused my father of misusing state funds, wrote a beautiful letter to my mother after my dad died. The letter writer admitted what he had done was very wrong, but instead of firing him as would have been appropriate, my father reached out to help in his personal and professional life over a period of many years. He called my dad the finest example of a Christian that he had ever come across.

There were many examples like this. I believe my dad thrived on opportunities to set powerful examples. After his death, we found in the

---

[12] Myrtle Beach: A History, 1900-1980 By Barbara F. Stoke. Pg. 168
[13] https://www.visitmyrtlebeach.com/articles-media/post/tourism-generates-7-billion-annually-for-myrtle-beach-area/
[14] Mr. Tom Brown, National Park Service, Association Regional Director. Statistics given on November 1, 1991.

trunk of his car his copy of "The Power of Positive Thinking" by Dr. Norman Vincent Peale. The book was worn, and all the pages were dirty. It looked as though it had been read hundreds of times.

My dad didn't do a lot of talking, but his few words were well thought out and often profound. He never lost his temper. I never saw him act in anger or say something negative about a person. In fact, he always managed to point out something good in everyone. When I did something wrong, he never responded immediately. Sometimes it would take weeks, and when he did it would be through a story that was amazingly similar to the situation I had been in. However, the story would show how the main character chose to do things differently, and positive effects followed. After a while, I figured out what he was doing. Humbled by the effort and patience he showed, I understood the real love behind it.

My father embraced everything about South Carolina, including its rich history. He loved to stop the car to read historical markers or point out an old roadbed. I have memories of him taking me to the South Carolina Tricentennial events of 1970. And while in college, I remember him recommending that I "broaden my horizons" by taking history electives. I would have nothing to do with that. Engineering, science, and the future were all I cared about. Two weeks after my dad retired, he was diagnosed with cancer and died four months later. Suddenly, a huge part of my life became history.

I was taken aback at my father's funeral when someone called my father a workaholic and said that living with that must have been such a sacrifice for my mother, sister, and me. How wrong they were. My father was always there when we needed him, more so than any other father I knew of. His dedicated work ethic gave us a good living and provided jobs for many South Carolinians. He helped many others along the way in their own personal lives. I was so proud him but, sadly, never told him that. Repeatedly through the years, I've asked myself the question, where did all the motivation and good in my father come from?

A clue to that had come to me early in life through two profound things my father revealed to me. One was on the eve of my ninth birthday. My mother was in the hospital, and a terrific lightning storm popped up. I verified this event by finding the newspaper archive, which recorded the storm damage done in our neighborhood that night. While the lightning and thunder were raging, I sought refuge in my dad's bed, where he told me I had nothing to fear and that God would take care of us.

THE STATE — Columbia, S. C., Monday, June 30, 1969

City Power Is Disrupted By Storm

Thunderstorms Sunday in and around Columbia disrupted electric service and ripped limbs from trees in scattered areas.

Among the worst damaged areas was Old Dominion subdivision where a late afternoon lightning storm deposited large limbs in front yards and on the roofs of homes. Residents thought the storm was a small tornado, but the Columbia Weather Bureau said it was just a vicious thunderstorm. Electricity was disrupted.

A spokesman for the S. C. Electric and Gas Co. said the repair service faced "a lot of problems that kept them working throughout the day." The spokesman said no problems were major.

He said the crews replaced 15 transformers Sunday — most of which had failed because of overloads in the heat. About a dozen more transformers had to be repaired.

A 5 a.m. storm also caused spotted damage in Cayce, Forest Acres and Edenwood.

Some hail was reported near the State House and in Cayce.

Figure 4: The State newspaper records the 1969 storm damage to our Forest Acres neighborhood.

My dad sometimes only shared a special moment in his life to one person. Sometimes my mother. Sometimes my sister. But it was then that he told me the story of when God spoke to him. Now that got my attention. He said he was about my age and leaving school one day when God told him, not through his ears but somehow in his head, that something terrible had happened. God promised my dad that He would take care of him and everything would be alright. For an unknown reason, he took a different route home from school that day and discovered his mother's lifeless body on the edge of a pond, where she had been trying to get water for the farm animals.

My dad was the oldest of three children, and, with his father working and living in the city during the week, he would now mostly be responsible for watching the younger siblings. Late in their lives, my aunt and uncle recalled another time when God may have spoken to my dad. My aunt and uncle retold the story of how the three siblings were walking through an open field one sunny, cloudless day when my aunt and uncle witnessed a direct lightning strike to my father's head. Although knocked out cold, he showed no visible signs of injury. His life, however, would take a dramatic change, and he dropped out of high school to join the Navy in 1943. The Navy saw something unique in my father and chose to place him in the role of a lifesaver.

The second profound thing my dad revealed

28

to me came at the age of 13 when he allowed me to read his 1945 uncensored letter to his father about his experience as a Navy Corpsman working the beach in the initial invasion of Iwo Jima.

These revelations didn't directly account for the motivation and lifelong good deeds of my father, but they pointed me to the people and things that would eventually provide the answers.

Chapter 4 – The History Begins: Attack Transport APA-154 (The USS Lowndes)

The summer of 1970 ended with another family move back to Myrtle Beach, where my dad would again run the Chamber of Commerce. The public-school system in Myrtle Beach was poor compared to Columbia. I found myself faced with a rough bunch of kids. I did, however, get my first work experience, and by the summer of 1973 I was working 13 hours a day, seven days a week, in the arcade at the Grand Strand Amusement Park. These hours were not unusual for a 13-year-old in Myrtle Beach. My mother would take me to work at noon, and my busy father would pick me up at 1 a.m.

Most of the kids worked so many hours that they didn't find time to spend their money until the summer was over and they were back in school. Looking back, I can see the dangerous opportunities this set up for the kids. Specifically, this opened the door to drug use. Remember, this was 1973. Long hair, love, and drugs were everywhere. Undoubtedly when my dad was then offered the top job at the South Carolina Department of Parks, Recreation, and Tourism in Columbia in 1973, he also saw it as an opportunity to get my sister and me away from the temptations of Myrtle Beach. My sister had just finished high school, so the timing was also right for her to go to the University of South Carolina in Columbia. So, for the fourth time in my short life, we packed up things and made another move.

While unpacking in Columbia, I came across an old box which had always lived in the attic. Inside were photo albums from 1943-1945. A wooden box contained glass bottles with sand from the islands of Guam, Saipan, and Iwo Jima. There were letters written in Japanese along with Japanese coins and bills. To my shock, another small box contained a gold tooth with the full root.

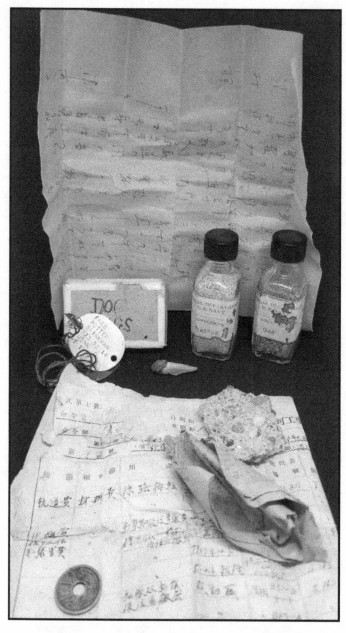

Figure 5: Fred Brinkman's Iwo Jima items (Dog Tags, gold tooth, bottles of island sand, concrete, Japanese documents and a coin).

I had many questions for my father. Many would not be answered except through the most important item, a 40-page letter my father wrote to his father. The letter's envelope indicated it was sent from San Francisco in April of 1945. Years later, I learned that a letter with this content would never have made it through a military censoring process on a ship. My father through his entire life believed in paper trails to document the truth. He apparently smuggled this letter to shore and mailed it to his father, and then he later saved it for me.

In writing this book, I came to realize this project was something my humble father could not have done himself. He didn't like talking about himself or his experiences except in one-on-one encounters. Saving his war letter was clearly an attempt to move its publication to another generation. Maybe he hoped I would be the one to handle it.

When my father hosted his WWII Navy Reunion in Myrtle Beach in 1996, my wife and I were eager to help and meet the old shipmates he had surprisingly become so friendly with since the reunion group found him in 1990. My dad was not one to reminisce about his war experience, and it was evident that he was avoiding war stories and more interested in the post-WWII lives of his shipmates.

In just a few months, my dad would be diagnosed with what proved to be a very aggressive form of non-Hodgkin's lymphoma. He would be leaving us in just six months. Because of his lifelong good health and incredibly positive attitude, I had always thought he could beat something like cancer and would probably outlive all of us. In fact, I worried about who would take care of him in the end with the rest of us gone.

After my dad succumbed to cancer, I was heartbroken to find a file cabinet full of items related to his Navy Reunion. Many notes and ideas showed he was looking forward to a very active role in the reunion. I never thanked my father for all he had done for me, but now there seemed to be an opportunity to begin doing that. My mom, wife, and, in two years, what would be the first and only grandchild started representing my father at the reunions.

I first began to compile all the great WWII documentation and accounts of the sailors and started a website, which I believe has become the best compilation of literature of any WWII ship.[15] One thing would lead to another, and unlikely developments would solve WWII mysteries. I was probably working several hours every night for ten years in this labor of love. In the end, I now see how a historian was born, and it was all from an attempt to thank my father and keep his memory alive.

But let's go back to that 1945 letter and the ship my dad would call his home during WWII.

One of the most significant forgotten feats of WWII happened in the United States, mainly through the efforts of American women. In 1942, President Roosevelt vowed that the United States would build hundreds of large invasion troop ships, and it would take only ten days to make each one.[16] Dozens could be built simultaneously. The Germans laughed at Roosevelt's dream, saying the feat was impossible. Nevertheless, shipyards around America began doing just that. The Oregon Shipbuilding Company was one of the original nine emergency shipyards and was capable of building 11 troop ships every ten days.

Figure 6: The USS Lowndes (APA-154). Credit US Naval History and Heritage Command, photo # NH 98739. Donated by Boatswain's Mate First Class Robert G. Tippins, USN (Retired), 2003.

---

[15] USS Lowndes: http://www.dobrinkman.net/lowndes
[16] Earth Tales: New Perspectives on Geography and History By Henry T. Conserva. Pg. 217

Figure 7: The Lowndes museum model commissioned by the Brinkman family and built by Raven Arts. Christening by Jeremy Brinkman in 2003.

Figure 8: Henry Kaiser's Oregon Shipbuilding: Keel to Launching in ten days.
Public Domain WWII Military photo.

At its peak, Oregon Shipbuilding employed over 35,000 people, 30% of them women, and 455 ships were built there during the war. Henry Kaiser, who ran this shipyard and others, recruited workers, including large numbers of women and minorities, from across the United States. Kaiser is considered the father of modern-day shipbuilding as well as the father of child day care, which became a necessity at the shipyards where many of the workers were young mothers.

Figure 9: A celebration of the first ship built in 10-days. President Roosevelt (bottom right) and Henry Kaiser (second from the left). "Record Breakers", published by the Oregon Shipbuilding Corporation in 1945.[17]

The city of Vanport, Oregon was built to handle the homes for over 40,000 of these Oregon workers and their families, making it the second largest city in Oregon. As a side note: On May 30, 1948, Vanport would be completely destroyed by flood when a 200-foot-wide section of a dike broke. No warning was given. The entire city was washed away in an instant. Miraculously, only a few of the 20,000 residents were in the town

---

[17] http://www.dobrinkman.net/lowndes/oregon/OregonShipBuilding1.htm

because almost everyone was taking part in Memorial Day ceremonies outside of the city.[18]

While my dad was completing training in 1944, the USS Lowndes (APA-154) was built at the Oregon Shipbuilding yard. The job of an APA (Attack Transport) ship was to carry assault troops and support equipment to the sites of amphibious operations. The USS Lowndes was 455 feet long and 62 feet wide. It carried 86 Naval officers, 480 ship's company, and 1,475 troops (U.S. Marine Corps/Army).[19]

She and the other 33 Haskell Class Attack Transports built in this yard all survived their WWII missions and safely returned home. The Haskell Class APAs were the pinnacle in the WWII evolution of troop ships. They were preceded by the Liberty and Victory troop ship designs. Although a few Liberty and Victory ships survive today as museum ships, sadly all the Haskell ships have been scrapped or intentionally sunk.

The APA ships were named after counties in the United States. The Lowndes had a triple distinction, taking its name from Lowndes counties in Alabama, Georgia, and Mississippi. All these counties were named after the distinguished South Carolina statesman William Lowndes (1782-1822.) Lowndes was a highly respected Congressman nominated for the office of President of the United States in 1821. While traveling to England in 1822, he became ill and died. He was buried at sea.

My dad would write his Iwo Jima letter while on board the Lowndes, probably several weeks after the Iwo Jima experience. To set the stage for my dad's letter, I'll provide background on a few of the heroic characters whose names are mentioned. After basic training in Farragut, Idaho, my dad's accelerated training was completed at Camp San Luis Obispo, California. It was there that he bonded and trained with what would become a Beach Battalion of men.

A strong friendship developed with 19-year-old Norman Richards. Norman was the oldest son from the Richards family of Nebraska City, Nebraska. Norman had a religious upbringing (Christian), and this may be the reason

---

[18] Oregon Disasters: True Stories of Tragedy and Survival By Rachel Dresbeck. Chapter 6: The Vanport Flood 1948
[19] http://www.dobrinkman.net/lowndes

for him becoming a lifesaver. My dad divided his leave time between his hard-drinking Navy buddies and Norman, who led him to church services instead of bars. Donald Bowman was probably my dad's second closest friend. Donald also had a strong faith in God and love for his country. Donald was the oldest in the group, at 26, and the humorous one. He would be given the job of leading the Beach Battalion's Hospital Corps unit. Rounding out the close working friends were Corpsmen Wesley Follett and Jerome Frieder.

The Lowndes was launched on July 18, 1944. On Sept. 9, 1944, my dad and the Beach Battalion boarded the ship. After shakedown, they departed on Oct. 23, 1944, for amphibious training in the Hawaiian Islands. They continued landing rehearsals for the rest of the year in preparation for the Iwo Jima and Okinawa operations.

Despite dropping out of high school to join the war effort, my father was already an experienced writer. In the area near St. Louis, Missouri where he grew up, he wrote a neighborhood newspaper in his youth. He would take the one copy by each house, giving everyone a chance to read the local news and, in doing so, would gather information for the next issue. Shortly after his experience at Iwo Jima, he was well prepared to put the horrific details of the battle into words. There is no better way to show this than in those 1945 words of my father in his letter home. We have donated this letter and my dad's M-1 carbine rifle to the South Carolina Confederate Relic Room and Military Museum. The museum director, Allen Roberson, calls the letter one of the best accounts of Iwo Jima he has ever read.

Figure 10: The USS Lowndes (APA-154) Beach Battalion - 1944

Figure 11: The Beach Battalion heroes.

Below are excerpts, with a few additional revelations inserted in italics, from Fred Brinkman's letter: "Somewhere in the Pacific, En-route to Stateside":

Dear Dad and Family:

On February 15 of this year (1945) we lay in Saipan harbor, ready to get underway for our first invasion. Since last October, we had been on training maneuvers practically all the time in the area of the Hawaiian Islands. Our ship developed into one of the best assault transports in the fleet and we were well trained and fully-prepared for action.

Being in the Beach Party, I was on maneuvers with the Marines practically everyday on Maui Island in Hawaii. It was a rugged training cruise; but we were a well-organized beach party.

In late January we left Pearl Harbor with 1500 Marines and a full load of assault cargo, ready to make the invasion on Iwo Jima, a small Japanese held island in the Northwest Pacific. After making a step at Eniwetok in the Marshall Islands for additional cargo and supplies, we made our last stop at Saipan. Three days before D-day, we left this island in our convoy which included approximately forty other assault transports, 20 A.P.A.'s and 20 A.K.A.'s and were escorted by a number of destroyers. Meanwhile our battle-wagons, cans and cruisers began to shell all parts of the island today, while minesweepers combed the beaches and carrier planes attacked from overhead.

Enroute to Iwo we encountered a few enemy subs and planes, but had no attack. We manned our battle stations frequently, however and received little rest. At this time, I was anxious to land on an enemy beach, but I have never felt that way since.

We were given a Briefing of all the known details of the nature of the island, the enemy defenses and positions and all information which had been obtained during the previous months. We were given the complete plan of our attack and operations.

Our Marine troops, veterans of Saipan, Tinian and Tarawa were cramped into the hot, non-ventilated close quarters of the troop compartments - 1500 of them. It was the last cruise for many of them. Everyday, I worked out with the Marines in Physical drills up on deck. Otherwise, I may not have been fortunate enough to be aboard this ship today, since I was never in better shape just before we landed on Iwo.

There were forty-three enlisted men and four officers in our Beach Party. We were scheduled to debark from the ship on February 20, or "D plus one." Our medical section consisted of Lt. (J.G.) "Doc" Eastham and eight corpsmen. Don Bowman, Ph M1/c, 26 of Pueblo, Colorado was our leader. Besides myself, our only other rated man was G. F. Buck, 19, a 225 lbs. Ohioan. Wes Follett, Jim Pierce, Jimmy Anderson, Norman Richards and Jerry Frieder completed the remainder of our medical section. We were all 19, except Pierce and Anderson who were 20 and 21 respectively and Bowman. With the exception of Buck, who had recently joined us, we had all been together for nearly a year - in San Luis Obispo and Oceanside and aboard the Lowndes since last September. They are the best bunch of guys I ever knew.

Iwo Jima is a tiny island between Saipan and the Jap homeland only five miles long and 2 1/2 miles wide at its widest point. We expected to capture the entire island within five days. We knew it was well fortified, but did not expected what was in-store for us.

On the way to Iwo, we prepared all our equipment for action. Besides our weapons and personal equipment, our medical gear alone consisted of about fifty packs and cases, averaging seventy-five pounds each.

We approached our destination early on the morning of February 20th. All battle-wagons, cans and cruisers, and smaller craft were pouring a continuous barrage of shells into every part of the island. From Mount Suribachi on the southern tip of the island to the rugged mountains on the northern end, the entire island was in smoke. Navy planes from our Carriers were strafing and bombing likely targets. The Japs were replying with rocket and artillery at our ships, but little damage was inflicted upon our fleet. While we were at Iwo, only one of our ships were sunk. Very few of our planes were lost. I didn't see more than ten of our planes get knocked down.

The whole ocean around Iwo was covered with ships - nearly one thousand of them. We pulled in off the Eastern side of Iwo.

Two hours after daybreak, we had all our troops unloaded and into our boats. The waters around the A.P.A.'s were now completely covered with boats loaded with Marines. About 0900, the first wave of boats headed for the beach. By this time, there wasn't a piece of any Japanese ships still afloat around Iwo. At the Northern end of the beach was the Japs only boat base on the island. Every boat was completely destroyed by our shelling. Along the beach a few Jap luggers and landing ships were smashed to hell.

There were three airfields on Iwo, a big bomber field just above the beach, a fighter plane airstrip in the middle of the island and a new airstrip which was under construction. From here, the Nips were intercepting and attacking our B-29's headed for Tokyo, and were also making raids on Saipan and our other Mariana islands. But not one plane left the ground from Iwo's airfields. All 350 of them would soon be a heap of wreckage. The pre-invasion barrage of our warships continued throughout the invasion. All Jap mechanized equipment was totally smashed. Not a single building was anything more than ashes by the time I hit the beach. Even the super blockhouses with five feet thick concrete walls were blown apart.

There wasn't anything above ground on Iwo which was left standing after three days of pounding.

But the Nippons were far from being defeated. They had held the island for over a century and it was now the strongest fortress in the world. The Japs knew we would strike at Iwo sooner or later. They never thought it possible, however, that all our troops could ever penetrate its beaches. The only possible landing place on the island was only about one - half mile wide. Besides the even smaller beach on the other side, the remainder of the shore line is a rugged cliff.

The Japs were very well prepared. The entire island was covered with blockhouses and pillboxes with gun emplacements from all sides. All the pillboxes were excavated deep into the islands with numerous compartments underground and were lined with concrete walls. There were no openings facing the ocean, making it impossible to score direct hits from our ships. We were not fighting men - they were rats. The volcanic Mount Suribachi was a giant blockhouse itself containing many dug-in pillboxes containing thousands of gun emplacements. From here, the Japs could set their artillery, mortar and rocket fire to reach and target anywhere on the beach or the whole island within a few feet. There were even more underground Jap emplacements in the northern hills.

Iwo Jima would never have been captured without an amphibious landing. All the ships of the U.S. fleet and our entire Air Force could not have taken the island by shelling and bombing. It had to be done the hard way.

The Japs would never surrender- it was necessary to kill nearly every one of the 22,000 troops. Fighting like rats in their holes, the yellow-bellies committed "hari-kari", their famous act of suicide, before being taken prisoner.[20]

---

[20] DC Locke (artist, photographer, historian, and archaeologist): Seppuku or "Hari-kari" as it is known in the West is suicide using a Wakizashi (Japanese short sword) or Tonto (a Japanese dagger). Many Japanese soldiers used grenades to blow themselves up or stuck a rifle under their chin to kill themselves rather than using swords or daggers esp. if they were low ranked and not officers and/or descended of Samurai class. Full-size swords at

The first day (February 20), the 4th Marines landed on Iwo. Then the fireworks began. From everywhere the Japs opened up. About twenty yards from the beach of black sand, a jagged terrace had to be crossed. Many Marines were mowed down before they reached the top. Others were killed in the boats as they landed on the roughest beach I've ever seen. But through blood and shells, the leather-necks smashed through. After a rugged battle, the Marines had captured the first airfield and crossed the island on the first day.

Still aboard ship, we will land early tomorrow morning. At about 1000 (10 o'clock), the first casualties were brought from the beach by our boats. We received about forty seriously wounded Marines, Beach Party men and boat crewmen aboard ship the first day. As we observed the condition of these wounds, while-giving plasma and giving the best possible treatment, I realized we were going to have a rough go when we hit that beach the next day. Ordinarily, even though we are having a hard time, there's always a "bull session" or somebody's got something humorous to say or a

---

that time, usually machine-made Shin Gunto's, were typically issued to Officers or NCOs. Some officers purchased a special commissioned hand-made sword from a traditional sword maker or carried into combat older family heirloom swords such as the earlier Katana or Tachi styles. Occasionally a Japanese officer might have impaled himself on his long sword or used that to cut himself open. Some others also had a subordinate officer behead him after he cut his belly. There were, however, exceptions as there were cases of Japanese officers shooting themselves instead. These suicides were all about not losing "face" or honor, esp. if the earlier Samurai warrior or WW-II soldier thought he had failed in his duty. A good example is: General Mitsuru Ushijima, commander of the Japanese 32nd Army at Okinawa turned down a personal appeal from the American General Simon Bolivar Buckner Jr. to surrender. Instead, hearing the sounds of destruction on nearby Hill 89 of Japanese positions, Ushijima and his second-in-command, General Isamu Cho committed suicide, each disemboweling himself with a short sword followed by his beheading by his principal aide. As for Tadamichi Kuribayashi, the Japanese commanding General at Iwo Jima, no one is sure of his final fate. Most likely he was killed on the morning of March 25th while leading an attack with his surviving soldiers against sleeping Marines and Army Air Corps ground crews. The assault climaxed in a hand-to-hand death clash between the men of both armies. After that fight ended, Kuribayashi's body could not be identified for he had removed all of his officer's insignia to appear as an ordinary soldier. However, it is also believed by his son, based on his personal interviews after the war with Japanese survivors, that Kuribayashi was actually taken down by an American artillery barrage during the final assault.

wisecrack to make. Today was different, everybody was silent and serious.

All day long and most of the night, we all worked like hell. The only comment (there wasn't many) any of the casualties made was: "That beach is hell." Tomorrow, I would discover that a truer sentence was never spoken.

Before sunset, the battle was becoming worse all the time. Jap troops counterattacked and recaptured most of the airfield. There was no fixed battlefield. Every part of the island was a front line. But the hottest place on Iwo was the beach. From Suribachi and from the Northern mountains, Jap mortar and rockets exploded continuously. The beach was their best target. Here, our troops were pouring ashore. Boats, tanks and DUKWs jammed the beach. Our ammunition dumps covered the beach. Most of the troops were pinned down here.

A beach party like our own was also operating on every beach. (The beach was divided into seven "beaches.") But tonight there was no beach party remaining on "Yellow Beach One." They had been completely wiped out.

Early on Tuesday morning, our Beach Party went over the side. There were two boatloads with twenty-three of us in each boat. If one boat were lost, one-half of our outfit could still operate. In the first boat, I had three corpsmen with me, Follett, Anderson and Pierce. In the second boat, there were Bowman, Buck, Richards and Freider.

At the USS Lowndes 1995 Reunion in San Antonio, Texas, my father added another profound addition to this debarkation while he was paying tribute to Norman Richards. He said that as they stepped down into the landing boats, Norman prayed out loud and asked God to bring his buddies back safely. But for himself, Norman prayed that if it is your will for me to die here today, I am ready, and I accept that.

In another recollection by USS Lowndes' Dave Frederick - "I was on the boat deck when the Beach Party was loading, and Don Bowman said to me

'Here Dave I don't think I'm coming back.' He gave me his billfold, keys to his locker and penknife."[21]

Figure 12: A page from Fred Brinkman's WWII photo album
showing Norman's family and his dog.

Figure 13: A DUKW was a six-wheel-drive amphibious modification of the CCKW trucks used by the U.S. military during World War II and the Korean War. They were not effective at Iwo Jim as most of them became stuck in the volcanic black sand. The above Iwo Jima USMC photograph shows one of them turned upside-down and almost completely buried in the sand.

Figure 14: The 16th annual (2004) USS Lowndes Reunion in Branson, MO ended with some of the members taking a ride in a WWII DUKW (top). Jeremy Brinkman and his father, David, enjoy the land portion of the ride (lower left). After moving into a lake, Jeremy takes to wheel (lower right.)

Continuing with my father's words from the 1945 letter:

> After loading both boats with all our equipment, the boats were lowered into the water and we went down the nets. From up above, some of the crewmen gave us some "Good Luck", "Take it easy", etc. Wishes, and we headed for the beach.
>
> A steel helmet and liner, Marine greens, Marine jacket, field shoes and socks constituted my clothes. My field pack contained everything from rations and mess kit to tent canvas and poncho, but this soon disappeared after I hit the beach. I also carried a gas mask and decontamination bag and my "Unit #3", which is a field medical kit, containing sufficient material for the treatment of any emergency battle casualty. My dog tags and a few identification

tags were my only personal effects. Two water canteens, a shovel, cartridge belt, carbine ammunition, a knife (the one Dad gave me last summer) and a carbine rifle completed my personal outfit.

Doc Eastham and Bowman were armed with .45 pistols while the remainder of our corpsmen, including myself had carbines.

The entire beach was covered with the remains of bodies, many of them blown to pieces. Some of them were Japs who were wiped out as we attacked the beach yesterday. But most of them were our Marines, beach party men and sailors from the landing craft. It was not possible to step very far without stumbling into these badly-mangled bodies, most of which were partly or completely buried in the sand.

Before we had landed, there was nothing left of our other beach party from another ship which had landed yesterday. The same catastrophe occurred on the other five beaches. There had been no one available to treat and evacuate the hundreds of casualties, which were now piled up on the beach. Some of them were killed here after being wounded. As the terrific bombardment continued, additional casualties were being produced all around us.

Figure 15: David Brinkman's GI Joe U.S.N. Corpsman
wearing the Unit #3 medical bag.

Between the rounds of firing there were groans of agony from our wounded men. We were going to have a hell of a job - only nine of us in the medical section. The other men of our beach party had a tremendous job also in the defense of the beach and handling the many broached boats and DUKWs and bringing in the cargo and ammunition for our guns.

It was impossible to have any organization of our setup. Our only choice was to work like hell in giving the roughest and quickest treatment and evacuate those casualties off this damn beach in the quickest possible way and at the same time, we had to fight for our own skull.

In order to have a partially protected place to work, I began to dig some corruption from a mortar shell hole to use as a foxhole. But all I could do was dig into the skull of a dead Jap. On the beach, it was hard to locate any place beneath the sand without digging into a body.

In a few magazines, I noticed pictures of the cemetery at Iwo which was erected after the fighting had stopped. Upon each cross, the name of one of those who had his life inscribed. Beneath each cross, the name of supposedly the body of each man. I regret to say that this assumption is entirely false. There are no bodies under those crosses, except those who were killed in that location. After the fighting had almost ceased, some of our boys were probably buried there. But during the five days we were on Iwo, those who died remained where they were until covered by a shell hit or the bulldozer tractors which were put into operation to clear the beach. Most of our men who were lost were unidentified. It was impossible to examine or bury them. The battle was too intense for anything of that nature.

I think it was impossible for any correspondent to get the straight dope as to what actually happened on Iwo. When a battle is hot, there aren't going to be any photographers or news correspondents to make some close shots or jot down some fresh news. People just simply don't do such things - not on Iwo. I recollect one exception. As a boatload of troops landed on our beach, some pressman dashed up on the beach with a portable typewriter and began clicking away. I don't know what happened to this poor chum, but a few minutes later a piece of this typewriter landed alongside of me. As far as photographers went, I didn't see any, except a couple of them who soon abandoned their cameras not long after they hit the beach. There were just too many other things to think about on Iwo.

I saw a few newsreels of Iwo Jima, but they seemed pretty vague. It was plain to see that none of the announcers had been there. I don't mean to criticize anyone on their viewpoints of Iwo, or the newsreels. In fact, they did a wonderful job in being able to pick up what they did. However, it is absolutely impossible for anyone to actually know what happened. Besides the things we individually experienced, one guy's opinion is as good as another. All I know are the things I actually experienced. Anything else other than these are merely my opinions, which may or may not be true.

There was no time to lose in taking care of all our casualties. I headed for the guy nearest to me which I remember was an unconscious Marine with one leg practically torn off. I cut the remaining cords off with my big knife, slapped on a large battle dressing over the stump after dusting it with sulfa powder, gave him a syringe full of morphine in the arm and Freider and I brought him out to one of the boats which had just beached. Bowman and all the rest of our gang were hauling other casualties in to the boat. We jammed all the stretchers we could into the boat, and every casualty who could stand up, we also piled in. It was a hell of a job loading one of those damn boats on that beach. There weren't nearly enough boats to begin to handle our casualties and it was almost impossible to land them without broaching. After a boat once broaches, it didn't take long for the rough breaker waves or a mortar blast to smash it to pieces. Then too, there was hardly an open space to bring a boat in.

I don't remember how many casualties we handled that first day or the next three days. I can remember very few of them individually. All I do know is that it was a continuous rushing job for all of the guys day and night.

Our medical work on the beach would have better represented a slaughter house than a hospital. Every wound was covered and packed with the instruments, all we could use was our dirty field and jack-knifes. Sometimes it was necessary to sew up a chest wound to prevent air from escaping a punctured lung. Against all laws of surgery, all I had time to do was make a quick stitch, jam the needle through each side of the flesh and tie a knot with my fingers. It was never practical for us to sew a wound of any other kind. The main idea was to stop bleeding and pain and keep a guy breathing until he could be given proper attention aboard ship.

Battle dressings were used by the hundreds along with sulfa powder. They were the most important weapon against death we had. We gave every casualty a full shot of morphine, with the exception of a few with bad head wounds. We used plenty of plasma too, although we didn't have time to administer this blood-restoring fluid to everyone who required it. We didn't have time to immobilize any fractures on the beach. It was mainly a matter of keeping a guy living.

A number of Marines around us were killed the first morning. We had some of our casualties lying just next to the surf, waiting for boats to come in. Most of them were killed by a series of mortar shells and others were further wounded. From the middle of the island, the Marines continued to bring in more wounded men. Three of our beach party men were wounded before noon the first morning. Red Buzzard, a radioman, was seriously wounded in the gut. "Chips" Guimont, carpenter's mate, was hit through the leg. One of our officers, Lt. Laudesbach had a leg blown off. We evacuated all these fellows safely. There were a number of other minor casualties among our Beach Party that morning, including two of our corpsmen, Anderson and Pierce who received shrapnel wounds but stuck with us.

Figure 16: Donald Bowman

I don't know what happened to

Buzzard or Lt. Laudesbach, although Guimont is back with us today.

Just after noon, things got hotter than ever before. Just behind us was a battered Jap pillbox which had been smashed in. But suddenly a Jap sniper poked his head out a hole and opened up fire with his rifle. Don Bowman was only a few feet away, giving plasma to a wounded Marine. Don never knew what happened. He had been our leader and performed a job that couldn't be surpassed by anyone. He gave the supreme sacrifice, but he won't be forgotten. I was just next to Don when he was hit. He fell against me and knocked me down. The Jap continued to fire and a couple other guys were wounded. Had it not been for Don, I would have been directly in his line of fire. Of course, the Nip didn't last long. Everybody who saw him opened up with their rifles. I grabbed my carbine, and even though about ten other guys must have hit him first, I kept my finger on that trigger until my ammunition clip was empty. I'll bet enough shells went into that Jap to keep every hunter from St. Louis supplied for one season. After we had ceased firing, I was so mad, I jammed the butt of my rifle into his face as hard as I could. That's where my gold tooth came from.

This occasion was my only opportunity to fire my carbine, but she was a mighty handy baby. We had numerous other sniper attacks, even up until the fourth day. Some of our beach party fellows made some bags on other Nip snipers.

I'm going ahead a little, but I almost mistakenly killed one of my buddies the second night. Unidentified boats were spotted off the beach and we were on the lookout for Japs attempting to swim ashore and counter attack us. The Japs never came ashore but someone jumped down against me from off a smashed tank. My first thought was a Jap and I had my carbine against his guts. I couldn't say anything, but my finger was squeezing that trigger. The supposed enemy identified himself as one of my buddies. I'm thankful that something must have been wrong with that trigger. Due to the close battlefield on Iwo, there were numerous occasions where our men were killed in a manner similar to this.

In the same pillbox where we killed that first Jap, some of the Marines spotted two more live enemy soldiers attempting to come out. They dashed back under their holes and refused to come out. They couldn't be seen to hit with a rifle. Then we put the flame-throwers into action. A shot was heard, which meant that one Jap evidently committed "hari-kari". Another body, flaming with fire, soon came rushing out. A barrage of shells brought the burning figure down.

Another Jap sniper was seen setting up a radio inside the wreckage of a Jap ship buried into our beach. He had been directing the firing of Japanese mortar and artillery from the hills of Suribachi and the northern end of the island, enabling them to find our best targets. Other snipers made banzai charges against us on the beach, but all were wiped out. They did kill a few Marines and wounded a couple of our beach party.

However, it wasn't the snipers that really worried us. A sniper could be located and wouldn't cause much trouble. Our problem was dealing with a hidden enemy. They knew exactly where we were, but we couldn't possibly locate their positions. All we could do on the beach is hope that the next mortar shell would miss.

The mortars were blasting terrifically by mid-afternoon. Within two hours fifteen men of our Beach Party were wounded. Two more were killed and two missing. Norman Richards, while carrying a casualty out to a boat was killed along with the wounded man and the Marine on the other end of the stretcher. Like Bowman, he had done a brilliant job and was a great loss. There was nothing we could do for either Don or Rick. Before Rick was hit, it seemed that he wasn't worried about anything. He just kept pitchin' in his quiet way.

In a letter that Norman Richards' mother wrote to my father after the war, she stated that Norman's dog "Red, howled so one night." Later, after learning that Norman had been killed, they realized that the dog howled at the same time as Norman's death on the other side of the planet.[22]

---

[22] USS Lowndes Memorial: Florence Richards

Figure 17:
Norman Richards

Going back to the 1945 words of my father's letter:

I don't know what happened first or last - except that they did happen. Doc Eastham, our medical officer, had been right with us all the time. There was no way to apply his professional medical skill other than the same way the rest of us did. Eastham was 25, married with one baby, and hailed from Nebraska. He was giving plasma to a casualty during the heavy barrage. I was working on another guy next to him, while Pierce was mixing a bottle of plasma. The beach was now loaded heavier than ever with casualties. Between each blast, someone could be heard howling "Corpsman". Pierce and I just lifted up our casualty to drag him to the beach when a direct blast hit directly on the wounded man, sinking him in the ground. I didn't know whether I was still alive or not. I was covered with sand, but managed to force my way out. I don't know why, but I wasn't even scratched by shrapnel from the blast. However, I couldn't hear a sound for the rest of the day. The only way I knew a shell was blasting was when someone fell or made a dive for a hole.

Meanwhile, Doc Eastham had received a shell concussion from the blast. He wasn't hit either, but was so mentally affected that we later lost his services. Pierce received numerous shrapnel wounds on the back, but we evacuated him safely. Anderson was shot in the foot by another shell. We also lost the services of Buck, who was wounded alongside of one of our ammunition dumps which the Japs hit.

Pierce, Andy, and Buck have now recuperated and are back aboard ship with us. Doc Eastham still remains in a hospital. They performed a great job on the beach that first day. Even after being wounded, Pierce and Andy stuck right with Follett, Freider, and myself before we evacuated them. Buck was reported as missing in action, but fortunately he had been evacuated by some Marine corpsmen. Bowman and Rick gave more than all of us. But now there were only three of us left on that beach, Follett, Freider and myself. There was more work to do now than ever before. There would be no rest for a long time.

Besides our doctor and four corpsmen, whom we lost the first day, there were eighteen other casualties among other members of our beach party. Besides Bowman and Richards, a seaman named Morton was lost and another seaman is missing. We managed to evacuate all the other sixteen casualties, and as far as I know, all of them are living today.

After that first day, our beach party suffered only a few more casualties - in fact, only two minor ones. The Jap barrage kept up continuously, day and night, but that first afternoon on the beach was our worst experience.

However, our evacuation work for Jerry (Freider), Wes (Follett) and myself had hardly begun. I'll never forget that first night. There were only three of us to handle the day's casualties from Iwo. All night long, however, the other members of our beach party were serving as stretcher-bearers. Fresh Marines were helping us all night, too. It was now absolutely impossible to land a boat on our beach. All casualties had to be carried 500 yards down to the next beach where boats could still land. It seemed like an endless procedure. There was a cold rain all night long. It wasn't hard to see, however, as our ships rocketed starshells over the island all night. Our ammunition dumps were burning all night too.

Wes and Jerry really went through hell in carrying out their job on the beach. So did everyone else. I'll never forget either of these boys. They had been in the beach party for one year and were not awarded a rate. It required an occasion like Iwo Jima before they finally were awarded a meritorious advancement to PhM3/c[23] for their services on Iwo. I mean they earned their services on Iwo. I mean they earned it, too.

---

[23] Pharmacist's Mate Third Class (Corpsman)

Wes was in bad shape all the time. He had a slight shell concussion and lost about twenty pounds, but refused to quit until our job was completed. It didn't seem to bother Jerry very much. His big, sloppy frame was the same as always when he returned to the ship.

When the flag went up on Suribachi the 23rd of February, we never realized it would be a historic occasion. No one did at the time. It was merely just another thing that happened.

It wasn't till the night of the 23rd that we were able to get some rest. The flow of casualties had decreased considerably by now. Most of the Jap gun emplacements had been knocked out and there wasn't too much mortar hitting our beach. The Fifth Marines had taken Suribachi after a bloody battle. The third and Fourth Divisions had the No. 1 Airfield well in hand and were smashing around No. 2. It was a costly battle all the way. Flame-throwers, rifles and hand-to-hand combat was necessary to exterminate the rats of Iwo.

It rained almost continuously all the time we were on the beach. We were cold and water soaked all the time. The odor from blood and bodies penetrated all through us. It would have been impossible for anyone to attempt to sleep the first three nights on Iwo.

However, I was able to dose off in my foxhole about an hour on the night of the 23rd. The three of us, Jerry, Wes and I crawled into a shell hole. We had one case of brandy left from our medical units, which we broke open and consumed that night. A case consisted of only twelve small bottles, containing about one-third of a pint a piece. It really pepped us up. I was then able to eat about three meals of K rations. Plenty of rations had reached us amongst the cargo which was continuously coming ashore. My appetite and general condition mentally seemed to be in good shape by this time. I suppose I just didn't give a damn anymore.

Cigarettes had also made their way ashore. Ordinarily, I seldom smoked even though cigarettes cost only a nickel per pack, but I "ate 'em" that night.

All Wes could do was smoke. At every shell burst he jumped and quivered. Even today, Wes becomes nervous at the sound of gunfire or an explosion. My nerves didn't affect me until after I had been aboard ship a few days afterwards. Jerry sprawled out as comfortable as he used to on his high school football field in Cleveland. That's the kind of guys a beach party needs on Iwo. A strong back and a don't give a damn for anything.

I don't know what kept us from being hit. With the help of God, the law of averages just didn't catch up with us. We stuck as closely together as possible. Some of our casualties whom we were carrying down the beach were killed on the stretchers. A number of Marines who were hauling casualties on the other end of our stretchers were killed and wounded. I was always wondering when it was our turn. But rotten eggs never seemed to crack- at least three of them didn't.

On the morning of the 24th, we were still waiting for our relieving Beach Party. By now, our Marines had all of Iwo Jima well in hand. New troops were heading to the front lines. Our artillery and other guns were blasting from all parts of the island into the Jap positions. Tanks and other vehicles were rolling across the sand. Bulldozers were plowing roads through the island and covering the remains of the beachhead battle. Our ammunition was being cleared from the beaches as quickly as the boats came in. The wreckage from all the beaches had been cleared and our boats were landing rapidly and easily. Our ships were concentrating their bombardment into the northern hills.

The Marines were even bringing field ambulance trucks ashore now. An occasional Jap mortar or rocket shell would hit near us, but opposition on the beach was almost over. It would require over three weeks more to complete the battle of Iwo, but sooner or later, every Nippon on the island would meet his fate - 22,000 of them. There was still a big battle ahead for our Marines and there would be many more casualties, but the worst of the fight was now over.

On the morning of the 29th, we set up a real evacuation station- one such as we have been training and working at for the past eight months. The bulldozers went into action and we reinforced the sides of the dug-in station with sand bags. It was now the only evacuation station from shore-to-ship on the whole island. We lined up all on the medical gear on the ground, ready for immediate use.

The casualties continued to come in, but we were now able to provide excellent first-aid attention and a smooth evacuation to the boats. One mortar blast hit our station, but little damage was done.

Finally, our relief Beach Party came ashore. We were a happy bunch of guys. I was so stiff and sore from cuts and scratches I could hardly walk. There weren't many of us left now- plenty of room to spare in this single boat. Wes, Jerry and I, of course, were the only corpsmen. I'll never forget the fellows who couldn't come back to the ship with us, and those whom we evacuated as well as we could. "Platoon 15 of Beach Battalion "A", and later called the "U.S.S. Lowndes Beach Party" is one outfit I'll never forget.

The other beach parties, or at least most of them, who landed on Iwo included many guys whom I knew very well in San Luis Obispo and Oceanside. Many of them were lost on D-Day, the day before we landed on Iwo. Considering the heavy losses of those seven beach parties, we actually were quite fortunate. It was a hell of a job bringing my legs up that net on the side of U.S.S. Lowndes, but I could have climbed the Empire State Building. The old girl was heaven compared to that blasted island.

Souvenirs are something that everybody seems to want, but no one was interested in these things after he had been on Iwo. I never once thought of a souvenir while I was on Iwo, although I did bring back a Jap revolver I took from an enemy sniper, who was wounded at the time, and a few coins, cigarettes, and a couple bills. I still have the gun aboard and also my own carbine, and if I ever have a chance, will send them to you.

Everybody was happy to see us, as the rumors aboard ship had us tabbed as "cooked pigeons." That steel deck really felt good. Before I knew it, we were sitting on the Pharmacy deck with Chief Biggers breaking out a bottle of "Old Overholt". After a few shots of this delicacy, the rest of the gang had three trays of good chow from the officer's galley sitting before us. Even Wes had now regained his appetite.

After Wes, Jerry and I spent about half-an-hour under the hot shower, the Chief gave us two tabs of Sodium Amytol which put me to sleep for twenty-four hours.

While we were on the beach, our ship had been busy as hell too. It was one of the many A.P.A.'s around the island of Iwo which was taking care of the many casualties we were evacuating from the beach. About one-hundred seventy-five wounded Marines and sailors had been brought aboard when Wes, Jerry and I arrived. All the ship's doctor's and the thirty corpsmen attached to the ship had also been performing a big job, as well as the rest of the crew.

We worked night and day aboard ship, treating the wounds of our patients. Most of them were in serious condition and required constant attention. Most of the wounds were the result of Jap mortar fire- large, gaping wounds, ranging everywhere from the head to organs of the abdomen. But this was play compared to the nightmare on that blasted island.

Only eight or ten of our patients died before we arrived in Guam on the 10th of March. Our load of casualties was transferred to a base hospital on Guam. From here we proceeded back to Saipan. The U.S.S. Lowndes had weathered her first battle.

My father's letter was very impressive for a 19-year-old. The one thing, however, that does not come across is the deep personal pain my father would endure in losing his buddies Norman Richards and Donald Bowman. A few patches of Lowndes shipmates would remain close throughout the years, but the reunion group would not form until 45 years after the war.

Before the reunion, my dad's only two WWII contacts were the Richards and Bowman families. In fact, every Christmas he wrote to Norman's family, and he visited them on several occasions. Norman's mother would live to be 104 years old. When my dad died, an outpouring of love came from their family. They told me my dad was the only person from the ship who had contacted them before the reunions started.

Over the 13 years we were involved with the reunion, I would learn that many of the virtues of my father were actually in place well before he joined the Navy and then reinforced by his war experience. But how could such a horrific experience turn into something good? I believe it all came down to a responsibility to live a good life. An opportunity my dad was given by Norman, Donald, and the hundreds of other men my dad watched die on Iwo Jima. His saving of dozens of lives on that horrid beach and a Navy citation would not be enough. The remaining part of his life would have to be dedicated to helping others and setting the right examples.

One of my early tasks with the reunion group was to find missing sailors and introduce them to the reunion. After Iwo Jima, the Lowndes needed many replacements in its medical section. One man I found was one of these corpsmen who transferred from the European war front. My dad had, many years before, left quite an impression on this newfound reunion member.

When we first talked, he asked me to tell him what my dad had done after the war. I went down the list, telling him how my dad had always been the boss everywhere he went as he took on jobs of greater responsibility. I told him that everyone loved my soft-spoken, unassuming dad. When I was done, the old corpsman said, "I knew it." He said he knew my father was a born leader but very different than most leaders we think of. His patience was unmatched, and he calmly worked with every sailor to make sure they understood their jobs. Although my dad was out-ranked by other members of the medical section, everyone viewed him as the leader. The corpsman said he frequently thought about my dad even 50 years later and was so satisfied to learn he had succeeded in the best of ways.

My father had many opportunities over the years to make himself monetarily rich, including a chance to partner with a man in the development of Hilton Head Island, South Carolina, and another opportunity to be an instant millionaire as a vice president of a huge property holding company in Myrtle Beach. In both cases, my father's response was an instant "No." Instead, he dedicated his life to high-responsibility jobs, at relatively low pay, that would improve the lives of those in his adopted state of South Carolina and make him a mentor to hundreds of employees and colleagues. He thrived on a stage where many watched his every move and witnessed his powerful examples. In honoring my father, I began to understand what made him what he was.

Of course, a huge part of what made my dad a great man was my mother, Roberta Weaver Brinkman. In their 49 years of marriage, my mother was by his side through it all. She talked my dad into going to college, and she worked and paid for it. My mother was a strong woman with a strong faith. My father's death was only the second time I saw her cry. As in the years before, she would attend the Lowndes reunion the year following my father's death, but that would be the last one, as her health declined. She had always wanted to be a grandmother, and I feared that would not happen. Odess and I had tried for years with no luck and only miscarriages. During the grieving for my dad, I just stopped thinking about it and gave up hope.

Christmas of 1998, however, brought news of a miracle. Odess was pregnant, and we passed the point where the previous miscarriage had occurred. My mom's life was energized with the hope of a grandchild. On August 3, 1999, labor was induced as Odess was already two weeks late. A full 12 hours later, she was struggling. The baby was unexpectedly large, and Odess was ripped opened (accidental episiotomy). Things were becoming critical as a C-section was quickly arranged. I was there, and I soon held our 10-pound baby boy Jeremy.

Odess, who was utterly exhausted, only had the energy to ask me: "Is he complete?" He was complete and well, despite the traumatic delivery. Odess, however, would develop a staph infection. Having never held a baby in my life, I would have to take care of Jeremy. I was overwhelmed and did the only thing I knew to do. I asked my 79-year-old mother if she could help me. The new grandmother said she didn't remember how to do this baby stuff but that we would figure it out.

While we were busy with Jeremy, Odess' condition would worsen. After almost a week in the hospital, the infection was finally beaten. Odess was soon back home and our lives as parents began to settle down. If, that is, you could ever call the life of a parent being settled.

We loved our Jeremy, and my mom loved being a grandmother. She would occasionally babysit to give Odess and me a break, but after a couple of years, she informed us that it was taking her days to recover from just a few hours of babysitting. In the spring of 2002, while gardening, she injured her shoulder and was given a shot of cortisone. It seemed this suppressed her immune system enough that it allowed shingles to develop. In a worst-case scenario, the shingles caused permanent nerve damage in my mother's abdomen.

She would soon move in with us. Desperate for pain relief, she went so far as to have three epidurals in one week. Each one had less of an effect, and the last one did nothing. More and more pain drugs did not help. Applying pressure to her abdomen with a pillow, she broke ribs. She was almost completely bedridden. Nevertheless, she insisted on having her hair done every two weeks. One day, after a trip to the hair salon, she probably had a heart attack, but the only symptom was nausea. Over the next few days she would become too weak to get out of bed, and I took her to the hospital.

Within minutes of her attachment to an EKG, an alarm sounded. An ultrasound technician, who had a bad habit of talking to herself out loud, gasped at the ultrasound reading of my mother's heart and mentioned severe problems. She then asked my mother if she had had rheumatic fever when she was young. This is what had led to the early death of my father's mother, so it caught my attention. Rheumatic fever is the stage of illness that occurs if strep throat is not treated. It almost always causes major damage to the heart and premature death. My mother's response to the technician was "I may very well have had it. During the Great Depression, our family could not afford to go to the doctor."

The way my mother responded, and her expressions, left no doubt in my mind that she had always suspected this. As I thought more about it, the pieces of the puzzle came together. Just like with my father's mother, my mom developed respiratory problems as a teenager, which can be caused by heart damage. By 19, she had to give up violin playing because of severe arthritis. In her 20s, her doctor recommended that she move from Virginia to Florida to help alleviate the respiratory problems. It was in Florida that she met my dad. I began also to realize that I had never seen my mother do anything that would lead to physical exertion. All these years, she knew she had heart damage from rheumatic fever. Her careful lifestyle, or maybe a miracle, is how she had lived to be 81.

My mother was quickly admitted to the ICU, where doctors reassured us she would be fine, and they inserted a temporary pacemaker. They would not be able to move forward with more extensive tests, however, until they figured out why my mother's hemoglobin count was so low. After my mother had been in the ICU for a few days, my sister arrived from Myrtle Beach. We both worried about how my mom would be able to recover from this new issue after being so weakened by the shingles complications.

Unknown to us on this Sunday, many of my mother's church friends had stopped by to see her, and she gave them all the same message. It was a goodbye message. She was ready to go. That night, my sister Terri Stevens, Odess, Jeremy, and I stayed with my mom until visiting hours came to an end. We all told her we loved her and would see her tomorrow. I was the last to walk out. After several steps forward, something stopped me. I walked back and pulled the curtain back. No words. I just simply smiled at my mom, and she smiled back.

Early the next morning, I headed over to the hospital. Based on what my mom's nurse told us, I was probably parking my car as the nurse brought breakfast to my mother. My mom loved to have a banana for breakfast, and that just happened to be on the plate. She asked the nurse if she would peel it for her. As the nurse handed it back to my mom, my mom thanked her and said, "You know, I think today is going to be a good day." Only a minute or two after she left the room, the nurse said alarms sounded on equipment monitoring my mother's vital stats.

As the elevator door opened for me to the ICU, my mother's room was directly in front of me. It was full of doctors and nurses who were frantically working on her. I broke into a run toward her but was intercepted by hospital employees who said I could not go there. They carried me to a room where an ICU administrator tried to calm me down and informed me my mother had just had a massive heart attack. I could not speak. My throat was constricted from the emotional stress. I jotted down on a piece of paper to have someone call my sister and tell her to come.

As the staff was continuing CPR on my mother, I thought about her Living Will and the many times in life she made her will clear to me. Every time she saw or heard of someone being kept alive by a machine, she would tell me to never let that happen to her. She even once told me to unplug the machines myself if necessary. My sister also knew this. When my sister arrived at the ICU, a doctor described the situation. There was nothing left of my mother's heart. It had been ripped to shreds. Only a heart transplant could save her, although he admitted not even a young, strong, and otherwise, healthy person could survive something like this. My sister and I shared a glance with each other, and we instructed the doctor to stop the CPR. My mom died a few minutes later on Nov. 18, 2002.

I still had not gotten over the grieving of my father's death five years earlier. The grief for my mother was more intense but would not last as long. Odess and I thought about moving into my parents' house but changed our minds at the last minute and sold it. I realized later that my father would have strongly recommended against keeping their home, saying that we needed to break away and live our own lives now. I would never be able to do that entirely, but my mom and dad did leave us with something that would help. We would later use money from their estate to buy our "Lot of History" (Chapter Six).

I had promised my mom I would keep working on the Lowndes reunions. My efforts led to a website of 750 pages of the ship's history and more than 1,200 photographs. I located about another 40 missing sailors, including ship's officer Dr. Stuart Hyde, who had spent his life as an author and teacher and would take this information and turn it into papers on the Lowndes's invasion of Iwo Jima and Okinawa.

I acquired the blueprints of the ship and commissioned a team to build a detailed scale model of the Lowndes, which would be on display at the South Carolina State Museum for the 60th anniversary of D-Day Iwo Jima.[24] The tedious, detailed work, as well as the reunions, began to slow down as the old sailors and their wives could not muster a large enough group to make the trips. During this time, the real detective work brought new excitement to the Lowndes project. There were new horizons in sight, with more to learn and more mysteries to solve.

---

[24] USS Lowndes Blueprints and Model: http://www.dobrinkman.net/lowndes/ship.htm

Figure 18: The 8th annual (1996) USS Lowndes Reunion in Myrtle Beach, SC.
Hosted by Fred Brinkman.

1. David Brinkman	17. Earl Robertson	33. Lebbie Dyer	49. Stan Dunn
2. Odess Brinkman	18. Sally Cary	34. Arthur Rauseo	50. Richard Jones
3. Ruth Ann Trostel	19. Cliff Schraffer	35. Don Lorenzi	51. Charles Ross
4. Don McPherson	20. Bill Taylor	36. John Dyer	52. Iris Ross
5. Bud Kautz	21. Leo O'brien	37. Shirley Lorenzi	53. Jackie Umbarger
6. Joan McPherson	22. Margaret O'brien	38. Joe Freitas	54. Clark Martin
7. Dallas Stratton	23. Fred Brinkman	39. Loreta Freitas	55. Joanne Long
8. Frances Robertson	24. Frank Wanits	40. Agnes Bensie	56. David Long
9. Harold Brunner	25. Howard Chappel	41. Jack Hovey	
10. Eileen Murray	26. Alice Wanits	42. Dorothy Weaver	
11. Mike Michalski	27. Roberta Brinkman	43. Evelyn Hovey	
12. Lorene Stratton	28. Mims Grody	44. Mona Dunn	
13. Jerry Michalski	29. John Vernale	45. Jim Ross	
14. Emily Cary	30. Lois Chappel	46. Ina Ross	
15. Amelia Taylor	31. Marjorie Rauseo	47. Roseanna Jones	
16. Mary Schaffer	32. James Chilcote	48. Walt Umbarger	

Chapter 5 – Researching the Greatest Generation: A Historian is born

The other Joe Rosenthal Iwo Jima Photo:

While searching through my dad's WWII Iwo Jima items, I came across a familiar canister containing different WWII training photos and publications. How I wished I had paid closer attention to this before my father's death. Once again, typical of my humble dad, he had a very significant item hidden among the mixture. Numbers had been drawn on grainy newspaper pictures from Time and Life magazines of a horrific scene on Iwo Jima. In the mix of documents, my dad's hand-written notes identified things and people in the photo.

Although these were relatively low-quality prints, my dad was identifying his Yellow Beach evacuation station and members of his Beach Battalion. He was relatively sure he had identified himself and the other two surviving Lowndes' corpsmen, based on the placement of their "Unit #3" medical bags. Shortly after hitting the beach, my dad sensed that the Japanese were targeting the corpsmen, and he instructed his two corpsmen (Jerome and Wesley) to change the placement of the only item that could give them away.

By this time in the war, the United States had stopped placing the red cross on corpsmen because it had become a target. While I was doing consulting work for the movie "Flags of Our Fathers," I had learned that at Iwo Jima the Japanese were trained to spot corpsmen by the upper body placement of the medical bag.[25] The Japanese knew that, if you killed a corpsman, wounded Marines would die. They also understood the loyalty between a Marine and a Navy corpsman. A downed corpsman would bring Marines into a dangerous open position in an attempt to save the corpsman. The bottom line was that corpsmen were easy targets, and their loss was very costly to the cause.

It should be understood that the primary goal of the Japanese at Iwo Jima was not to necessarily win the battle but for each Japanese soldier to kill ten Americans before they were killed. The Japanese believed that killing

---

[25] Flags of Our Fathers By James Bradley, Ron Powers. Chapter: Armada, pg. 140

200,000 Americans in a battle would cause an uproar in the American public, which might lead the United States to pull out of the war. The brainwashed enemy had also been programmed to kill themselves before being taken prisoner. Instead of a 10-to-1 kill ratio, the United States reversed it to a 7-to-20 ratio, and the American war effort gained even more momentum.

The wise medical bag placement change by my father from the upper body to the belt may well have saved the lives of Jerome, Wesley, and himself as well as dozens (maybe hundreds) of wounded Americans these three corpsmen saved over a period of four days. Out of the Lowndes Beach Battalion and hundreds of supporting crewmen on the ship, these three men would be the only ones to receive a Navy Citation. Many years later, during the Lowndes reunions, my dad would make an official statement on the citation. As he had done all his life, he gave the credit to others, stating:

> While we considered the citations a great honor, Wes, Jerry, and I didn't understand why we were singled out for this recognition. We didn't do any more than anyone else. Whatever took place on the beach at Iwo Jima was a team effort by all members of the Beach Party. And our Beach Party couldn't have functioned without support of all of our U.S.S. Lowndes boat crews and all of those with other responsibilities aboard ship. We were all on the beach when Don Bowman and Norman Richards died and others were wounded, and all of our Beach Party members, the boat crews and others on the ship were involved with the many Marine casualties. Follett, Frieder and I had adjacent foxholes in the black sand of Iwo. Follett was Catholic, Frieder was Jewish, and I was Protestant. Several times we repeated the prayer we all knew beginning with "Our Father who art in Heaven." We weren't "heroes." (I was downright scared). All three of us were thankful that we were alive and unscathed when we returned to the ship with the remaining members of our Beach Party. I'm sure that all three of us believe that those citations we received in 1945 belong to all members of the Beach Party and our other shipmates on the Lowndes. In summary, if we were able to rewrite those citations of 1945, I firmly believe that Wes and Jerry would want to join me in replacing our names with all the members of the U.S.S. Lowndes

who contributed to the important role of our ship in the battle of Iwo Jima.[26]

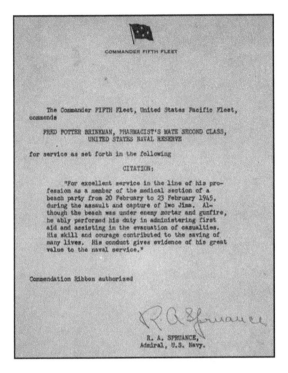

COMMANDER FIFTH FLEET

The Commander FIFTH Fleet, United States Pacific Fleet, commends

FRED POTTER BRINKMAN, PHARMACIST'S MATE SECOND CLASS, UNITED STATES NAVAL RESERVE

for service as set forth in the following

CITATION:

"For excellent service in the line of his profession as a member of the medical section of a beach party from 20 February to 23 February 1945, during the assault and capture of Iwo Jima. Although the beach was under enemy mortar and gunfire, he ably performed his duty in administering first aid and assisting in the evacuation of casualties. His skill and courage contributed to the saving of many lives. His conduct gives evidence of his great value to the naval service."

Commendation Ribbon authorized

R. A. SPRUANCE, Admiral, U.S. Navy.

Figure 19: Above: Commendation. Below: Two months before Iwo Jima, and happy in Hawaii, (left to right: Follett, Brinkman, Frieder, and Follett.

---

[26] USS Lowndes Recollections of Iwo Jima: Fred Brinkman: http://dobrinkman.net/lowndes/iwostories.htm

The discovery of the Iwo Jima photo and my dad's notes would become the first real history mystery for me to solve. Who took the picture? Exactly when was it taken? Could I verify it with other living crew members?

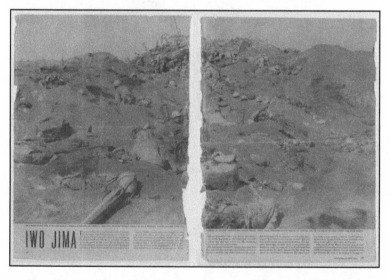

Figure 20: Old Magazine pages that were saved by Fred Brinkman

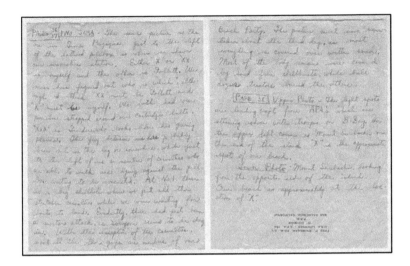

Figure 21: Fred Brinkman's notes about the Lowndes crewmen in the photo.

The photo and notes identified members of the Lowndes Beach Battalion at their evacuation station on Iwo Jima on D-Day+1. It didn't take much research to discover that the photo had been taken by none other than Joe Rosenthal just a few days before he would snap the most famous war photo ever; the flag-raising on Mount Suribachi. I contacted the Associated Press, and they sent me an 8X10 from the original negative. My mother and I were stunned and certain that my dad had correctly identified himself.

I sent a copy of my dad's notes to an address I found on the internet for Rosenthal, and he called me up and talked to me for about 45 minutes. He made it clear that he never usually responded to requests like this, but he was compelled this time when he saw my dad was a Navy Corpsman on the beach. Rosenthal knew the statistics. Iwo Jima was the bloodiest battle in Marine Corps history, with one in three men being casualties. But Navy Corpsmen on Yellow Beach at Iwo Jima? The casualty rate for that was five in six! During our talk, Rosenthal confirmed from his notes that the photo was taken at Yellow Beach, and he said it made perfect sense that this was an evacuation station.

I had also done some shadow measurements in the photo and determined the time was 3-4 p.m. The only sunny days during the first week of the invasion were on D-Day and D-Day+1, so I was pretty sure it had to be one of those days. Rosenthal checked his notes, and the photo was taken at 3:45

p.m. But his records showed it as being D-Day, not D-Day+1. The Lowndes group landed on D-Day+1. Rosenthal told me that many people over the years had seen themselves or a relative in his photos. "I'm sorry David, but it's very unlikely that that could be your father," he said.

I was very disappointed, but what else could I do? The only surviving Lowndes crewman that my dad had identified in the picture was Rhonal Shy. That's when I sent him a copy of the photo and notes, and we talked on the phone. Rhonal said the scene could have been their station, but he couldn't be sure because the memories had faded over the years. At that point, I set the photo aside and went on to do other research about the Lowndes.

Later, while preparing a presentation about the Lowndes for the local library, I had a fantastic revelation. The corpsmen from another ship that manned Yellow Beach on D-Day were completely wiped-out within a few hours of hitting the beach. The photo shows three corpsmen working the station. This could not have been true on D-Day at 3:45 p.m. There were no corpsmen at the station then. On D-Day+1, however, the Lowndes had lost five corpsmen and their doctor within a few hours of hitting the beach. At 3:45 p.m., this left the three corpsmen my dad had identified in the picture.

Adding to this was that my dad identified in his notes the three corpsmen in the grainy photo not by the faces but by the way they were wearing their medical bags. My dad had noticed that the corpsmen in the photo were wearing the bags in that exact fashion. Further examination of the hi-resolution version of the photo also shows a facial resemblance to a second corpsman. I could now conclude that Rosenthal's date was wrong. The picture was really taken on D-Day + 1, not D-Day.

USS Lowndes Beach Party
Invasion of Iwo Jima
Corpsmen: Fred Brinkman,
Jerome Frieder, and
Wesley Follett give plasma
to wounded Marine.
Photo by Joe Rosenthal (AP)

Figure 22: Original Rosenthal (AP) photo and enlarged area of Corpsmen. Fred Brinkman's notes identified himself as the corpsman on the left, then Frieder, and Follett (standing) on the right. Use by license with AP Images.

There are other facts in my dad's letter that have proved to be more accurate than other accounts. A Lowndes seaman named Morton was completely unaccounted for in the official history of the ship and not mentioned in modern-day accounts. The Navy was unable to determine what happened to Morton. My dad's letter clearly states that Morton, not a part of the beach party but a seaman on the ship, was killed on the beach, and we finally were able to prove this. This was another reason for me to have high confidence in my dad's notes about the Iwo Jima photo. Also challenging

Rosenthal's D-Day date on the picture is another observation in my dad's letter where he noted that the only reporter he saw was soon hit by an enemy mortar. He pointed out how the battle was just too hot for the action to be covered by the press on D-Day + 1. The conditions were much worse on D-Day.

> Fred Brinkman – 1945: I think it was impossible for any correspondent to get the straight dope as to what actually happened on Iwo. When a battle is hot, there aren't going to be any photographers or news correspondents to make some close shots or jot down some fresh news. People just simply don't do such things - not on Iwo. I recollect one exception. As a boatload of troops landed on our beach, some pressman dashed up on the beach with a portable typewriter and began clicking away. I don't know what happened to this poor chum, but a few minutes later a piece of this typewriter landed alongside of me. As far as photographers went, I didn't see any, except a couple of them who soon abandoned their cameras not long after they hit the beach. There were just too many other things to think about on Iwo.

The fate of Ellis Morton

Ellis R. Morton 1944

Figure 23: Photo of Ellis provided
by the Morton family.

As well as the Lowndes crewmen had documented their experience during and after the war, no doubt, there would be facts that would be lost. Tragically, one of them would be a fellow crewman who was killed at Iwo Jima but only listed as missing in action. This was a sad mystery to solve but very necessary.

Ellis Robert Morton Jr. was a Seaman 2nd Class on the Lowndes from Richland, Washington. Ellis was the oldest of 10 children from the Morton family. Born in December 1926, Ellis was one of the youngest on the Lowndes and turned 18 just two months before being killed on Iwo Jima. After the battle, he was officially listed as MIA, but months later that was updated to KIA. The official ship's log showed he was missing, with no other details. My father's Iwo Jima letter and his war log, however, said a sailor named Morton was killed on the beach. This was strange because Morton was not part of the ship's Beach Battalion. He should not have been on the beach at Iwo Jima.

I believe the best way to tell this mystery is through a letter I wrote to a man who I thought might be a surviving brother of Ellis:

8/23/06

Dear Mr. Morton,

My name is David Brinkman of the USS Lowndes (APA-154) Reunion group, and I am contacting you regarding Ellis Robert Morton, Jr. who gave his life for our country at Iwo Jima in 1945. My father (Fred Brinkman 1925-1997) was a WWII Navy Corpsman (PhM2c) in the Lowndes Beach Battalion that went ashore at Iwo Jima. For almost two years now, we have been searching for the family of Ellis. Records in the ship's log (which I just obtained a few years ago) only state that Ellis was missing in action, and other reunion crew members that I have talked to could not remember any details surrounding his disappearance. The name Morton seemed to ring a bell with me, and I went back to a 40-page uncensored letter that my dad had written shortly after the battle at Iwo Jima and discovered that my dad had recorded the real facts. He mentioned that they (the Lowndes) lost Norman Richards, Don Bowman, and a Seaman named Morton. Richards and Bowman were fellow corpsmen and close friends of my dad's. They were killed, and my dad recovered their dog-tags, but not Morton's dog-tag. In another sentence, he mentioned that one man was missing but this must have been another missing man that we found in the ship's log, and it turns out that he was picked up by another vessel and transferred. In a third sentence, my dad mentions 18 wounded men from the Lowndes. In short, he separated the casualties, and it was now clear that Ellis had been killed on Iwo Jima with the two corpsmen. Further searches using the Navy ID of Ellis (found in the Ship's log) led to the discovery of his name in a Hawaii memorial and a KIA memorial at the Tahoma National Cemetery.[27]

In our search for Ellis' family, we keep hitting dead ends. Just last week we held the group's 19th annual reunion in Seattle, and we visited the memorial to Ellis at the Tahoma National Cemetery. I hoped to invite some Morton family members to the reunion dinner last Saturday night at our hotel in Renton, WA, but my last-minute phone calls failed to find them, and the Tahoma Cemetery would only tell us that the memorial to Ellis was set up by a brother. They could not give us his name or contact information.

I was about to give up the search, but then when I was explaining the last failed attempts to the reunion crewmembers, a quiet member of the group (who had not attended a reunion in many years) raised his hand and said he knew Ellis and he knew what happened to him at Iwo Jima. We were all stunned. It turns out that this reunion member had slept in the bunk under Ellis on the ship.

I began to wonder if any of his shipmates had ever contacted Ellis' family. My dad remained in contact with the Richards and Bowman families all his life, but Mrs. Richards (Norman's mother who just recently died at the age of 104) told us that, until the reunions started in 1988, my dad was the only one that had contacted her family, so I fear that Ellis' family may not have been visited/contacted by a single shipmate, especially given that most of the crew was not aware that he was killed. I think most of them assumed he was wounded and returned on another ship.

[27] Tahoma National Cemetery: Ellis Robert Morton:
http://www.interment.net/data/us/wa/king/tahoma/tahoma_mopa.htm

You might wonder why my dad never mentioned the Seaman Morton after the war. The experience for my dad was horrific. Four days and three nights of non-stop lifesaving (others and himself), death, and gore. He never talked about it again after writing the letter, and I think he blocked it out until there were no more memories.

Through the years of the reunions, the group has done special tributes to Norman Richards and Don Bowman. The family members of these boys have participated in some of the reunions. Now that we know the fate of Ellis Morton, we see that the story of the Lowndes is not complete. We have no pictures of Ellis. No stories of what kind of young man he was, and we know no one in his family. Families are a big part of the reunions, and everyone is invited. My wife, seven-year-old son, and I attend each reunion. My dad hosted the reunion in Myrtle Beach, South Carolina in 1996 just before being diagnosed with the cancer that would take him six months later. My mom attended the next reunion, but poor health kept her from the next few, and she joined my dad in 2002. Before she died, she encouraged me in the building of a Lowndes Internet website, which has become one of the best ship sites with hundreds of pictures and videos. Thousands of pages of documents, recollections, letters, and diaries. All of them are of the Lowndes and her crew. It's a continuing labor of love that is made available to everyone for free and is a tribute to the Lowndes men, their wives, and that whole great generation.

Two years ago, Ensign Stuart Hyde of the Lowndes discovered the website and he embarked on an effort to write the story of the Lowndes. Two years later he has finished chapters on the Lowndes at Iwo Jima and Okinawa. It was Stuart that pointed out the fact that Ellis Morton was listed as missing in the deck log which I have on the website. Dr. Hyde is a writer and taught at San Francisco State University for 45 years. His work is not for profit, but it is excellent, and he wants to get the story straight and make sure that Ellis' courage and sacrifice is documented.

I don't want to keep rambling on (which I could do because I've learned so much about these Lowndes guys and it's great stuff to talk about), but I was just hoping that we could finally learn more about Ellis and include him in Stuart's writings and on the memorial page on the Lowndes website. I have included a copy of the Memorial page, so you can see the kind of information we include about the other two young men that were killed at Iwo Jima. I have also included some other ship documents and a page from my dad's letter. I have also included the newspaper articles from the 1960s about what I think are some of your family members. This is what led me to you.

I hope you are related to Ellis and, if you are, please let us welcome you to the Lowndes reunion family. We hope this is the beginning of a friendship, and of discovery.

As I said before, it would be great if we could get some stories about Ellis and a copy of his picture for our Memorial. Please call me if you would like to talk about Ellis or the Reunion group. Thank you and God Bless.

David Brinkman

As I had hoped, the letter did fall into the hands of Ellis' last surviving two brothers and sister. They informed me that all of Ellis' seven brothers honored their fallen brother by serving in the Korean and Vietnam wars. As I had feared, the Morton family never heard a word from a shipmate of Ellis until they received my letter over 60 years later. They had assumed, since Ellis was a Seaman (and not in the Beach Battalion), that he was killed on board the ship, maybe by a kamikaze attack. I informed them that not a single Lowndes crewman was killed on board the ship. I then relayed the story from that "quiet" Lowndes crewman who had recently revealed the fate of Ellis.

During those intense first four days of the battle of Iwo Jima, this sailor and Ellis volunteered to help deliver much-needed supplies to the Beach Battalion at Yellow Beach. When their landing boat hit the beach, Ellis picked up a spare carbine rifle and turned to his friend and said, "I'm going to get me a Jap!" His shocked friend watched as Ellis ran up the steep black sand mound that the Japanese had made to slow an assault. When Ellis reached the top and raised his gun to fire, he was immediately gunned down by enemy fire.

Another previously unnoticed account of Lowndes crewman Chuck Munson backed up this account. He said that while on the beach they observed an unknown Lowndes crewman running out of a boat in the direction that only attacking Marines would follow. They tried to stop him but could not.

After 61 years, the Morton family finally learned what happened to Ellis. They couldn't provide much personal information on Ellis, but they did share his photograph, which was added to the Lowndes memorial page. My historical research had taken a very different turn on this mystery. Although sad, it was probably the most significant accomplishment of the countless hours I would spend on the WWII work.

Lowndes Boat #21

The Lowndes work sparked lots of little interesting side projects. I spent many hours transcribing and indexing the entire Lowndes ship's deck log. This was a 24-hour recording of ship and crew movements as well as any unusual activity. The index is available in chronological order and by crewman names, which is an easy way to see what interesting things your favorite crewman did on the ship. It can be humorous, especially in the case of the boys who partied hard on shore leave and got themselves into trouble. Penalties for inappropriate behavior were also recorded in the deck log, including a few cases in which crewmen were placed in the brig with only bread and water for several days. I had a lot of fun with this side project.

Figure 24: Above: Marine Corps photo (USMC 109604) of broached Lowndes LCVP #21. Below: Another USMC photo (also with the USS LSM-202 in the background) probably also shows the abandon boat #21.

For the Lowndes, I will close with a footnote to what might be the most famous picture related to the Lowndes. In 2005-2006, the production team of the movie "Flags of Our Fathers" found the Lowndes website. The film was based on the book by the same title by James Bradley, whose father was a Navy Corpsman who went in with the Marines at Iwo Jima. Of course, I read the book and was very excited when the movie production team contacted me for some consulting and permissions questions around the Lowndes web content. Like all my history work, I was not paid for this, but I got something more important: A signed movie poster from Director

Clint Eastwood to my son. And, even cooler, the movie's ending included a photo of Lowndes Boat #21 broached at Iwo Jima.[28]

Recorded in the Lowndes' "Recollections of Iwo Jima" by the late crewmen Clifford Schaffer, whom my family and I came to know well at the reunions, is the story behind the photo. Coincidentally, Boat #21 was also the boat that delivered Ellis Morton to his fate on Iwo Jima:

> My Iwo Jima Memories: The morning of the attack, we were up before dawn. Ships and planes were shelling the island, all I saw was the outline of the island and smoke. I was the engineer on boat No. 21 on No. 4 hatch. We went over the side loaded with Marines and circled around waiting for orders to attack. When I saw all the smoke and heard the explosions, I thought nobody would be left alive on the island. (Boy was I wrong.) When we got the signal to attack, all the boats lined up and headed for the beach. When we hit the beach, I dropped the ramp and the Marines disembarked with lots of shelling around us. We were broached, and the ramp wouldn't go up. Ensign Chuck Munson was on my boat. Instead of being sitting ducks for the Jap mortars we abandoned the boat and got separated. At this point, I was real scared. I remember wishing I was back in Limeport. Then I crawled up on the beach next to a Marine and said to him "This is real rough." He didn't answer me. I looked at him, and he had been shot in the head. Then I saw a jeep bogged down in the sand nearby. I crawled to the side and used it for shelter. That was a terrifying night. The next day I saw a boat from the Lowndes, think it was No. 12. I got on and returned to the ship. I was then assigned to another boat. That night we were out and the "R" boat with an officer aboard ordered us to take our boat and scout the south end of the island and look for a disabled boat which we could not find. A ship nearby fired several shells over us into Mount Suribachi. The noise was the loudest thing I ever heard. Later we went back to look for the Lowndes but could not find it. Another boat informed us that it might have gone out for night retirement to avoid an attack. We were told there was a supply ship where we could get fuel for our landing craft. We found the ship, and they threw down two lines and we tied up. I filled both tanks. They asked us to come aboard for a hot meal. We climbed up the

---

[28] Photo # USMC 109604: Beach scene on Iwo Jima, 20 February, 1945

lines and had a hot meal and an apple. It was a storage apple, but I had not had an apple for such a long time and it sure was a treat. The next day we located the Lowndes and loaded on supplies to take to the beach. On our return trip, we took on wounded troops and brought them back to the Lowndes. It was an experience I will never forget. When I saw the American Flag on Mount Suribachi, it lifted my spirits.

The Bayfield Archives

During work on the USS Lowndes project, I thought it might be possible to locate some WWII film footage of the Lowndes in the vast holdings of the National Archives. A partial electronic index had been recently created at archives.com, and this became my search portal. I made no direct finds on the Lowndes, but I came across a collection of many films shot by a couple of photographers on the USS Bayfield (APA-33). The Bayfield was a Coast Guard ship and did not have any combat photography restrictions like the Navy ships. I remembered seeing references to the Bayfield in the Lowndes deck log. The Lowndes traveled with the Bayfield on a couple of occasions and was next to the Bayfield throughout the Iwo Jima invasion. Could some of these films contain footage of the Lowndes? Some of the film descriptions looked very promising.

In requesting permission to access the films, I learned that because no intermediate copies of the films existed most of this footage had never been viewed since the end of WWII. I took a chance and spent several thousand dollars to have the footage copied and transferred to digital video. The results were far better than I expected. Some of the 35mm black-and-white footage had the quality of broadcast film media of today. Some of the Iwo Jima footage was in color. The footage covered the Bayfield from pre-D-Day exercises in Scotland to the actual landing footage at the D-Day invasion at Normandy. More footage showed incredible scenes of the invasion of Iwo Jima. Still, more footage followed the Bayfield through operations in the Korean and Vietnam wars.

During volunteer work that I did to save the last APA ship of WWII, the USS Gage[29], I learned that a historical study had been done on the WWII ships and that the Bayfield was considered the most historic of all the

[29] The Last APA: USS Gage: https://en.wikipedia.org/wiki/USS_Gage_(APA-168)

Amphibious type ships. The Naval Historical Center logs the following information on the Bayfield:

> USS Bayfield, the first of a class of 16,100-ton attack transports, was built at San Francisco, California. The Bayfield was completed and commissioned in November 1943, with a U.S. Coast Guard crew, and sailed for the British Isles. The following three months were spent preparing for the invasion of France. Her conversion had fitted her with special command facilities, and during the June 1944 Normandy Operation, she was flagship for the "Utah" Beach landings. Moving to the Mediterranean in July, a month later Bayfield participated in the invasion of southern France. The transport returned to the U.S. for overhaul in September 1944.
>
> The Bayfield went to the Pacific in November and spent the next two months in amphibious training in Hawaiian waters. In February 1945 she landed Marines on Iwo Jima and, at the beginning of April, took part in the Okinawa invasion with a force that simulated landing operations to confuse the island's Japanese defenders. The Bayfield was employed for the rest of the Pacific war on logistics functions. During the last four months of 1945 and in early 1946 she supported the occupation of Japan and Korea, as well as bringing war veterans home as part of Operation "Magic Carpet."
>
> In June and July 1946, the Bayfield was present for the atomic bomb tests at Bikini, in the Marshall Islands. She remained active in the Pacific until nearly the end of the decade, then went to the Atlantic. However, in mid-1950 the Korean War brought her back to the Far East, where she operated off the embattled peninsula until May 1951. She made a voyage to and from Japan in September 1951 and deployed again to Korea during 1952. Bayfield continued to cruise regularly to the western Pacific during the rest of the 1950s and nearly through the 1960s. Her involvement with events in southeast Asia began with participation in Operation "Passage to Freedom" in August and September 1954, resuming in 1967 when she served as a floating barracks at Danang, South Vietnam, carried Marines to and from the combat zone and took part in landing operations.

This short bio on the Bayfield leaves no doubt this ship, and her mission were historic, but yet no detailed history of her had ever been written. Telling the Bayfield's story through the footage seemed to be the proper thing to do.

After some investigation, I located Joe Williams, the past president of the Bayfield Association, in York, South Carolina. Joe and his wife Faye became immediate friends with my family. Joe and Faye were so energetic and young at heart it was difficult to believe they were old enough to be from the Greatest Generation.

Joe was quite a character. He, my wife, and I were all guitar players. Joe was a welder and musician on the Bayfield during WWII. He carried his guitar with him on the ship through the invasions of Normandy and Iwo Jima. After the war, he would perform for many years with a band, The Carolina Hillbillies.

Figure 25: 1944: Joe Williams (left) playing guitar in the Bayfield band and Joe (right) welding repairs on the ship. Credit USCG.

After marrying Faye, Joe started a stereo sound business that provided the public-address systems for NASCAR tracks. He and Faye would later become very successful in real estate. Through the years, Joe also took parts in any local movie productions that popped up. Among them were "The Color Purple" and "The Last American Hero."

For the WWII film project, Joe gave direction on what archive footage should be included in our video production. I edited the footage, and we produced a two-volume video collection of the Bayfield Archives. We kept the price low, $10, with the idea we would just try to break even.

Figure 26: Joe Williams and David Brinkman and their
Bayfield Archives film project.

Almost 500 copies of the DVD/VHS were produced and sent to members and friends of the Bayfield reunion group[30]. More than a hundred also were sold through the USS Lowndes website. I received more than 200 letters from the Bayfield WWII crew members and families thrilled to learn about and see this footage that most of them never knew existed. Among the most touching letters was one from the wife of a crewman who had died a year earlier. In a segment of the best film shot, a close up of her husband, 18 years old then, was shown on the ship's deck as he was struggling to light a cigarette. She said they did not have a single picture of him from the war or his youth. His only child was now 18 years old, and she was seeing her dad again but now at the same age as herself. Sadly, the wife said that in all the pictures they have of him, and now this footage, he was always holding or

---

[30] Both volumes of The Bayfield Archives have now been made available on youtube.com at:
https://www.youtube.com/watch?v=6xWt7GWX2iA and
https://www.youtube.com/watch?v=Fb-jrVy0S6Q

reaching for a cigarette. He died of lung cancer just about the time I found these films.

Figure 27: Billy Muse (lighting cigarette), Marvin Perrett to the right of Muse. Credit USCG and National Archives.

Joe was not the only colorful character on the Bayfield. A boyhood baseball friend of my dad, Yogi Berra, was a rocket boat pilot on the Bayfield. Boy, how I wished my dad could have been around to learn this.

I would soon have the pleasure of meeting another famous Bayfield sailor. Marvin J. Perrett[31] was a Coxswain on the Bayfield. He drove one of the landing boats -- a Higgins boat, also called an LCVP -- that took the troops from the large Attack Transport ship to the shore. When they hit the beach, a ramp would drop open to allow the men and equipment to be removed. Marvin's job was as dangerous as those being dropped off. The boats were easy targets, and they were prone to get broached on the beaches. Marvin would repeat this work in the invasions of Normandy, southern France, and Iwo Jima, where his boat was hit and sunk.

Marvin was a history buff, and after the war, he took on the mission to educate the public on the role he and the Bayfield played in WWII. He was probably the best spokesperson the USCG ever had. If you watched any of the 60th D-Day Anniversary specials on TV, you saw Marvin. He appeared on almost every network. Joe and Faye Williams were very close friends with Marvin, but it would be another discovery of mine that would bring Marvin and me together.

---

[31] Veterans History Project – Library of Congress – Marvin J. Perrett:
http://memory.loc.gov/diglib/vhp/story/loc.natlib.afc2001001.07902/

The APA ships of WWII carried 20 to 28 LCVP landing boats. Marvin drove boat #21. While going through some of those untouched films in the National Archives, I found incredible footage of a practice run of three LCVP boats of the Bayfield just before the Normandy invasion in 1944. The cameraman on one boat was focused on the boat next to his, which happened to be boat #21. Joe Williams confirmed that it was Marvin at the wheel of the boat. More footage from the deck of the ship, just before the Iwo Jima invasion in 1945, showed Marvin. Like many of the Bayfield crewmen, Marvin was unaware of this footage, and he also did not have a single WWII photograph of himself on the ship or in his boat. Suddenly, we had almost two minutes of high-quality film of both.

I made a special VHS tape with the footage and mailed it to Marvin. He happened to receive it while being interviewed by Voice of America. He stopped the interview and had the news team view the footage with him. While still holding the interview, he called me and told me that I was his hero. I was taken aback by that one, but it would prove to be a great motivation as I continued working on both the Bayfield and the Lowndes projects.

Figure 28: Marvin Perrett driving his Bayfield boat #21 in training before the Normandy invasion. Credit USCG and National Archives.

Marvin worked almost nonstop in his final years in his mission to educate the public on WWII and promote the USCG. He spent his last few days giving rides to the public on a replica of his Bayfield boat #21. On the evening of his last ride, on May 6, 2007, Marvin went home and reclined on his sofa. When he was a few minutes late for another assignment the next morning, the USCG sent people to check on him. They found Marvin had died peacefully in his sleep.

Figure 29: Marvin J. Perrett in 1943 (top right) and just days before his death in 2007. Credit USCG.

Another significant story to surface from this project was the discovery of the last known images of Admiral Donald Moon. Just before the D-Day invasion in France, under the command of Admiral Moon, the United States and Great Britain held landing exercises off an English beach town (Slapton Sands in Devon) that had been vacated for reasons of secrecy. This was called "Operation Tiger." The results were disastrous. Several hundred American troops were killed in landing exercises because of a miscommunication with the English, who fired live ammunition into the exercise area. Later, unknown to the Allies, the Germans found out about the event and sent some torpedo boats into the area. Because of another miscommunication, the English pulled out their ships, leaving several fully manned American LSTs unprotected. The German boats moved in and sank the LSTs. As many as 1,000 Americans drowned. Many of them had improperly attached life preservers, and many of them could not swim.

All the survivors in this operation were told that they could never talk about these events. In Joe's words in The State Newspaper "We were told: You will not write home about it, you will not talk about it, and we will escort you to prison if you do." Some years back, however, the BBC learned of this and several men came forward to tell the story on television. Most of the Bayfield crew would still not talk about it, but Joe was haunted by the cries and moans of the drowning men. Not included, however, in his State Newspaper article was a profound revelation that Joe gave to me. He told me that it was the duty of the Bayfield men to bury all the hundreds of dead men in a mass and unmarked grave.[32] I can't help but feel, like in the case of my dad's Iwo Jima letter, that a responsibility was given to me to make this information known.

Admiral Moon apparently felt responsible for this great loss of life. Not long after Operation Tiger, Moon was on board the Bayfield, which was a lead troop ship at Normandy. Some of the great untouched footage I found shows Moon inspecting the Normandy beach just after the invasion. His large entourage seemed upbeat, but you can tell Moon was a broken man. Not long after this, while in his cabin on the Bayfield, Moon became the highest-ranking American Officer to take his own life during a war. Moon left behind four children under the age of ten.

During the final editing of the film, I was contacted by one of Moon's daughters, who was planning a 60th reunion of his death in Washington D.C. I sent her a copy of the footage of her dad, and she used it in the ceremony. These are the last images the children have of a father they were so proud of.

---

[32] Clover-area WWII vet remembers historic landings, loss. The State Newspaper, November 10, 2013: http://www.thestate.com/news/local/military/article13828679.html

Figure 30: Admiral Donald Moon just after D-Day at Normandy, shortly before his death. Credit USCG and National Archives.

Sadly, the United States and England have never made any attempt to locate and memorialize the site where the hundreds of Americans, lost in Operation Tiger, were buried in a mass grave. Locals have testified to witnessing the burial of these men on a nearby farm, but action was never taken. Today, archaeologists could verify the mass grave in a matter of a few hours. Instead, the only monument to the Operation Tiger exercise is a stone pillar placed by the United States Army giving thanks to the residents who allowed their town and beach to be used in the military exercise. The monument has been vandalized over the years, and the American flag has been removed. Is this the way to honor those who made the ultimate sacrifice?

Both CNN and Voice of America have used footage of the Bayfield Archives in specials done for the 60th Anniversary of D-Day.

As I look back on all this WWII research, I can see how it took me from nothing to the point of having many of the necessary skills to solve history mysteries. More importantly, it gave me confidence to hang tough when a dead end is reached and to expect there may be a good reason behind the search for the truth. In moments of struggle, something good will come along to help. For these WWII projects, that goodness and faith came through my friends of the Greatest Generation. Most of these beautiful people have now left us, but they will always live in our hearts. My old Bayfield friend Joe Williams and his wife Faye recently passed away within a few months of each other. As Joe would always say: "If we don't see each other here again, we'll see you on the top-side one day."

Figure 31: The Bayfield ship under construction. Photo
rights purchased from the AP.

At the end of the movie "Saving Private Ryan," Captain John Miller (played by Tom Hanks) is mortally wounded. His mission to find and save Private James Ryan (played by Matt Damon) had cost his team many lives. In his last breath, Miller tells Ryan, "James...earn this. Earn it." The movie moves forward to over 50 years later. James Ryan is standing over the grave of Captain Miller, remembering his last words. In tears, Ryan says to his wife, "Tell me I've led a great life. Tell me I'm a good man."

These WWII survivors were not only worthy of the lives sacrificed, but their continued lives would also earn them the title "The Greatest Generation".

Chapter 6 – A Lot of History on the River

The fall of 2004 brought some new excitement to our family. Our son Jeremy had just started K5 kindergarten at St. Peter's Catholic School in downtown Columbia. At five years old, Jeremy was already a seasoned sci-fi moviegoer, and on Labor Day 2004, we took him to see the new Alien vs. Predator movie. After the movie, Odess and I got on the topic of where we could move in the Columbia area that would be an easy and quick trip between home and Jeremy's school. I thought about the Skyland neighborhood on the Broad River just northwest of Columbia.

I had never really explored that area except for a couple of high school adventures to the infamous Green Hole, a pre-Civil War quarry that was accidentally flooded when the workers broke into an underground stream. There were many tales of the Green Hole and the many items and bodies rumored to have found their way to its cold, deep bottom. The Green Hole would be a future history project, but on this Labor Day, my attention turned to figuring out if the Skyland neighborhood had any homes for sale.

As we drove down Skyland Drive, I wondered if one of the side roads led to homes on the Broad River. We decided to take a turn down a street called Castle Road, which was a circle. About halfway around, to our surprise, there were two adjacent lots for sale. We stopped the car and got out. Because of the thick growth, we couldn't see the river, but we thought we heard flowing water. A small path maintained between the two lots took us down a steep slope. I wondered if the slope was too steep for a house and, if not, would the expenses involved in building a house on it be too much for us.

As we finally made it to the bottom of the lot and out of the brush and trees, we were overwhelmed by the untouched beauty of the river. It was difficult to believe we were less than two miles from downtown Columbia. It seemed too good to be true. All the homes in the neighborhood were at least 40 years old, and only a few were built on the river. What was wrong with these lots? Was there something that made it impossible to build here?

Figure 32: Our first visit to the "Lot of History."

Later that day, I learned the price was $60,000 on the larger lot and $100,000 on the other. For 7/10 of an acre of riverfront property, $60,000 seemed like a reasonable price. Little did I know that in six months riverfront property in Columbia would go through the ceiling, with lots going for as much as $300,000 for 1/10 of an acre.

For now, the main problems were several questions that had to be answered. Why had these lots been on the market for so long? Would there be problems getting the necessary permits to build? The steep slope would require a basement excavation, and what would happen if we ran into the granite abundant in the area? Would the house be in the floodplain? Would we be able to find and afford a builder who could handle this job? There were so many questions to answer. I thought it would take months to get the answers. The property had been on the market for some time without a sale, so I really wasn't worried about someone else taking it.

We returned to the lot the next day, and as I worked down the path under a beautiful canopy, my eye caught something through the thick brush. As I pulled back some branches and vines, I revealed an odd opened area that seemed unnatural compared to the nearby terrain. A strange feeling came over me, and I immediately felt something human had been here and altered that place, maybe many years ago. Being near the river, I thought perhaps it was something Native American. From that point on, the feeling became a curiosity and grew on me. At this point, there was no question about which lot we would buy. At $60,000, it was the best price, and it held a mysterious feature just waiting to be explored.

After a few weeks, the only progress made on the unanswered questions was to get the name of a builder who had constructed homes with basements, but none of those homes were on a steep lot like this one. Again, I was not too concerned and thought we had plenty of time. But then, one night at about 3 a.m., I woke up in a cold sweat, overwhelmed with an urgency to buy the lot. I could not get back to sleep; I had to get the lot now. I called the real estate agent early that morning and told her I wanted to sign a contract and did so within the hour. Later that day, I wondered what came over me to do something that, just hours later, would seem so irrational?

As the days passed waiting for the final closing to occur, I met the man who would be our builder. He answered my questions and assured me that a house could be built on the lot.

At the lot closing, I finally met the seller. I was curious about why he had chosen to sell the lot. I'm not sure if he was serious, but he said he had decided to become a monk and was getting rid of all his possessions.

As we walked away after all the papers were signed, the real estate agent approached me. She said she was compelled to tell me how this was the strangest sale of her career. In almost a year, we were the first people to contact her about the property, even though it was a beautiful lot at a great price. Then came a moment of chills down the spine. She said the morning I woke her up to sign the contract for the lot, minutes after I completed that contract, a prominent Columbia businessman came in and offered cash (at full price) for the lot. I had not offered full price for the lot, and my contract was not legally binding until the seller signed it. The agent said she called the seller to give him the great news. The seller instructed her to sell the lot to me. She told him that he didn't understand, that the second offer was the full price. The seller said to her that he understood perfectly and told her to sell the lot to me at the lower price. I walked away from our closing with the feeling that maybe something supernatural was behind us getting that lot.

The next day, our builder had his clearing and excavation team on site to begin the job. Within a few hours, the workers came running up from the edge of that "mysterious" area at the bottom of the lot. Their equipment had ripped away English ivy, exposing a man-made stone structure. After all the excitement died down, a neighborhood teenage boy, without any knowledge of our find, happened to pass by. He approached me and pointed down to the area of the stone structure. He said a few years ago he found a Civil War era rifle in those rocks.

So began the local history discoveries. The idea that our stone structure was possibly the lost Broad River Confederate Bridge site grew as I started researching the area's old river crossings. A few months later, in February of 2015, Joey Holleman of The State newspaper wrote a story about the anniversary of the burning of Columbia. He included an 1865 illustration showing Union Army General Sherman's men crossing the Broad River on a pontoon bridge constructed next to the burned bridge. I quickly noticed the similarity of the terrain in the illustration and the terrain around our stone structure. I contacted Joey, and he would write stories about this and my other discoveries to come. In an eight-year period, seven of these stories would appear on the front page of South Carolina's largest newspaper.[33]

I felt sad in a way that my WWII work with the USS Lowndes (APA 154) might become second fiddle to this. But a few days after the lot excavation, the city informed me the 170 Castle Road address on our lot was a mistake. The correct address was 154 Castle Road. Old 154 (USS Lowndes APA-154) was still with me, and my dad's remaining shipmates also felt something from above was at work here. The street name would take another ten years to figure out, but that's in another chapter.

After clearing and excavating the lot, it was time to start building the house. Our builder had been in dire need of a job. In a previous partnership, he was left with a large debt and could not get a construction loan to build again. He saw our project, where I was getting the construction loan, as a way to get money up front to purchase his own lot and build a second house at the same time as our house's construction. Many people would say what I did was insane. I gave, upfront, the entire builder's fee and prepayment for some of the work yet to be done, about $50,000. However, it wasn't in my opinion that big of a risk. This man was a U.S. Marine. He had also been

---

[33] Sherman's Crossing? By Joey Holleman, The State Newspaper: http://historysoft.com/news/newspaper_2007.htm

doing volunteer construction work for his church in Columbia and in distant mission locations. If you can't trust someone like that, who can you trust?

In the end, our builder did a lot more work than planned. His builder's fee, paid up front, was only 7% for the project, and other builders would have charged 25%. We saved money, and he could build his other house in parallel. The profit he made between the two projects eliminated his debt, and he would go on to be a very successful builder.

In hindsight, that miracle with the real estate agent was pivotal in everything to come in this book. A low-priced, beautiful riverfront lot on the market for almost a year, and within 30 minutes, two buyers showed up to sign contracts. Against his real estate agent's advice, the seller chose to go with me and the lower price. Had things gone the way they should have, I'm sure my historian days would have quickly faded away with the USS Lowndes project.

Chapter 7 – A Story of Broad Crossings

After the discovery of the apparent bridge abutment, I focused on educating myself about the basic local history. This meant finding the best sources, including the South Carolina Department of Archives and History, the University of South Carolina libraries and the local public library. Internet search engines were the quick-and-dirty start. My laser focus was on the lost Confederate Bridge site and Sherman's Union Army pontoon bridge crossing as shown in the 1865 Harper's Weekly illustration by William Waud[34]. Multiple period maps of the river and a historical marker, however, seemed to contradict themselves. It was clear the research would require learning about all the area river crossings -- fords, ferries, and bridges.

Fortunately, the South Carolina General Assembly required a chartering process for ferries and bridges. Luckily, all these records had been moved out of Columbia before the burning of the city in 1865, so I had access to all of them at the state archives. It wasn't easy, however, as the cursive handwritings were challenging to read, and the microfilm copies were often very poor. The tedious and painstaking process would go on for several years.

One thing I learned early on with historical research is that you need to log and file every interesting detail you come across. At the time, these may seem insignificant and not related to the task at hand, but you will likely come back around to them. Using information from the archives, the U.S. Geological Survey, and South Carolina Institute of Archaeology and Anthropology, I built a database of the hundreds of river crossings through history in South Carolina. In the short term, I focused on the lower Broad River around Columbia, and I called the project Broad Crossings.

---

[34] William Waud: https://en.wikipedia.org/wiki/William_Waud

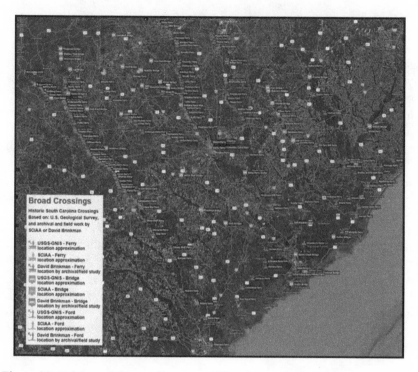

Figure 33: Brinkman's interactive map of historic South Carolina river crossings.

Although I was continually frustrated at solving the Confederate Bridge site, a fascinating story about the earlier period on the river and development of the new capital city of Columbia arose from the old General Assembly documents. An interesting and involved court case from the early 1800s, which involved two of the primary ferry crossings, provided further details almost impossible to obtain from other sources.

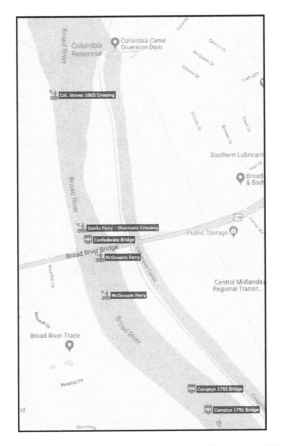

Figure 34: River crossings near today's Columbia, SC.

It would take several years to turn all the archival pieces into the story of life as it was on the Broad River in our young country. In fact, the story begins with the American Revolution and the Frenchman who built the first bridges over the Broad River.

The military portion of the American Revolution began in 1775. The French were still reeling from their loss to the British in the French and Indian War. For revenge, they would support any effort to weaken the British in the American Revolution. In 1778, 28-year-old Frenchman John Compty, like hundreds of his countrymen, came to America to be a soldier of fortune.

Compty befriended Charles-Francois Sevelinges, the Marquis de Bretigny and a captain in the French Army, who was also a soldier of fortune. Bretigny sent petitions to Benjamin Franklin, George Washington, and the Continental Congress offering the services of the French soldiers. Frustrated by the lack of response from these men and Congress, he befriended South Carolina's John Laurens and was able to build his regiment under the government of South Carolina. In April of 1779, a letter from Compty shows Compty's engagement in the same effort with Bretigny.

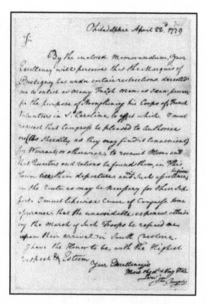

Figure 35: Compty's letter requesting he be allowed to organize Frenchmen in South Carolina. Historic letter: Public Domain.

Compty originally came to Philadelphia, where he built a home in 1779. While waiting on his South Carolina regiment to develop, Compty would team with Joseph Clunn, a well-known Revolutionary War hero and the first postmaster of Bucks County, Pennsylvania, to purchase a Pennsylvania sloop called Two Friends. In 1995, Patricia Clunn Jones published her history "Stories of the Ancestors," which documents details of the Two Friends. The sloop had two guns and a crew of 12. Clunn and Compty posted a $20,000 bond on the sloop.[35]

Their mission was spelled out in a letter written by Clunn, stating "the officers and crew thereof, by force of arms to attack, subdue, seize and take all ships and other vessels, goods, wares and merchandizes, belonging to the Crown of Great-Britain." Compty and the sloop made trips to Charles Town until the war reached a critical stage in 1780.

---

[35] Stories of the ancestors: Clunn, Horan, Robinson, and Mackintosh families of New Jersey and Pennsylvania Paperback – 1995 by Patricia Clunn Jones

Figure 36: 1913 photo of the Brig Niagara, which had just been raised and restored after being sunk for almost 100 years. The Brig Niagara was a Revolutionary War Pennsylvania Sloop like the one John Compty owned in 1780.
Historic photo: Public Domain.

Some historians believe that, following the American Civil War, there was an effort to downplay the critical role of South Carolina in the American Revolution. One only has to look at the battle map of the Revolution to see that the war was turned around and won in South Carolina.

The selection of the Carolinas by Bretigny and Compty put them in the middle of the action, although no archival details have been found on Compty's role between 1780 and 1783. After the war, Compty in 1783 purchased land north of Granby, South Carolina, where he built a house on the Congaree River and married Elizabeth Rugborck. Compty's selection of this location might have had something to do with brothers Richard and Wade Hampton, who lived in this area and possibly fought alongside Compty in the war.

For the first few years in his new South Carolina home, Compty did his shopping at the Congarees store in Granby, about two miles south of his home on the other side of the Congaree River. Granby was located in what currently is the city of Cayce. A few years ago, Leo Redmond, director of today's Cayce Historical Museum, was happily surprised when a local resident brought in the account book of the Congarees store from 1784 to

1788[36]. Leo purchased the priceless piece of history. The book shows us John Compty's purchases, many of them items for his wife. By far, the primary customers were Richard and Wade Hampton. Not far behind were brothers James and Thomas Taylor, who owned the high ground on the other side of the river near Compty's home.

This brings us to a significant historic moment in South Carolina. The state's population had grown much since the first push of Europeans into the backcountry in the early 1700s. The trip to Charleston, then the capital, was a long and hard one for many of the residents of the state's interior. The logical solution was to move the capital to a central location. If you look at my map of historic South Carolina crossings (Figure 33), Friday's Ferry is dead center. The lawmakers of 1786 saw the same thing. Friday's Ferry was in the town of Granby. However, the new General Assembly had concerns about flooding and public health in Granby. The link between mosquitoes and Yellow Fever hadn't been discovered yet, but people recognized the connection between poor health and low-lying areas like Granby.

Rumors began to circulate that a new city might be created on the high ground just north of Granby on the other side of the Congaree River. Legend has it that[37] Thomas Taylor and Wade Hampton discussed this possibility over a beer at the tavern in Granby owned by Timothy Rives (my first cousin, seven times removed; see Chapter 16 for more on that). They planned to purchase all the land in the expected area so they could profit from a sale to the state if the area was selected for the new capital. Timothy Rives was not interested in becoming rich, and he happily settled for a lot with a Tavern and Inn that would be across the street from the new State House. Thomas Taylor, Rives' brother-in-law, promised Rives he would give him that land and build a tavern and inn for him.

With properties sold and purchased by the Hamptons and Taylors, the investment paid off, as the General Assembly approved the location and the purchase of 2,471 acres of land. About half of that area was owned by the Hamptons, Taylors, and John Compty. The new city would be known as Columbia.

---

[36] Congarees Store Account Book: Cayce Historical Museum and University of South Carolina: http://library.sc.edu/digital/collections/congaree.html
[37] Forest Acres by Warner Montgomery, Ph.D.

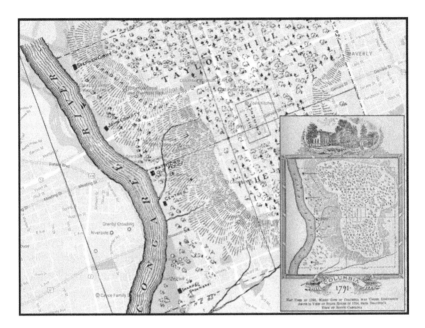

Figure 37: The first plan for the City of Columbia showing Compty's property. The larger image shows an overlay of this old map onto today's map.

As Columbia began developing, Wade Hampton realized the importance of being able to move people in and out of the new city. By water, a channel already was maintained through the Congaree, Santee, and Cooper rivers that connected Charleston and Granby. The two miles between Granby and Columbia, however, were a problem because of the fall line, which occurs between the foothills of the Appalachian Mountains and the Coastal Plain. In the Congaree River, the fall line creates an area of a rocky river about four miles wide. It cannot be traveled by boat. Supplies had to be unloaded in Granby and moved overland to Columbia.

The more significant problem was for people traveling to Columbia from the west. They needed to cross the Congaree River, which was over 800 feet wide at Columbia and 500 feet wide at Granby. Ferries existed at these locations, but they could not be operated for several days after a heavy rain. For Hampton, the obvious solution was a bridge at Granby, where the Congaree river is narrower. Back in those days, the government did not build bridges or run ferries. It was up to private citizens to build these and pay for them with tolls.

The Hampton brothers had recently purchased Friday's Ferry from the Friday family. Changing a ferry charter to a bridge charter would be relatively easy to do. In 1790, the General Assembly approved the building of a bridge by Wade Hampton, but they would not allow the bridge tolls to be higher than the ferry tolls. Hampton accepted that he would have to shoulder the burden of the extra capital expenses of a bridge compared to a ferry.

John Compty kept a close eye on his friend Wade Hampton and began to consider building his own bridge. Compty owned and operated a ferry on the Broad River about one mile north of the new Columbia. The Broad River moves north to south and joins the Saluda River, which runs west to east, at Columbia to form the Congaree River, which then runs north to south. The Saluda River blocked travelers from the northwest from going down to Hampton's new bridge, making Compty's crossing convenient for them. Within a few months of Hampton's bridge construction, Compty got his approval from the General Assembly in 1791 and started to build the first bridge across the Broad River.

Compty and Hampton were building these bridges, but they were only paying for the operation and overseeing it. African-American slaves were doing the back-breaking work. The General Assembly required that all area landowners donate the use of their slaves toward these projects. Also, the owners of the lands leading to the crossings had to build and maintain the roads to the crossings.

By the fall of 1790, activity was bustling in the new city of Columbia. The State House and Rives Tavern and Inn were completed in time for the first legislative session. The residents were excited about President George Washington's visit, scheduled for the spring of 1791. The General Assembly made a special provision in Hampton's bridge charter that allowed for free passage of the President, but Hampton's bridge was not finished in time. Washington had to take the ferry in Granby to cross the Congaree River.

After passing through Granby and Columbia, President Washington noted that Columbia was rather thin and not as developed as Granby. The President may have also been a little biased, as he was aware of the Revolutionary War heroics that occurred at Granby. Adding to this may have been the apparent population advantage Granby had over Columbia, but that was quickly changing, as a decade of terrible mosquito-borne illnesses was beginning. With the President's trip and stay at Rives Inn completed, Columbians pulled out the blueprint for the first planned capital city in the country and continued the work.

The Hampton and Compty bridge work also continued. They were not bridge engineers, and their building resources were limited in the scant new city of Columbia. Their bridges were entirely made of wood except for the end abutments, which were a mass of granite stones. In 1792, Compty's bridge was being finished, but the road to it had not yet been completed, while Hampton's bridge was in full operation. Then disaster struck, and both bridges were washed away by a flood.

Another thing we take for granted today is the maintenance required on bridges. When floods occur, trees and other debris fall from the river banks into the raging water. Flowing debris hangs up on the piers of a bridge. A chain reaction occurs, and other trees and debris build on top of that. As the debris mass gets larger, the force of water on the mass becomes so great that it threatens the piers of the bridge. Even today, with steel reinforced concrete piers, it is a severe threat.

Hampton and Compty sank more of their money into rebuilding the bridges while their ferry operations continued to move people into Columbia. The next generation of bridges would be bigger and stronger, but still with wooden piers. Compty chose to move a few hundred feet north to build a higher abutment on the west side of Broad River. Physical evidence shows he kept the same abutment on the east side of the river, so his bridge was not perfectly perpendicular to the river as we are used to seeing.

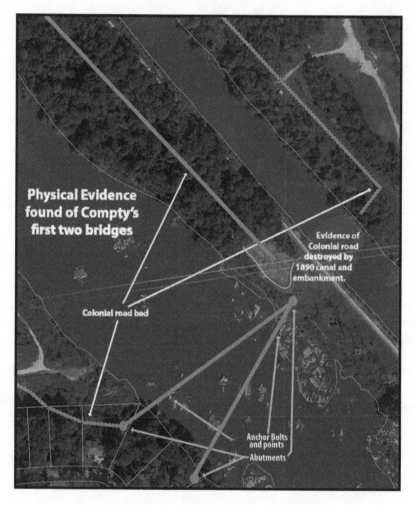

Figure 38: Archaeological evidence of Compty's
first two bridges and old road beds.

For several years, the new bridges brought people into Columbia faster than ever. But then came the great Yazoo Freshet in January of 1796, when 16 straight days of heavy rains gradually raised the levels of the Broad and Congaree rivers to within inches of the tops of the piers of both Compty's and Hampton's bridges. John Belton O'Neall's "The Annals of Newberry" (part one) tells the fate of Compty's bridge:

Compte's bridge across Broad river, three miles above Columbia, just finished in apparently the most secure way, went. It is said the owner, a Frenchman, was upon the bridge, looking at the raging torrent, and impiously exclaimed: "Aha, God Almighty does tink we build bridges out of corn-stalks." Scarcely were the words uttered, until the cracking timbers gave notice that its end was at hand. With difficulty, the owner reached the land.

The remains of Compty's bridge floated down into the Congaree River where they struck and destroyed Hampton's bridge at Granby. It was back to square one, and Compty and Hampton would go back to ferry operations while planning the third generation of their bridges.

John Compty and his wife Elizabeth Rugborck welcomed their third child, Charles, later in 1796. Their other two children were 11 and 8 years old. As Compty finished his third, and final, bridge, Elizabeth took ill and passed away. The average life expectancy during this time was below 40 years. The South Carolina epidemics of the 1790s made this even worse. Living near the river, and mosquitoes, was downright dangerous.

Wade Hampton was more determined than ever and not ready to give up on the bridge-building. His third bridge was a huge covered bridge said to be the largest building in South Carolina. Jedediah Morse's "The American Universal Geography" (1796, page 675), gives the following description of Hampton's final bridge:

A bridge has lately been erected over the Congaree river, at a small town called Granby, about two miles below the confluence of Saluda and Broad rivers. This bridge is remarkable for its being built in a curvilinear direction with the arch up-stream, which contributes much to its strength and also for its height, being 40 feet above the ordinary level of the water. The bridge is supported by wooden pillars, which are strong, framed into water sills, which are bolted into a solid rock that extends across the river. These bolts are secured in the rock by running into the interstices round the bolts large quantities of melted lead. The great height of the bridge was requisite to secure it from the freshets which rise here to a great degree, the current of which is so rapid as to carry before it everything which should present to its fury any considerable surface. The center arch is upwards of 100 feet in the clear, to give a passage to large trees brought down by the flood in great abundance, and would otherwise, by lodging against the bridge, prove fatal to it, as was the case with one, some years since, which had been erected in the same place. For this useful work, the country is indebted to an enterprising and valuable citizen, Colonel Wade Hampton, who has a right of toll secured to him by the legislature for 100 years.

The great floods of the 1790s were now behind them. These final bridges of Compty and Hampton were not washed away. Instead, it seems they faded away, and the future owners let them fall into decay. The days of individuals taking on tasks like bridge building were over.

The next generation of river crossers was about to step in. Elizabeth Stanley was engaged to Henry McGowan. The lovers "had a falling out," and Elizabeth "in a fit of pique" found the first willing man and married him. That was widower John Compty. Elizabeth was 23 years old, and Compty was 47 years old and referred to by most as "old man Compty." He managed his bridge operation and probably educated Elizabeth, who took on the role of mother to his three young children, on how to continue the business if something happened to him. In 1799, after a short illness, John Compty passed away at the age of 49.

Within a few months of Compty's death, Columbia resident Captain Swanson Lunsford passed away. Lunsford was a member of Lee's Legion during important events of the American Revolution and apparently was a very popular man in Columbia. Today, he remains the only person to be buried on the South Carolina State House grounds. His death in 1799 brought many people to his funeral service. Among these people were the former lovers, Elizabeth Stanley Compty and Henry McGowan. Within hours of reuniting at the funeral service, they were married by a local minister.

Henry and Elizabeth McGowan honored John Compty and raised his children. Court records show the McGowans became the legal guardian of the younger son, Charles Compty, and made the older son, John Compty Jr., an apprentice. There is no trace of John Jr. after he entered the service for the War of 1812. Charles Compty can be found in some court records of the 1850s, but it appears he had no children. No records were found on the Compty daughter, so all traces of the Compty family have been lost. For the

McGowans, their union was just the beginning of a successful business and long line of descendants.

In November of 1799, the newly married McGowans washed their hands clean of the Compty Bridge charter and requested a charter for only a ferry. In their petition to the General Assembly, the McGowans noted that the old Compty bridge was falling apart and that they would like to start a ferry at the same location. Elizabeth inherited the ferry landing property on the east side of the river, but Captain Mazyck owned the land on the west side of the river. Despite this, their petition was granted, and McGowan's Ferry began its long and successful run. The property ownership on the west side of the river would lead to many problems in the future. For now, however, they were safe with a 14-year charter. These were good years for Henry and Elizabeth as they started their family and developed friendships among the neighbors.

Hampton's last bridge appears to have lasted a few years longer than Compty's, but it befell a similar fate. Hampton sold the bridge/ferry site to Nicholas Hane of Granby, and within a few years, only ferry service was offered at the site. Once again, the flow of people from the west into Columbia was hampered by the inability to cross the rivers in volatile conditions.

In 1806, Alexander Bolin Stark purchased Captain Mazyck's property located across the Broad River from the McGowans' property. This property started in the southern tip of Dutch Fork, the fork of the Saluda and Broad Rivers, and went up to just above today's Broad River Bridge. Stark later purchased land on the east side the river.

> Historian note: The southern border of this east property was adjacent to the northern boundary of the McGowans' land. I know exactly where this property line was because of an 1832 document, which shows that Elizabeth McGowan sold this land to Jacob Coogler. An 1870 canal survey shows the upper boundary line of this Jacob Coogler property in relation to common landmarks of today and 1870. This is an example of how important it is in historical research to note all locational information you come across. This information can be used for future archaeological proof of a site.

According to many accounts of Alexander Stark, the McGowans and Stark were initially good neighbors and friends[38]. There was a verbal agreement between Henry McGowan and Stark that there would be no ferry charge for Alexander and his immediate family in return for letting the McGowans use the west landing area on Stark's property for McGowan's west ferry landing. Stark was all right with this agreement but maintaining the road through his property was a lot of work.

Back in those days, landowners were responsible for maintaining public roads through their property. Henry McGowan, recognizing the sensitivity of the situation, gradually offered more benefits to Stark, and the free ferry service was expanded to all of Stark's family, friends, tenants, and people carrying produce from Stark's farm area to the market in Columbia. Stark said he was happy with this arrangement, and the friendship between the McGowans and Stark grew over the first few years.

During these years (1800-1810), Elizabeth and Henry had two children, Henry Jr. and Sarah. Nothing specific is known about Stark's family, and it appears he was single. Stark's interests grew from being a farmer and surveyor to building a road from Columbia to Augusta, which also required the construction of several bridges.

Many of the land plats of early Columbia and the surrounding area show Stark as the surveyor. It appears that during his surveying jobs he carefully and wisely selected certain properties for himself as investments. He acquired land on both sides of the Saluda just above today's Riverbanks Zoo, where he would own and operate Stark's Ferry for many years. It appears Stark was thinking about doing the same on the Broad River, as he bought the land just above McGowan's Ferry on the east side so that he owned land on both sides of the Broad River. In those days, running a ferry could be very profitable, especially in a growing area like Columbia. During this same time, Stark studied law, became a lawyer, and served in the House of Representatives from 1802 to 1808.

The McGowans probably noticed a certain power building around Stark during these years, and they must have been concerned that Stark would challenge them when it came time to seek a re-charter for their ferry.

---

[38] S.C. Department of Archives and History: Series: S165015 Year - 1818 Item - 00042

In 1811, Christopher Sharp submitted petitions to the General Assembly asking for a charter for a ferry about three miles above McGowan's Ferry[39]. The first petition included a drawing that showed Sharp's Ferry two miles above McGowan's, but this was corrected in the petition to be three miles. The critical thing to note in this drawing is that there was a new ferry just 200 yards above McGowan's. This would later be documented as Stark's Ferry which would be in violation of McGowan's charter. We know from the 1818 court case of McGowan vs. Stark that Stark in 1811 purchased the land just above McGowan's Ferry on the east side of the river. In Stark's mind, owning the property on both sides of the river was all he needed to justify starting his own ferry.

Sharp's ferry charter was approved, and in just one year the Columbia ferries on the Broad River tripled. For the next few years, the McGowans would not attempt to stop the illegal Stark's Ferry, despite gross violations of the law by Stark. Maybe the McGowans felt it was only fair to let Stark run his ferry since he owned the land on both sides of the river, but this was putting the McGowans out of business. It left them with no choice but to seek help in the courts.

After several years of research, I felt I had come to know these old neighbors on the Broad River. The evidence says a lot about these people, and I have formed my own opinions of their character. You will see this mixed in with the facts.

In 1811, more than a year before the lapse of the 14-year charter the McGowans had on their ferry, Henry McGowan applied for the re-charter. Apparently, it was given immediately without following the usual procedure of notifying the Commissioner of Roads, at least according to petitions from A.B. Stark and the court case of McGowan vs. Stark. The plans for re-chartering were also normally advertised so the general public would be aware of the plan. Why Henry McGowan and the government official did not follow the standard process is not clear, but I'm sure Henry was concerned the aggressive Stark would likely take the charter from the McGowans if he had the chance. Stark was a man who always got what he wanted, and he would stop at nothing to get it.

---

[39] S.C. Department of Archives and History: Series: S165005 Year - 1811 Item - 00087, Year - 1811 Item 10703

Stark was outraged when he learned of the re-charter. Sharp's proposed ferry was three miles north of McGowan's, and the laws at that time stated ferries could be no closer than two miles from each other. In the drawing, Stark's Ferry was only 200 yards above McGowan's Ferry. For the next several years things were quiet as far as petitions to the General Assembly, except for one petition from the McGowans asking that the road to their ferry be reopened. Around 1815, the petitions start rolling in again. This time Stark is the petitioner, and he is doing everything he can to shut down McGowan's Ferry and have his ferry vested/chartered. By 1818, Stark had a personal vendetta against the McGowans, and the petitions contained personal attacks.

It wasn't clear to me what was happening until I found two documents covering an 1818 case and appeal of McGowan vs. Stark. According to the court's investigation, Alexander Stark in violation of the law started his own ferry in 1811 about 300 yards above McGowan's Ferry without a charter to do so. He was charging the same fare as McGowan's Ferry. In 1812, at the road where a fork would take you to either Stark's Ferry or McGowan's Ferry, Stark cut down trees blocking the road to McGowan's Ferry. He also cut down several trees on the bank of McGowan's Ferry and dropped the trees into the water to block McGowan's Ferry landing. He also placed a fence across another part of McGowan's road. He posted a sign at the fork stating McGowan's road was not accessible, the Road Commissioner had refused to work on McGowan's road, and it would soon be closed. Unbelievably, this situation lasted for three years. In that time, the McGowans paid more money to their ferryman than they made in gross proceeds from the ferry tolls.

It's hard to understand Stark's extreme actions. A man that had accomplished so many positive things in the previous 15 years seemed to have cracked. The General Assembly forced the reopening of the road in 1815, but the legislators required that the McGowans make road improvements. There was no indication in the records that Alexander Stark had done anything wrong. No doubt the required road improvements came about from the many petitions of Stark in which other members of the public were complaining about the steep slope down to McGowan's Ferry on the west side of the river. Stark's petitions had many signers, often around 50, and the statements in the petitions clearly showed these people thought Stark's road was much safer and easier to travel.

This must have been a difficult time for the McGowans. They seemed to do all they could to avoid confrontations with Stark, but something had to give because they were losing money and going out of business quickly. They were left with no choice but to take Stark to court so the facts of the case would come to light. It never appeared the McGowans wanted to shut down Stark's Ferry. They just wanted to have their ferry back in operation and have a little peace on the river. The higher court would not be kind to Stark.

Despite Stark being a very well known, hardworking, and respected citizen of Columbia, the court would show him no mercy[40]. It seems the judges who dealt with the case were appalled that Stark had the nerve to start a ferry without the government's approval. I don't think the McGowans were seeking anything more than a half share of the profits during those three years, but the court decided what the award would be.

One of the two court documents goes into details about the money normally taken in at Stark's Ferry. They did this by interviewing the ferryman. He stated the average gross proceeds were about $15 a week -- sometimes only $4 a week, and sometimes as high as $30. Because Stark went to such extremes to cut off the chartered McGowan's Ferry, the court decided that Stark should pay the McGowans the gross proceeds based on a much higher than average crossing rate, almost $25 per week. This came to $4,000, a considerable sum. All the land Stark had managed to accumulate on the Broad River for his ferry was not worth $4,000. The case was a huge loss for Stark, and the appeals court backed the original judgment.

This was probably Stark's greatest defeat, and it came at the hands of a simple husband and wife who wanted nothing but to operate their ferry in peace. I would guess the McGowans themselves were shocked at the judgment and maybe even thought it was too severe. In any case, the McGowans now had money to improve their road. Stark, in his final response to the court, as noted in the case documents, said McGowan should be vacated and canceled and should be restrained by the court for his manifold acts of fraud.

Stark would not give up. The petitions continued, with Stark still stressing that a ferry owner must own the land on both sides of the river. Stark's

---

[40] Harvard Law School Library: Reports of Cases Determined in The Constitutional Court of South Carolina by Henry Junius Notf & David James McCord: Vol 1, 1820

petitions rambled on and on about how much better his road and ferry were, claiming McGowan's Ferry could never be improved to match his. On the personal side, Stark accused the McGowans of cheating the children of John Compty. Stark said if the McGowans were decent people, they would have split the Compty land among Compty's children. He said the Compty children were really the owners of the land on the east side of the river and should have the rights to the ferry.

I wonder if the people back then believed Stark. The McGowans were humble folks, and they never seemed to respond to Stark's negative remarks. The truth is, as I have found in many different documents at the South Carolina archives, the McGowans did all they could for the Compty children. They became the legal guardian of one. They made the older child an apprentice. In the handling of the Compty estate, I found where money was set aside for the education of Compty's children. These were things the McGowans did on their own, as it appears John Compty left no will or instructions. As one last note on this, none of Stark's petitions were signed by the Compty children.

Despite the court victories for the McGowans, the South Carolina General Assembly stalled until 1821 before passing the act to officially reopen the road to McGowan's Ferry and make it a public road once again. That was nine years after Stark blocked the road to McGowan's Ferry. Henry McGowan never got a chance to make those road improvements, as he died on February 1, 1821, at the age of 48.

It appears that later that year, the woman described as one of the best Christians in her church, went out of her way to allow an exception to the law. Even though it was unheard of to have two chartered ferries just a few hundred yards apart, it looks like Elizabeth McGowan allowed Alexander Stark to have his ferry and his charter.

There were no more petitions from Stark, just finally peace on the river. I guess Stark could now relax and look back on his life and all his accomplishments. Maybe it was then that he realized what he had missed out on. On March 16, 1822, the 55-year-old Stark was married (for the first time) to 39-year-old Sarah Ann Lamar.

On June 30th, 1823, Alexander Bolan Stark died at the age of 56. Documents show that Sarah Ann was his sole heir. The river now belonged to the women.

In 1825, the McGowan and Stark ferries each had their own public road entering on the west side of the river. Based on the "Mills' Atlas of 1825," a single road on the east side came in at McGowan's Ferry, so the two ferries shared the same east road. It had been several years since the deaths of Henry McGowan and Alexander Stark, and it seems that both ferries were running smoothly with no complaints surfacing at the General Assembly. Elizabeth McGowan and Sarah Stark were bringing people across the river better than ever.

Later in 1825, the construction of the first bridge over the Congaree since Wade Hampton's bridges of the 1790s began under the control of the Columbia Bridge Company, which was owned by private citizens. As in 1791, there was a push for a Broad River bridge, but how would this work with the charters for the McGowan and Stark ferries? And where would this bridge be built?

I found documents that show the initial study, requirements, and cost for a new Broad River bridge. The proposed site, at that time, was at or near McGowan's Ferry, although the design states that the road to McGowan's Ferry is too steep. The document also mentions that some compensation must be given to the owner of the Stark property for the use of the land for a road.

More documents from the archives showed the location of the bridge shifted to "at or near" Stark's Ferry. The apparent reason was that it simplified the land ownership. If the bridge were built at McGowan's Ferry, then there would be two owners to compensate for the road. At Stark's Ferry, one owner, Sarah Stark, owned the landing on both sides of the river.

In 1827, state legislation created the Broad River Bridge Company, making Elizabeth McGowan and Sarah Stark principal stockholders, with each getting 4% of the stock in return for giving up the rights to their ferry charters. Sarah and Elizabeth would continue to operate their ferries for another two years while the bridge was being built.

On August 11, 1829, after 30 years, the Broad River would once again have a bridge thanks to Elizabeth McGowan, Sarah Stark, and the other stockholders of the Broad River Bridge Company. Elizabeth must have had mixed emotions. It meant the end of her ferry, which was a big part of her life with Henry McGowan, but it also must have been a good feeling to see the last mission of her first husband, John Compty, realized again after so many years. This time the bridge had stone piers and was bigger and much stronger than the bridges of John Compty. Most importantly, it had an insurance policy. The insurance companies would lose on these Broad River bridges, but they were a very profitable business for the stockholders.

On December 9, 1843, at the age of 61, Sarah Ann Lamar Stark died. Between the Starks, McGowans, and Comptys, Sarah is the only one whose gravesite is known. She was buried in a small cemetery in her hometown of Lamar, South Carolina. Sarah never remarried after Alexander's death. She handled Stark's Ferry and the bridge project, probably better than anyone would have expected. She never relinquished the Stark property on the west side of the river. This was the land that had given life to at least three ferry operations and four bridges. The land now, however, was up for grabs, and the locals on the west side were excited about the auction of this long-held riverfront property.

The Huffman family had been in the area for a while, and a young Jacob N. Huffman was the high bidder, grabbing all three tracts, totaling 641 acres, of the Stark estate for $10,427[41]. Jacob had a great life on this land and brought in a new and large generation of Huffmans. His large home was occupied, and spared, by Sherman's troops in 1865 only to meet its end generations later to make room for a Food Lion grocery store.

One of the last records found about Elizabeth McGowan shows her getting a loan, using her Broad River property as collateral. In one Columbia history book, Elizabeth was described as a very wealthy woman, mostly from her Broad River Bridge stock holdings and her boarding house on the northwest corner of Gervais and Assembly streets. It's not clear why she was seeking a loan in 1832. In 1833, papers showed she is trying to divide this same property into three parcels. Her son and daughter, Henry and Sarah, are also listed in this document as though they had something to do with the transaction. That's the last record we found on Elizabeth. We know

---

[41] Sarah Stark to Jacob N. Huffman transfer: Lexington County Assessor's Office, Lexington, S.C

she lived on the northeast corner of Assembly and Taylor, and that her son would occupy that residence through the Civil War.

Two living descendants of Elizabeth have done extensive genealogy work into her family but have found no information on her death. Since Elizabeth lived in the city and she appears in the 1830 census, but not in later decadal censuses, it must be assumed she died sometime between 1833 and 1840.

Her church cemetery records were searched, but nothing was found for her or her husband Henry. Looking at the things we know about Elizabeth, I guess it should not be surprising that she made a quiet and humble exit. She lived a great life. She had the brains and heart to do things in a special way that none of her male contemporaries could match.

Her son Henry had three girls: Olivia McGowan, Henrietta McGowan, and Agnes E. McGowan.

A photograph of Olivia is the only image we have of the McGowans of that era.

Only Agnes McGowan married, to Jacob Hildebrand Hydrick, and had children. Today this Hydrick family is quite large, although none of them are in the Columbia area. Elizabeth's siblings and cousins in the Stanley family had many descendants, some of whom are still in the Columbia area.

I guess it's natural that the simple and humble people are the first to be forgotten over the generations. After all, there are no monuments to them. Their tombstones were small and simple, made to last not much longer than the lives of their children. The history books fail to include them because they were not among the influential people of their time.

Figure 39: Olivia McGowan, full-length carte-de-visite by Richard Wearn, Columbia, S.C. (Photographs 6552.5). Courtesy of the South Caroliniana Library.

121

It's sad to see it happen because we all know these are the people who set the real meaningful examples in life. As you continue through this book, you will see other instances of how these forgotten good people are brought back to life through Miracles to Yesterday.

Chapter 8 – Heaven drops a Survey

My initial goal on the backyard bridge abutment was to determine if it could be the site of the Broad River Confederate Bridge. The city of Columbia's most catastrophic event happened at the end of the American Civil War when General William T. Sherman and the Union Army invaded and burned the city. Sherman's march through the South was all about property destruction. Killing people was not working; it only gave people reason and purpose to continue the fight. But when you destroy homes, farms, and towns, you take away the ability of people to make a living, and their spirit is soon destroyed. Sherman's denial of intentionally burning Columbia makes no sense. He burned everything between Charleston and Columbia. Why not Columbia? After all, the original secession document was written in Columbia. Sherman and all his men knew this. There was not a city they would have wanted to destroy more than Columbia.

On February 16, 1865, all that stood between Sherman's right-wing of 30,000 troops and Columbia were the Broad River Bridge and Confederate General "Fighting Joe" Wheeler, with approximately 30 Confederates under his command. The conflict should have been over quickly, but entering Columbia proved to be one of the biggest obstacles Sherman would face on his march. Wheeler and company would be the last stand for the city. As big an event as this skirmish was, the location of the bridge and Sherman's crossing would be lost over the next 75 years.

The research on the backyard abutment ultimately brought a who's-who of local historians to the site. With another anniversary of the burning of Columbia approaching, I contacted Joey Holleman of The State newspaper. It was Joey's article on this event two years earlier that sparked my research on the Confederate bridge possibility. Joey had quite a background writing about local and South Carolina history, and one of his contacts was State Archaeologist Dr. Jonathan Leader. Joey looked at the abutment himself and then set up a meeting with me and Dr. Leader. When Dr. Leader arrived, I began to lead him down my steep driveway on the side of our house. The sharp eye of the archaeologist spotted the top of the abutment without any directional clue on my part. Dr. Leader identified several key points about the abutment, including the old roadbed that led to it, the hand-drilled and machine-drilled holes in the quarried stones, and the unique features of chiseled stones.

Figure 40: Left: Machine cut hole (1800's). Right: Possible hand cut hole (late 1700's).

Figure 41: First abutment: Left: Looking down from my house at the top of the abutment. Right: hand-placed stones at the base of the abutment.

Figure 42: Old colonial roadbed that ended at the first abutment.

Figure 43: Second abutment (view from the river).

This evidence left little doubt that this was an old bridge abutment, but Dr. Leader would not put a specific date on it. He said more work was needed, and he gave me a list of things to work toward. Joey interviewed both of us and wrote a story that appeared on the front page of The State in time for the 2007 anniversary of the burning of Columbia.

Over the next two years, I continued the research and maintained communications with Dr. Leader. With the publicity of the newspaper article, I was also able to bring in a few local historians to inspect the site. Among them was Allen Roberson, the Director of the South Carolina Confederate Relic Room and Military Museum. Allen played a significant role over the next two years, including bringing in more local historians and leaders of historical organizations. The bottom line was that, although I had the support of many historians, no one was willing to put their stamp of approval on my abutment being the Confederate Bridge.

As my work continued, I traced the old roadbed and discovered another similar road on the other side of the river. I also found another abutment-like structure on the other side of the river and in the middle of the river an extremely old iron bracket that appeared to be for a rope to secure the midsection of the bridge.

Figure 44: Compty evidence that is normally under water: An iron tie in river rock. 1.5-inch hand drilled holes which are consistent with the Wade Hampton Bridges that were built four miles south of here at Granby during the 1790s.

I also began accumulating more evidence related to the original ferries and the three bridges of John Compty in the 1790s. My original theory was that the Confederate bridge was built at the last Compty bridge site. While doing inspections of the riverbanks along the lower Broad River, I discovered another abutment in my neighbor's yard, just two hundred feet down from my abutment. This certainly seemed to be another Compty bridge possibility. Further up river, just below today's bridge, I found roadbeds leading to the river bank on both sides of the river.

To operate a ferry or bridge in Colonial times, the state required that the ferry/bridge owner own the property on at least one side of the river. I had found all the General Assembly documents for Compty's ferries and bridges, but none of them gave details on the exact boundaries of Compty's property on the Columbia side of the river.

In total, the General Assembly documents showed three Compty ferry and bridge sites from 1790 to 1800. In 1825, the owners of McGowan's Ferry and Stark's Ferry sold their ferry shares toward the creation of the Broad River Bridge Company. This company built a bridge over the Broad River at a location described as being between the old Stark and McGowan ferry sites. The total evidence, including the Civil War sites, could be confusing, so my research was challenging.

Among the evidence was a historical marker from 1929 on today's bridge stating the Confederate Bridge and Sherman's pontoon crossing events took place downstream toward our abutment, which was half a mile downstream. The contour of the land at our abutment was very similar to that shown in an 1865 illustration of Sherman's crossing site. A staple for historians, the 1825 "Mills' Atlas," also showed landmarks that suggested the site was at our abutment. Those pieces of evidence all seemed to identify our abutment as the Confederate Bridge site. How could they all be wrong?

There was other evidence, however, that did not go along with the marker and "Mills' Atlas." A couple of other maps and a land survey, all done before the Civil War, showed the bridge within a few hundred feet of today's bridge. As one unbiased out-of-state historian put it: "It doesn't make sense that the bridge would be up there and then move half a mile down to your site in 1865 and then move back up to today's bridge site after the Civil war. Established roads don't move around like that." I could not argue with this opinion.

For several years, I could not make any sense of it. I tried to remain persistent and stay the course, but I had exhausted all the historical resources. Although my research had brought back to life many long-forgotten stories of early life around the rivers at Columbia and some clarity on the first Broad River crossings, it seemed the Confederate Bridge site might be something I could not find and prove. I was very frustrated and close to the point of quitting.

I decided to make one more trip to the South Carolina Archives and History Center. After a couple of hours, no new sources turned up. The only other place to look was in the old card catalog. I had several sections of interest in these old indexes. As I pulled the drawer out looking for "The Columbia Canal," something caught my eye. A new card amongst a sea of old yellow cards, and it was in the section for the canal. I honestly could not remember ever seeing a new card in these card catalogs. In fact, maybe this was the first one to be added in many years.

This new record was for an 1870 canal survey.[42] It had just been added a few days earlier. Surveys are always good sources because they are based on measured lengths and angles, and processed with basic mathematics. A survey from 1870 could be as good as one from today. I filled out a request to view the item but did not get my hopes up as I waited for the librarian to retrieve it.

I was soon presented with a rolled document that was about three feet wide. The librarian began to unroll it ... and unroll it. All the way out to 12 feet! The survey covered the full five-mile length of the Columbia Canal and the banks of the rivers around Columbia at a scale of 200 feet to the inch. I had never seen an old survey of this size and detail.

As I looked closer, my heart sank. There was the Broad River Bridge that had been rebuilt in 1870 on top of the undamaged stone piers from the Confederate bridge. And in the same relative position that Civil War artist William Waud had shown Sherman's pontoon bridge next to the burned Confederate bridge, there was a ferry site. The ferry matched exactly where I would have expected the old Stark's Ferry site to lie. A hot flash came over me as I noticed another landmark in the Columbia Canal that is still there today. I instantly realized the Confederate Bridge site and Sherman's crossing were half a mile above my bridge abutment. These were not in my backyard. I felt sick as if the whole project had been a failure. I took a few pictures and went home and into bed.

---

[42] 1870 Columbia Canal Survey by George C. Tingley. Held at the South Carolina Department of Archives and History.

After a long sleep, I woke up refreshed and realized this was not a failure. I must have been in a state of shock. I had found maybe the best piece of evidence yet, and it went right along with those other pre-Civil War maps and surveys that had dogged me for so long. However, it meant a reset on the research, a whole new investigation on why a historical marker and the renowned "Mills' Atlas" were so wrong.

It also led to the development of a process and technique to overlay old surveys onto modern-day aerial photographs. This overlay process would become a trademark of my projects through the years. To begin the overlay process for this survey, I needed to figure out how to get a high-quality scan of the large 1870 canal survey.

At this point, I met historian Patrick McCawley with the South Carolina Department of Archives and History. Patrick had handled the acquisition of the 1870 survey. For a small fee, Patrick had the survey scanned into multiple parts that I was able to stitch together. My next step was to capture just the outline of important man-made objects in the survey and key landmarks such as the outline of the river. I then did necessary calculations to get the right scaling and performed a rotation to match it to the standard rotation of aerial photography found with Google maps and county GIS systems.

When this was all done, the moment of truth came when I applied the overlay and lined up the two images using a couple of reference landmarks in both images. The result was stunning. The outline of the river, canal, and city blocks matched, all the way down to a train trestle five miles down at the bottom of the survey. No noticeable error anywhere! The survey showed the piers of the Gervais Street Bridge, the main bridge into downtown Columbia. The piers were all that was left of the original bridge in 1870. Those piers were just 20 feet north of today's bridge. Today, the decaying remains of those 150-year-old piers can still be seen when the river is low. They are precisely where the 1870 overlay showed them!

I now knew this was the best piece of evidence I could have hoped for. Now the job was to look for the Confederate Bridge location. I thought the overlay might show that the old bridge was in the exact place of today's bridge. It was not. It showed the old site to be about 150 feet north. Could there be anything left of it?

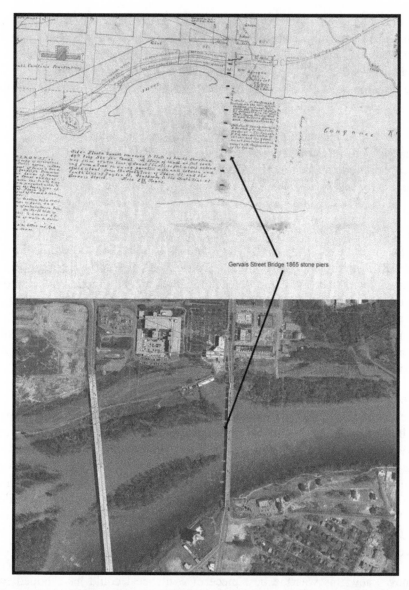

Figure 45: A portion of the 1870 Columbia Canal survey and overlay on a modern aerial photo. Permission and credit South Carolina Department of Archives and History and Richland County GIS.

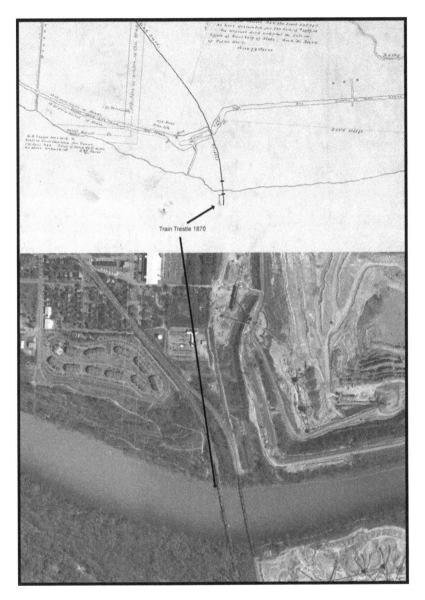

Figure 46: A portion of the 1870 Columbia Canal survey and overlay on a modern aerial photo. Permission and credit South Carolina Department of Archives and History and Richland County GIS.

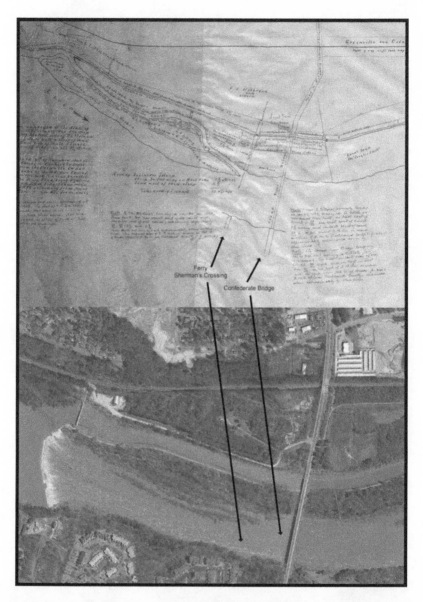

Figure 47: Portion of the 1870 Columbia Canal survey and overlay on a modern aerial photo showing the position of the old Confederate Bridge site and Sherman's ferry/pontoon crossing. Permission and credit South Carolina Department of Archives and History and Richland County GIS.

As luck would have it, the bridge site was easy to get to. In fact, there was a dirt road going down to it. Could it possibly be the old Colonial roadbed? I followed the road down to the elevation of the bridge as specified by the old Broad River Bridge Company in 1825. At that position, the current road took a sharp turn to the north, and directly in front of me was what looked like a replica of the top of the abutment in my backyard. I raced down the other fork in the road to get in front of the bottom of the abutment. Again, another replica of my abutment. I ripped away the English ivy, and there was the similar rough placement of stones that formed the support for the bridge. I had found it!

As if that was not enough excitement for the day, I crossed a creek and worked my way through the thick brush until I reached an opening. There on the other side of the river was a similar opening. I looked up at another bluff to the west and verified the site contour as being just like the one in the 1865 William Waud drawing of the site. This was where Sherman and his 30,000 troops built their pontoon bridge. Pulling out my Garmin GPS, I recorded the position, and I later verified I had navigated to the exact point of the ferry site in the 1870 survey.

Just a couple of days earlier, I was minutes away from abandoning the project and accepting failure. At that point, it seemed Heaven dropped a treasure map into my hands. I was now excited to learn more about this survey. Who donated this to the archives? Who was the surveyor that did this? And why was it done?

I would engage Joey Holleman once again, and he located and interviewed the donor of the 1870 survey. As Joey would learn, the survey should have been thrown away in the 1970s when the Richland County Engineering Department offices were moved. A county employee, Gordon Greene, was instructed to dispose of it. Greene's curiosity, however, had already led him to previously unroll the old survey and take a look. Instead of the trash bin, Greene took it home. Over the years, Greene and his son would occasionally pull out the survey when inspired by a canoe trip down the rivers going into and through Columbia.

While I was struggling to determine the Confederate Bridge site, Gordon passed away in 2006. His son Russell thought about framing the item that had been so special to him and his father, but he had no space on a wall for it. Russell then considered donating it, thinking others might appreciate it or find a use for it. I understood the attachment Russell had to the survey, as I had also struggled with the donation of my dad's WWII Iwo Jima letter and his M-1 carbine gun to a museum. In 2008, Russell made the decision and contacted the South Carolina State Museum. Maybe partly because Russell wanted the item on display and the museum had no place for it, Russell was redirected to the South Carolina Department of Archives and History. A few days after it was processed and entered into the card catalog, in a final desperate effort to keep my project alive, I discovered the new item. The significance and timing of the find was nothing short of miraculous.

As we looked more at the origins of the survey, we discovered just how important of a document it was. The people behind its creation were also not your average citizens.

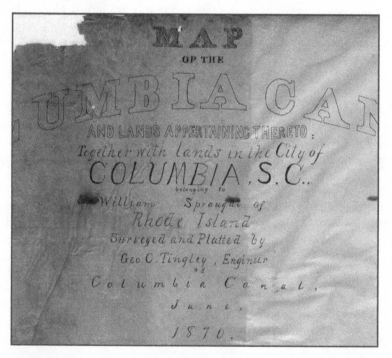

Figure 48: A portion of the 1870 Columbia Canal survey. Permission and credit South Carolina Department of Archives and History and Richland County GIS.

The first name on the survey was William Sprague from Rhode Island. Sprague had quite a life. He was born in the governor's mansion while his father was governor of Rhode Island. William's father was murdered when William was 13, and the family business of A & W Sprague Manufacturing fell partly into William's hands, along with his uncle, who also would serve as governor and U.S. senator from Rhode Island. William was elected the Rhode Island governor during the Civil War, and he even took part in the First Battle of Bull Run. At the time of the commissioning of the survey, William was a U.S. senator and one of the wealthiest men in the country. His marriage to Kate Chase, considered the belle of Washington and daughter of Secretary of the Treasury Salmon P. Chase, would capture much attention.

By 1870, William had the idea that he could turn the city of Columbia into the industrial capital of the southeast. He thought that by enlarging the Columbia Canal, he could use water power to drive new mills along the canal. The existing Columbia Canal, however, was only 16 feet wide and four feet deep. His engineers determined it would need to be ten times as wide and twice as deep. The 1870 survey was done to mark and calculate all the property Sprague would need to buy to widen the canal. While the survey was being completed, Sprague spent a small fortune buying up additional property for the mills. In total, he purchased 176 acres of land in the downtown area of Columbia.

The second name on the survey was Engineer George C. Tingley, who had been the state surveyor in Rhode Island. Sprague spared no expense by hiring the best surveyor he could find. Almost 140 years later, my overlay would prove the talents of Tingley.

In 1870, Columbia was suffering through the economic hardships of Reconstruction, and there must have been a real excitement over the promises of William Sprague. But the 1873 financial panic ended the dreams and hopes of many in Columbia. Sprague lost almost everything in the crash. He began to drink heavily, and his life with Kate turned into a soap opera, with affairs happening on both sides.

It took the city of Columbia almost 20 years to get back all the property Sprague had purchased. Somehow, that 1870 survey survived and found new importance in 1888. The new breakthrough of that period was electricity, and a new idea was born. Could the Columbia Canal be upgraded to drive electric generators? Using the 1870 survey, the city implemented Sprague's plan, except the canal now produced power in the form of electricity. The electricity powered a new textile mill, and the building that housed that mill today is home to the South Carolina State Museum.

In 1891, the new canal was officially opened. The original mill would become the first textile mill in the world to be powered by AC motors. Unfortunately, Columbia didn't have the money or private financial support to line the canal with mills and factories. That single mill would be the only one built. The generators continued to run until the October Flood of 2015 breached the canal dike just upstream of the plant.

I spread the word as fast as possible about the incredible survey find, and Joey Holleman produced another front-page story about it. [43] To my disappointment, many historians discounted the survey, saying "you can't depend on old maps" to prove a location. But it was not a map! It was a five-mile-long survey just as accurate as surveys of today. I just couldn't get the history jugheads to understand.

Dr. Leader said the survey was excellent, but it was circumstantial evidence, and I was making a big claim. He said I needed to go to the suspected locations and scientifically prove them through some type of archaeology work. So how was I supposed to do that? I was not an archaeologist, and I did not own the land that held the historic site. Once again, I had hit a brick wall.

I was depressed about the situation when one of my dad's longtime secretaries called to check on me. I told her I wished my dad was here to help me. Her response was firm and direct: "What are you talking about? You don't need your dad! He taught you everything you need to know! Don't you tell me you need your dad." I knew she was right, but I still had no answer. My dad was very creative in his problem solving, and I knew I needed to do something different.

Co-worker Ernie Corley mentioned the newspaper article to me the next day, and I relayed my frustration about the new find not being taken seriously by the history community. Ernie recommended I contact the national TV show "History Detectives" and ask them to investigate. "History Detectives" was one of those shows that I occasionally watched,

[43] A bridge to somewhere By Joey Holleman, The State Newspaper: http://historysoft.com/news/newspaper_2008.htm

maybe only a few times a year. I quickly found their website and the method for submitting a story idea. Right then I made the submission, but I really didn't expect to hear back from them. They must get thousands of story submissions a year. What would be the odds of being selected?

The next week, now late December 2008, to my surprise I received a phone call from a producer at "History Detectives." Stacey Young explained to me that the season shoot had just ended, but they still had a little money in the budget and were considering doing one more episode. Usually the stories were considered in the order they are received. Stacey did not have access to the earlier story submissions, but she noticed my new story arrival. Over the next two weeks, I went over the case with Stacey. She worried that the story was too complicated.

It was then that I contacted Dr. Leader, and Allen Roberson, who took on the role of a facilitator. In mid-February 2009, a conference call was set up with all four of us. The discussion got very detailed, with me giving maybe too many details. Dr. Leader muted the phone and asked me to leave the room. I stepped out and waited for about 20 minutes.

When they called me back in, it was a done deal. Dr. Leader had agreed, if we could get permission from the property owner, to do the archaeology at the suspected bridge and ferry sites. Allen agreed to make all the resources of his museum and staff available for the show. To this day, I still don't know what happened in that conference call, but I'm happy to leave it at that.

The pressure was now on me to get permission from the property owner. This was undeveloped land next to an apartment complex. The owner was a company in Michigan. I set up an appointment with the local manager, and I brought in a stack of research papers. I gave her my sales pitch, and I described our intended work as not being destructive. It would be geophysical surveying, not digging. Somehow, I was successful, and a follow-up meeting with "History Detectives" Assistant Producer Sarah Gregory (Messer) produced a signed agreement on the project.

We were now set to go, but the work was just beginning for me. I had no idea how much work went into making a TV show like this. It was a good thing I had a flexible day job because there would be many meetings and phone calls over a period of several weeks as the newly assigned producer,

Laura Marini, and I worked out the basic story. We focused on the Confederate Bridge site, Sherman's pontoon crossing site, and the incorrect historical marker. I sometimes wonder if our story would have been accepted by "History Detectives" without the historical marker mistake. The final production really revolved around that marker.

For our story, "History Detectives" would "rediscover" some of my work and complete their own research at the South Carolina Archives and History Center. Dr. Leader would assemble the archaeology team that, given the GPS coordinates I recorded, would test the abutment site and Sherman's crossing. I had no idea how these tasks would be done, and the crew and participants made sure it stayed that way.

Figure 49: Filming of History Detectives: Civil War Bridge" – 2009

By the end of March 2009, Laura and I had a basic script written and the participants of the show had been selected. In addition to Dr. Leader and myself, the cast included Joe Long, Curator of Education at the Confederate Relic Room and Military Museum, and Patrick McCawley and Dr. Tracy Power from the South Carolina Department of Archives and History. Local Sons of Confederate Veterans leader and Civil War re-enactor Dean Stevens would organize a group of Confederate re-enactors for a film scene.

At the last minute, Joe Long, an expert on the history around Sherman's invasion of Columbia, also completed a review of the script to make sure everything was historically correct. Of course, the script was not set in stone because there were unknowns like the results of additional archival research and the archaeology that would be done during the filming. A plan to do part of the filming in canoes on the river also would be highly dependent on the weather and river conditions. The final film crew assignments were completed, and the filming in Columbia began the next week.

This "History Detectives" episode, although fun to do, turned out to be very challenging for the team. I heard this from three different producers, and there were a couple of times when I was afraid the project might get canceled. There were so many pieces of evidence and narrowing this down into a 20-minute show was very difficult. I had spent two weeks with the first producer, helping her get her head around the story and the evidence. She wrote a basic script, and this is what PBS used to determine if the show could be done. After PBS approval, we were assigned another producer, and I had to go through the whole process again. This went on for three weeks, seven days a week!

About halfway through, an executive producer decided that we could not tackle the introduction, which had me showing the abutment on my property. Having multiple bridge sites could confuse the viewers, so the script had to be rewritten. I had memorized my part. I gave up on that because I could see this was going to be a very dynamic script. It would be changing daily.

The time for the shoot finally arrived after five weeks of preparation, which not only involved me but also many hours between "History Detectives" staffers and Dr. Leader, Joe Long, and Patrick McCawley. On Monday, March 30, 2009, the "History Detectives" crew arrived from New York -- host Elyse Luray, cameraman Dan Walworth, producer Laura Marini, and assistant producer Sarah Gregory (Messer), who was a Columbian and University of South Carolina graduate then working in New York. There were also a couple of local guys who did the sound and lighting. All the local participants were happy to learn that Elyse would be the host for this show. Elyse had already done a couple of shows in South Carolina, including one with Dr. Leader.

I had been monitoring the weather during the prior weeks and had a good feel for the river conditions. We had a big rain on Friday and Saturday, which I knew would raise the river above the anchor hooks, a key piece of evidence, on Monday and hold through Wednesday. The plan for Thursday was for me, Elyse, and a film crew to canoe up the river from my house to the bridge and pull the canoes over the rocky area to get into the river above the bridge. Elyse was not afraid to do stuff like this, but the cameraman was not too crazy about it.

For Monday, I was just going to take the producers on a tour of the suspected bridge site. I couldn't believe it when we got there. The river was higher than it had been in over a year, and the lower Riverwalk was completely flooded. But I was still hopeful it would drop back down on Wednesday.

The producers had already checked out the Confederate Relic Room and Military Museum and the State House grounds earlier in the day. Also, on Monday, we finally completed the clearance to film on the private property on the west side of the river.

On Tuesday, I went back to work while filming took place. I was really sweating about the river; it was still raging. Filming was completed on the State House grounds, First Baptist Church, where the original secession document was written, and the museum, where Joe Long was interviewed about the Union Army's 1865 invasion of Columbia.

On Wednesday, Dr. Leader and a bunch of University of South Carolina graduate students did their archaeology thing on the west side of the river. I was not allowed to see this or know about the results. I met Sarah to see if we could get to the ferry/pontoon site on the west side of the river. She told me the creek between this site and the bridge was swollen and could not be passed. I found my way in from the north, but it was not easy to do. The river was still raging. I looked out at the suspected pontoon site and noticed that, with the flooding, the tip of the old Bull's Sluice was easy to see now. It looked just like it did in the 1870 survey. I was now sure that I was standing at the ferry site shown in the 1870 survey.

I was glad I gave that GPS point to Dr. Leader. I was feeling lucky. The producer, however, said the crew would not be able to take my route from the north. Within a couple of hours, the river dropped dramatically, right on schedule, and allowed Dr. Leader to get to the second location of the ferry/pontoon site. Somehow, the film crew managed to squeeze in research and the two interviews at the South Carolina Department of Archives and History and then head over to the Cayce Historical Museum to film a scene with Dean Stevens and the local re-enactors. They provided some tremendous cannon-firing footage. At 9 p.m., the film crew took the re-enactors out for dinner, and Laura noted that not a single person in the restaurant took notice of the fully uniformed Confederates as they walked in.

Thursday arrived, and it was time for my parts. The show's intro scene in our "History Detectives" episode was filmed on the same day they shot the results scene. This is more efficient and saves money for PBS. The crew arrived at 8:30 a.m. The river was still dropping, and I estimated the anchor hooks would be visible by the time we could canoe upriver. But the bad news was it was now raining. What a mess it would be to pull the boats out at the bridge and then put them back in. Our producer had a backup plan. We would film the intro entirely from the back deck of my house with today's bridge in the background.

It worked out pretty well. Of course, we had to start with the knock on the door. This took about six or seven takes. On one take, out of habit, I locked the door and latched the deadbolt behind Elyse. I didn't know anything was wrong until the producer called "cut" and said, "We can't use that. That was creepy!"

Things seemed to go smoother as we went on and I got used to things. The process involved at least two shots of every segment. The cameraman would focus on Elyse on one take, and then we would repeat the scene with me as the focus. The crew was very professional and busy throughout the shoot, but they were also a lot of fun, so I was relaxed.

After the shoot, I came across Nielsen ratings for "History Detectives" from 2007. An average of 2.3 million people watched each show. I'm glad I didn't know this before the filming, or I would have been pretty nervous. That's a lot of people watching.

After the intro shoot, the crew went back to the bridge site to get footage of the anchor hooks which, sure enough, now were visible. Dr. Leader also met them there to get some video of Elyse with the unusual archaeological tool he had used. By the time everyone got back to our house, I had changed my clothes, and my wife (Odess) had prepared a nice lunch for everyone.

At this point, I had no idea what had been found at the archives or in the archaeology work, but Dr. Leader gave me a clue it was good. He merely said: "David, I hope you will come to realize and appreciate how the stars aligned for you on this one." It would be two years later (Chapter 10) before I could translate this to: "Miracle."

For the closing "results" scene, we decided to sit at my bar between the kitchen and the dining room. Once again, double takes on everything. I was getting really excited. I had an idea what Dr. Leader was looking for, but the results of his work were a real surprise.

The archaeology team had used a geophysical device called a Gradiometer. After the episode appeared on TV, I had many people, even my electrical engineering friends, pose questions about this invention. One even compared it to magic. A Gradiometer is actually a very simple electronic device. It has two highly sensitive probes about one meter apart. This creates an electromagnetic sphere capable of recording slight magnetic differences between the probes to a ground depth of about one meter.

The ground, on average, is about 4% iron. Over hundreds of years, these iron particles are charged to the orientation of the Earth's magnetic field. If something disturbs the ground, like by digging a hole or building a road, the particles get moved and rotated. It can take them hundreds, maybe thousands, of years to be "recharged" to the Earth's orientation charge.

A Gradiometer can detect this and display the disturbance. At the GPS coordinates for the top of the suspected Confederate Bridge abutment, Dr. Leader and his team detected horse carriage tracks on a road leading to and ending at the abutment. At the ferry site, it was a bit different, and they found massive ground disturbances that resembled a parking lot of carriages. As Dr. Leader put it, "Sherman's thousands of troops and hundreds of horses and carriages had no place to go while the pontoon bridge was being built, so they had to just park and wait."

The discovery that Patrick made in the archives, an 1840 plat with an image of the bridge, was also a surprise and provided a missing link. In summary, the circumstantial evidence of the 1870 survey and the 1840 plat were scientifically verified with the geophysical survey results. The historical marker and "Mills' Atlas" were proved to be incorrect.

It could not have turned out better, and I was speechless when this was presented to me on camera. I honestly had not thought about what I would say in this situation. Elyse asked me, repeatedly, what this meant to me. Each time the pressure to answer grew until it just happened, and I spoke from the heart. It was about my dad. I never expected to do that, but it happened, and I was glad it did. When I was done, the producer said, "That was great!" And she ran to the bathroom, wiping the tears from her eyes. I thought they would use this, but only a short part of it, without mention of my dad, made the final cut.

Almost done now with the filming, I changed back into my original morning outfit, and we headed back to the bridge to take photos and footage of Elyse and me in front of the incorrect historical marker. It was raining once again, so we got a little wet. Then we returned to the house, and the crew filmed me on the upper deck with a different angle of the bridge in the background. I say, "Sometimes history is in your own backyard." They admitted that was corny, but it still made the final edit.

Laura spent the next three weeks editing the video, and I think Dr. Leader also had a grad student do overlays of the 1870 survey as a sanity check of my work. After the three weeks of editing, it went to an executive producer at PBS. I think their edits went on for another two to three weeks.

In total, the planning, shoot, and edit took a total of 12 weeks of work for what would turn into less than 20 minutes on TV. At the writing of this book, PBS still had the episode available online. A Google search for "History Detectives Civil War Bridge" will find it.[44]

As the initial excitement settled down, I began to see how all the evidence fell into place to complete the puzzle. But there were two extra pieces left over. An incorrect historical marker and a flawed "Mills' Atlas." The historical marker error can be attributed to the 1929 account of an eyewitness to the 1865 event.

The old McGowan's Ferry site was opened shortly after the war, while the bridge was being rebuilt. The ferry site sat below the burned bridge and had not been used in many years. The old Stark's Ferry site sat above the burned bridge, as seen in the 1870 survey and 1865 illustration. It had been

---

[44] PBS History Detectives: Civil War Bridge video: http://www.pbs.org/video/history-detectives-web-extra-civil-war-bridge/

in use before the war, which is why Sherman used it. The 30,000 Union troops moving through would have made a mess of the site, which is probably why McGowan's Ferry site was later reopened.

I believe the eyewitness account to the 1865 event confused the two ferry sites, and the "downstream" wording in the marker really applied to the Stark's Ferry site. The word should have been "upstream."

As for the "Mills' Atlas," this map was based on the 1818 state surveys, which were accurate. There was a half-mile mistake made when creating the "Mills' Atlas." Of course, the atlas was more of a coffee table book than a navigation aid. This is an example of why old maps are not reliable. The lesson is that surveys should always be favored over maps for historical locations.

The success of finding the old bridge, and Sherman's Crossing, is what established me as a local historian. The Columbia Historic Foundation, which had also supported me through this venture, gave me the Historic Preservation Award for the year[45], and the South Carolina Department of Archives and History selected me as a speaker at their Civil War Symposium. Many more talks would follow, from neighborhood associations to Cub Scout groups, from the Sons of the American Revolution to the Sons of Confederate Veterans, from libraries and genealogical societies to the Explorers Club. I would be busy for a while, and it would all feed more inspiration and motivation.

---

[45] The Historic Columbia Foundation's Helen Kohn Hennig Award for Historic Preservation to David Brinkman for the PBS History Detectives "Civil War Bridge" nationally television episode.

Chapter 9 – The Story of Sherman's Crossing

On February 16, 1865, Union General William T. Sherman and his right-wing of 30,000 Union troops met Confederate General "Fighting Joe" Wheeler and approximately 30 Confederates at the Broad River Bridge. The official records of the Union Army did not include the details of this skirmish, probably because of the embarrassing trouble the Union had with Wheeler's tiny group. Wheeler and company would delay the 30,000 Union soldiers for almost 24 hours, enough time for other Confederates to move important items out of Columbia. This was the last stand for Columbia, as the Union Army burned the city the next day.

Figure 50: William Waud's 1865 illustration of Sherman's Broad River crossing from Harper's Weekly April 15, 1865.

As in the case of my father's Iwo Jima letter, the best sources for the details of this skirmish are the men who were in the battle. W.C. Dodson, who would become a historian, provided the following account in Volume 17 of "Confederate Veteran," published in 1909.[46]

46

https://en.wikisource.org/w/index.php?title=Page:Confederate_Veteran_volume_17.djvu/476&action=edit&redlink=1

Burning of The Broad River Bridge
By W. C. Dodson, Atlanta, GA.

The conflicts between General Sherman's army and Wheeler's Cavalry in defense of the city of Columbia occurred upon three distinct days and at three different points. The first battle occurred on the morning of February 15, 1865, at and in front of Congaree Creek, about five miles from the city on the State road. The second occurred on the afternoon of the 16th of February in the triangular space between the Saluda and Broad Rivers, formed by the junction of these rivers, and included the burning of the Broad River Bridge, which was burned late that afternoon. The third conflict was a skirmish with Sherman's advance guard after it had forced a crossing over Broad River on the morning of February 17 and took place between the Broad River and the city as Sherman advanced to take possession of the place. A short account of these engagements in the order in which they occurred will lead to a clearer understanding of the defense of Columbia.

The battle at Congaree Creek, which occurred on the morning of February 15, was brought about in this way: On the night of the 14th of February, 1865, Dibrell's Division of Wheeler's Corps went into camp on the State road about eight miles from Columbia, with General Sherman in their front and the doomed city in their rear. On the morning of the 15th at an early hour General Wood's division of Logan's Corps of Sherman's army moved forward toward the city, engaging our outposts hotly. Without waiting to complete even our scanty breakfast, which we were preparing when the firing began, we were ordered to move out of camp rapidly on foot by companies, not waiting for the entire regiment to form. We went to the front at double-quick, going into line of battle on the edge of a wood confronted by a cornfield through which Wood's Division of Logan's Corps advanced. They came in a heavy line of battle with skirmishers thrown out. The conflict became at once stubborn and sharp. Our men took shelter as best they could and refused to be driven. They held their ground firmly until overwhelming numbers forced them to retire. Our loss in killed and wounded here must have been quite heavy. I recall that Colonel Breckinridge's acting adjutant general, James W. Stoner, was mortally wounded; his aid, Lieutenant Hill, was seriously wounded, and never again was able for service. The Yankees with their superior numbers drove us steadily back for about one and a half miles, when we again went into line of battle at the bridge over Congaree Creek, about five miles from the city of Columbia.

We reached this point probably by 9 am of the 15th. Here the fight was renewed, our troops occupying temporary breastworks of logs and rails. Our line of battle was about half a mile long, running parallel with Congaree Creek, and about fifty yards from the creek. The center of our line of battle was the bridge over that creek. This line of battle was formed alone by men of Wheeler's Corps and was composed alone of Dibrell's Division, as I remember. Artillery was used on both sides freely. The conflict was carried on with great determination. Our lines held their ground until about 2:30 in the afternoon, when the Yankees succeeded in turning our right and crossed with pontoons over the Congaree above us. This forced us to fall back across the creek under a heavy artillery fire directed at the bridge.

In retiring we endeavored to burn the bridge, but its timbers were so wet and covered with mud that we found it impossible to do so. We occupied for a short time some earthworks which had been constructed on the north side of the Congaree; but these works were untenable, as they were enfiladed by General Wood's troops, who had reached the Congaree above our right. we now abandoned these works, mounted our horses. and fell back in the direction of Columbia. Dibrell's Division was really mounted infantry; we rarely fought mounted. We were armed with Enfield and Springfield rifles and navy revolvers.

As we fell back slowly in front of Sherman's advancing army we witnessed on the clear plain between Congaree Creek and Columbia one of the grandest pageants of arms that it was my privilege ever to see. Several thousand men of Sherman's army advanced over this plain in line of battle, artillery thrown out in front, with long lines of skirmishers in front of the artillery, and bands were playing and flags flying. It was a scene so impressive as never to be forgotten. While Dibrell was fighting

Sherman at Congaree Creek, General Wheeler with the other divisions of his corps was attacking Sherman's army in flank.

This ended the first day in defense of Columbia by Dibrell's Division of Wheeler's Cavalry Corps. That night our division crossed Congaree River into Columbia. We marched through Columbia, crossed the Broad River bridge, and went into camp about one mile from the bridge on the Atlanta road, I believe. Here we remained in camp until about two o'clock on February 16, 1865, when we were put in motion to meet General Sherman's army advancing on the Broad River bridge, having crossed the Saluda, although Opposed by General Wheeler's men on the night of the 15th and the morning of the 16th of February.

It must be remembered that Columbia is situated on the Congaree River, the Saluda and the Broad Rivers uniting just above Columbia to form the Congaree. Now General Sherman did not advance on Columbia in its front across the Congaree, but turned around the city, and marching somewhat west he forced a crossing over the Saluda above the junction with the Broad River. He then marched across from the Saluda to the Broad River bridge, which we burned to prevent his getting possession of it. He then on the night of the 16th forced the crossing of the Broad River below the burned bridge, marching into Columbia early on the 17th of February. The city was perhaps a mile away. About two o'clock on the 16th we were hastily mounted and marched to a point near the Broad River bridge. We were here dismounted and sent on foot down into the triangle formed by the junction of the Saluda and the Broad Rivers and placed in line of battle to meet General Sherman's forces, who were advancing to their objective point, the bridge over Broad River. Their aim evidently was to surprise us and capture the bridge by their heavy forces advancing rapidly on the position.

The Kentucky Brigade was placed in line of battle a full half mile from the bridge on the extreme left of Dibrell's Division. Howard's Corps advanced upon us in heavy force and the fighting was getting pretty active, when a courier came very hurriedly, ordering us to retire before the advancing enemy and to return to the Broad River bridge just as quickly as possible, as the left of Howard's advance was now close to it and would cut off our only means of escape. Heavy firing near the bridge told us more forcibly than words that we were in great danger of capture. We at once made for the bridge as fast as our legs would carry us, and we went in considerable disorder. Those of us who were on the extreme left retreated right up the bank of the Broad River, and encountered a good deal of rough and hilly ground over which we had to march; hence we were very much delayed in reaching the bridge. The right of our brigade and those who moved more rapidly had already arrived at the bridge before we did and passed over.

When our delayed detachment, composed of men from the extreme left of the line of battle, came in view of the bridge, to our astonishment there was considerable confusion at the entrance of the bridge, and men and horses commingled were being passed rapidly through. The advance of the enemy was only a few hundred yards away and was firing upon our retreating men. This delayed detachment at once took in the situation and constituted themselves into a rear guard, and without orders took possession of a high hill about one hundred yards from the bridge on the left of the road as we faced the enemy and opened fire on the enemy in our front. We at once saw that it was hopeless to try to pass the bridge while it was so jammed. This rear guard was composed of a few men and officers from all the regiments of the Kentucky Brigade and were under the command of no particular officer. General Wheeler, I am sure, did not know we were in the rear, and hence the trouble arose in regard to notifying us that the bridge had been fired. I suppose we held this position on the hill ten or fifteen minutes, when we noticed dark clouds of smoke issuing from the top of the bridge and from the entrance. The bridge was perhaps four hundred feet long, was built of pine, weather boarded on the sides, making it a closed bridge from end to end. The bridge was divided through the middle, thus making a double pass-way. We fully expected that someone would notify us when the bridge was fired; hence we lingered in its defense longer than we should have done. But no one appeared to give us notice because they evidently were not aware that there were any soldiers still on that side of the river. The increasing smoke and evidence of fire at the bridge convinced us that longer delay would be fatal so without waiting for orders we started on a run for the bridge. Every man seemed to feel that the time had come when his salvation depended on his own personal effort and that he could not help his comrade by delay. We rushed down to the entrance, saw the situation, and began a wild rush for life through the fired bridge.

It has been stated that the bridge was fired all the way through and that the men rushed through this fiery furnace. This is a mistake. If such had been the case, no living mortal could have passed through the ordeal alive. The bridge was fired' in both pass-ways; fired from the west end, the end from which we entered it again about twenty steps farther on, then again about halfway the length of the bridge. There was no fire from the center of the bridge to the eastern end or outlet on the Columbia side. But these fires were about fifteen feet wide, and were rapidly enveloping the entire bridge both on top and sides. The air was superheated and the smoke was dense and stifling, making a fearful place through which to run the gantlet for life. If we had hesitated for a moment at the end of the bridge or realized the danger before entering the fire, I doubt if any of us would have attempted it. I remember distinctly that when starting I pulled my hat down over my face, grasped the cylinder of my navy pistol with my hand, and rushed through the first conflagration at the west end of the bridge. I was horror-stricken to see another blaze just as bad a short distance ahead of me. I involuntarily shuddered and shrank and felt an impulse to retreat; but in a moment recovered my nerve and dashed into the next fire, hoping this would be the last. When I went through this fire, I felt as if I were almost burned up and as if my eyes were blistered. When I saw still another conflagration ahead of me, I summoned my strength and courage and rushed with all possible speed for my life. As I went out of this fire I fell flat over someone who had stumbled and fallen. I arose to my feet and ran for quite a distance and found that I was still in blinding smoke and hot air. I pushed on through this, hardly seeing anything, but feeling an impulse to push for daylight, which I finally reached, almost overcome with heat and suffocated with smoke. My hands and face and ears were blistered, my hat and clothing were scorched, and my brow and eyes felt as if they were on fire.

As I emerged from the bridge the first men I saw were General Wheeler and Colonel Breckinridge sitting on their horses peering anxiously into the smoke of the bridge, from which the men were emerging at short intervals. The first thing Colonel Breckinridge said to me was: "Are there any more men behind you?" I answered: "Yes, Colonel; but I do not believe any living mortal can pass through those flames after me and live." But as I spoke here came another run of men who were behind me nearly burned up. It was pitiable to see these men, some with the skin burned entirely off their hands and necks and faces, clothes scorched, eyelids blistered. Many of them, as stated, had to be sent to the hospitals or to private houses out in the country where they could be cared for. A few of them were never able for service again before the war closed, and many of them wore scars to their death.

No description of that terrible rush through those flames can do it justice. It is simply a marvel that we were not all cremated alive. One lived a lifetime in the few minutes which transpired in passing through that fiery expanse. The bridge was consumed entirely in a half hour and fell into the river. The burning of this bridge occurred about 4 PM. Our men were very soon compelled to fall back from the bank of the river, as the Yankees kept up a fire of small arms across the stream.

During the night of the 16th General Sherman's advance crossed in boats to an island in the Broad River. A pontoon bridge was made to the island. Early the next morning they crossed to the mainland on the Columbia side of the river under cover of their artillery. By eight o'clock they began their march for the city of Columbia, a mile or so away. Williams's Kentucky Brigade formed a line of mounted skirmishers in front of Sherman's advancing lines, and we fell back slowly to the city limits. A man in our line of skirmishers was killed just outside the city limits and was left there.

Just beyond the city limits we met the Mayor with a white flag, accompanied by a deputation of citizens, going out to meet the advancing foe with the purpose of surrendering the city. Near the city limits our brigade turned to the left and took up our line of march on the Winnsboro road, moving out of the range of the enemy. Lieut. Milton Overly, of the 9th Kentucky Cavalry, commanding the rear guard, passed through the city, clearing it of straggling Confederate soldiers, and joined us later. That night we, having learned of the burning of Columbia during the day, sent scouts back into the city to learn the fate of our wounded who were left in the hospitals there. Fortunately, the hospital in which they were placed escaped the flames, though it was very much endangered, and the wounded men were ordered out of the building.

In closing what I have written in regard to the defense of Columbia, I desire to say that no comrade can have a higher respect for Gen. M. C. Butler and his heroic soldiers than I. As a part of the Army of Northern Virginia they won imperishable renown; and if opportunity had been afforded them of meeting General Sherman's army before the gates of Columbia, without doubt they would have given good account of themselves; and I will further add that it was no fault of theirs that they were not at the forefront in the defense of the city, but such was not the case.

By the fortunes of war, it fell to the lot of other no less heroic soldiers belonging to the Army of Tennessee to occupy that position. I shall ever be proud that the Kentucky Brigade was of the troops chosen for that purpose, and we were but too glad of the opportunity of striking a blow at our common enemy in defense of the capital of South Carolina.

Four years later, in 1913, Andrew Sea provided his account in Volume 21 of "Confederate Veteran."[47] Andrew Sea was the man who had the terrible job of deciding just when to fire the cannons at a bridge that was filled with his own men. Sea is not as descriptive as Dodson, who had to run through the

---

[47]

https://en.wikisource.org/w/index.php?title=Page:Confederate_Veteran_volume_21.djvu/598&action=edit&redlink=1

burning bridge. Maybe Sea had blocked out memories of his fellow men who suffered and, undoubtedly, died from their burns. The Official Records of the Union Army did show that eight Confederates were captured because the bridge was destroyed before they had a chance to cross. The fate of these captured men might have been even worse, as they were probably sent to a prison camp where many Confederates died that winter.

Figure 51: David Brinkman's computer simulation of the Broad River Confederate bridge and Sherman's pontoon crossing skirmish. The bottom image is from the same spot where William Waud made his 1865 Harper's Weekly illustration of the burned bridge and pontoon crossing.

The accounts give great credit to the outnumbered Confederate forces, especially General Wheeler and his men, in defense of Columbia. The outcome might have been very different if the Confederates had even only one-tenth the troops of the Union Army. The Union, however, had worn down the Confederate Army, and the men and supplies were just not there. The destruction of Columbia, for all practical purposes, marked the end of the American Civil War. You could say this skirmish was the last stand for the Confederate Army. The Secession and Confederacy were born in Columbia on December 17, 1860, and they died there at the Broad River Bridge on February 16, 1865.

As I finished writing Miracles to Yesterday, I met with officials from the Richland County Conservation Commission, and the City of Columbia, to set a location for the historical marker which will replace the incorrect Broad River marker. I told them the story of Columbia's last stand while standing at the spot where it happened 152 years ago. It dawned on me then that the delay, that Wheeler and his men gave Columbia, may have been what saved those early South Carolina General Assembly documents from burning with the city of Columbia. Patrick McCawley of the South Carolina Department of Archives and History confirmed that, in fact, the 200 crates that contained these records were loaded on trains late in the evening on February 16, 1865 (hours after General Wheeler and men burned the bridge) and safely moved out of the city. My research could not have blossomed into anything without these documents. None of the South Carolina discoveries in this book would have happened without this little miracle of Wheeler's bridge defense.

Confederate General Wheeler would go on to be a U.S. Representative from the state of Alabama. In 1898, at the age of 61, Wheeler would return to fighting in the Spanish-American war as a Major General in the U.S. Army in Cuba. In 1899, he was back on a horse fighting in the Philippine-American war as a Brigadier General in the Philippines. He is one of only two Confederate Generals to be buried at Arlington National Cemetery where his memorial is the tallest in the cemetery.[48]

---

[48] https://en.wikipedia.org/wiki/Confederate_Memorial_(Arlington_National_Cemetery)

Chapter 10 - The Lourdes of Granby

During my four years of researching the area's old river crossings, a lost crossing on the Congaree River stood out. In 1786, Friday's Ferry of Granby was selected as a possible location for the new capital of South Carolina. Charleston had long been the state capital, but the people in the midlands and upstate wanted a more central location. Smack dab in the middle of the state were Friday's Ferry and Granby. Unfortunately for Granby, the people deciding the final location felt like Granby was an "unhealthy" place because of flooding and mosquito-borne illnesses. They decided to form a capital called Columbia on the higher ground on the other side of the Congaree River. Granby would die out over the next 40 years, and its location would be largely forgotten in another 100 years.

In 2010, historian Dean Hunt informed me that another local history buff, William Schumpert, had located what might have been a remnant of the Friday's Ferry structure in the Congaree River. I pulled out the notes I had compiled on Friday's Ferry and found it was at the end of a road that went through the center of the lost colonial village of Granby. I also used a combination of the 1870 canal survey and the 1818 state surveys[49] to pinpoint Granby.

The Granby community was gone by 1870, but a creek on the opposite side of the Congaree River was still there and was also shown in the 1818 surveys. After doing overlays of the surveys on modern maps, I had a high confidence in the location of Granby. Two-thirds of the old town was now erased by a granite quarry or covered by a quarry slag pile. The other third of the town, however, had been where a 250-home subdivision was built in 1962.

Visiting the area, I stumbled across a property foreclosure just a few hundred feet from the discovered ferry structure. Once again, an irrational force overcame my wife and me, and we decided to purchase the property with the intent of finding Granby. It was a horrible property investment, and by the time the house was repaired to the point of habitation, we had spent more than double the market value of the house and land. Our story of

---

[49] The state surveys of 1818-1820 completed in Richland and Lexington Counties by Blackburn and Coate. South Carolina Department of Archives and History.

Granby, however, was just beginning, and the event to open my eyes to miracles was about to happen.

After closing on the property, I met my history chronicler Joey Holleman and Friday's Ferry discoverer William Schumpert at the Cayce Historical Museum with Leo Redmond, the museum's director. Joey had written a story about our recent work to locate Friday's Ferry and Granby. All that was needed on this day was a photograph. The story, "This is where the history is," and picture would later appear on the front page of The State newspaper.[50] This would be the last photograph of me in that life as I knew it.

Later that day, Odess and I headed to our newly purchased property to do the first round of cleaning. The house was a mess. The previous owners were smokers, and the combination of cigarette smoke and a gas stove and gas heat furnace had left a thick yellow film on everything. Shag carpet from the 1970s had soaked up dog urine for decades. I wondered what kind of mold I was getting into. Just a couple of years earlier, I underwent allergy treatment for over a year only to have it backfire and trigger strange new allergies. What happened next would take a while to completely figure out.

At about 9 p.m., as we were wrapping up, I took one more load of garbage out. A yellowjacket in the garbage can decided to go after me. As I was going up the front porch steps, it stung me on the wrist. I would have completely forgotten about the incident, but Odess remembered me cursing as I walked in the house and stating that a bug had bitten me. I quickly forgot about the sting because my greatest fear that day was getting into dangerous mold and whatever nasty viruses were lurking in that old house.

Unlike most severe allergic reactions, this one seemed to have a five-hour delay. At 2 a.m., I woke up itching all over. I was shocked to find hives covering almost every square inch of my body. Initially, I was convinced it had something to do with mold or something I had gotten into while cleaning the house. Foolishly, I decided to wait it out. By noon, the reaction seemed to be subsiding, and it was at that point that I discovered a scab on my wrist. It was actually the stinger with a venom sack still attached. I

---

[50] This is where the history is By Joey Holleman, The State Newspaper: http://historysoft.com/news/newspaper2010.htm

scratched it off and apparently re-injected myself with the venom. The same pattern followed, in five hours the reaction occurred again, but with a vengeance this time.

Odess immediately drove me to the emergency room. The itching was so intense I felt I was going to have a mental breakdown. After an excruciating wait, my name was finally called, and a nurse walked me back. As she asked questions, my voice became hoarse as my windpipe began to close. The nurse placed me in a partitioned area and stepped out for a moment. I took the opportunity to scratch my legs. The stimulation from this seemed to overload my brain, and my legs started shaking out of control. The nurse was shocked to find me in this state, and she immediate raised my hand to look at my fingernails. The skin under the nails was dark purple -- a sign my body was shutting down.

I later learned this is often an irreversible process that leads to death. The nurse called a code blue, and I was rushed into another area where suddenly a dozen doctors and nurses gathered. They quickly arranged an IV mixture of steroids and an antihistamine. The nurse then said this was going to take my breath away and asked if I was ready. As the mixture was released, nothing happened. I felt nothing. Several minutes passed, and still nothing. The staff was no longer talking about a procedure or options. A gloom came over everyone, and one by one they started to leave.

I was immediately reminded of an African Catholic priest who had served at our church. Just months before, we gave him a going-away party at our house. One of the guests asked the priest what he thought was the most serious problem in the United States. He said the fear of death is the most serious weakness among Americans. He said he sees it everywhere. Commercials on TV are about looking younger and doing things to extend your life. In the hospitals, he said, every day he observed doctors making frequent visits to patients when they were doing well. But when death was near, the doctors disappeared, and instructions were left for the nurses to carry out the final work. The priest felt the doctors' behavior showed they took death as a failure and didn't want to face it.

The room was now empty except for me and the original nurse. I wondered what had happened to Odess. She was behind me when walking back to the emergency room. The nurse cried, knowing there was nothing she could do. I knew I was dying. Just 24 hours earlier, I was on top of the world. I had so many projects in the queue. I had a wife and son who depended on me to provide for them. Now I was losing everything, and I thought my life would end incomplete and be a failure. I had been blessed with so much but had done so little with it.

But at the point of falling to pieces I did take the time to do what had never failed me before in tough situations. I asked the question, what would my dad do? I guess I figured I could at least honor him one more time. As usual, with my dad being the great mentor that he was, the answer was obvious. It sure didn't seem like something that could help me, but I did it for him. I turned to the nurse and thanked her for helping me. That's what my dad would have done.

Some miracles take a while to figure out. Sometimes it takes months or years to realize something was a miracle. This was not the case. As those last words of thanks to the nurse came from my mouth, an indescribable peace came over me. I was done. I was ready to go. Looking back, it makes no sense. How could I in an instant go from losing everything to being at total peace? I closed my eyes. Nothing else mattered. My last prayer was simply: "God, I'm done. Do with me whatever you want."

With that, an easy-to-describe feeling came over me. It was like an electrical charge that started from the top of my head and slowly moved down to my feet. As it passed, all the overwhelming itching disappeared. I thought maybe my nervous system was shutting down. There was no tunnel or bright light, just darkness and peace. I thought this was death, and I accepted it.

It seems the electrical charge was not death; it was life. I'm not sure how much time passed, maybe only minutes. I came out of the darkness when I heard Odess' voice. I opened my eyes. Just beyond my legs, which were still shaking, I saw my rattled wife in shock at my condition and all the equipment connected to me. The nurse calmed her down and told her that they lost me, but I had come back and was now stable. While walking back to the emergency room, Odess had had a premonition and run outside with her rosary. She had been outside praying the rosary during the entire ordeal.

Just one hour later, the physical ailments were gone, and I walked out of the hospital. The peace that had come over me was, without a doubt, a miracle. The electrical charge also seemed to be a miracle, and for the next year I tried finding out if other people had experienced something similar. I thought for sure I would find something if this was a common effect of the IV mixture. But the electrical charge starting at the top of the head and moving down to the feet just didn't seem to make sense with a medical solution that entered through my arm. I tried, unsuccessfully, to come up with a scientific explanation, so it seemed the electrical charge was another miracle. Of course, the most important thing now was that I had been given another chance, and I began to realize that this journey into history was also about miracles.

As the next year passed, I continued researching the Colonial town of Granby. It became apparent that getting archaeologists on site was not feasible. We had already invested so much money in buying and repairing the property that there was no way we could afford to pay professional archaeologists to do the work. Odess and I decided to try our hand at a professional dig, with the idea that we might eventually lead the Granby archaeology work ourselves.

Along the way, I continued to keep my eye out for interesting historical items and projects. I had been on a committee to update the history of our church, St. Peter's Catholic Church in Columbia. While searching on eBay for old items that might be related to our church, I stumbled across an 1899 picture of the Grotto of Lourdes on the church's property. Lourdes is a town in southwestern France that is a major Catholic pilgrimage site. In 1858, it is said the Virgin Mary appeared to a local woman there. Over the years, the Catholic Church has investigated and accepted many miracles that have occurred at the site.

Figure 52: Grotto of Lourdes dedication day at St. Peter's
Church Columbia, SC - October 11, 1899.

Figure 53: St. Peter's School with Grotto in background – 1938.
Credit St. Peter's Church, Columbia, SC.

About the time of my near-death experience, the movie "Lourdes" was released in France. A year later, Odess came across a copy of it in the local public library and checked it out, knowing that I had been researching a re-creation of the Grotto of Lourdes at our church. The movie itself was centered on a fictional account of a woman who makes a modern-day pilgrimage to the site hoping to be cured of multiple sclerosis. As we watched the movie, reading the English subtitles, it came to a scene where the pilgrims are at Lourdes viewing a video of the testimony of a man, Jean-Pierre Bely, who was cured at the site. Try to imagine how I felt as the man describes his healing as occurring while others prayed for him and then the feeling of electricity moving from his head to his feet.

> Everyone was praying devotedly, repeating the words spoken by the priest.

> I was exhausted and felt unwell, so I couldn't pray anymore.

> I concentrated instead on a single thought: "Lord, may Thy will be done. Virgin Mary, pray for us."

> Suddenly, I felt a bolt flash through me from my head to my feet. Like an electric shock.

> I thought it was the end. But no, I was kneeling in front of my wheelchair, upright, with my hands together.

> I don't know what happened but I knew that I was cured. The pain was all gone.

> And my limbs, which had been paralyzed and flaccid, were full of renewed strength.

When I started writing this book, I decided to watch the movie a second time to make sure I remembered things correctly. I also wondered if the character and testimony of the man was real or fictional. Not only was it real, but the miracle also was investigated by doctors and scientists, who had never seen such a cure and had no explanation. The Catholic Church also investigated it and declared it as a miracle. Some people consider it to be one of the greatest of modern-day miracles. The man, despite having medically confirmed severe multiple sclerosis and paralysis, was permanently cured. Additional documentation also shows that his healing experience was preceded by a moment of indescribable peace. Over a year after my experience, it seemed almost like another miracle from our 1899 Grotto of Lourdes had been presented to further prove my near-death miracle.

So, what does this miracle mean to our stories of yesterday? Certainly, surviving the ordeal let me continue the history work. But why did it happen? Why did I have to go through this? The answer is that the miracles are behind all of this. This event is what made me understand that. I had already documented the historical finds in different places. What needed doing was to tie it all together, with the miracles, in a way that could be both interesting to read and inspirational. As more projects came along, I would become hypersensitive to "signs" as though my brain had been rewired to a new sense. It made me look back over all the history work and, as Dr. Leader hoped (Chapter 8), "come to realize and appreciate how the stars had aligned for me."

As far as Granby goes, on Memorial Day weekend 2012, Odess and I gathered a group of history-loving friends (Cooper Banks, Ken Banks, Jeremy Brinkman, Art Coogler, Dean Hunt, DC Locke, Fred Morrison, David Reuwer, Alma Robichaud, Andrea Robichaud, and Clover Robichaud), and the digging began. Even though most of Granby was made up of farmland, our little lot happened to hold features and artifacts of multiple historic home sites. Lots adjacent to ours held nothing. In five years, with the help of over 120 volunteers, we have found over 15,000 Colonial period artifacts from Granby in the front yard of that poor real estate investment. Almost 1,000 artifacts have been found related to the home site of Thomas Brown, who was the first area European trader from a 20-year period before Granby. And more than 500 Native American artifacts have been found, some of those dating as far back as 10,000 years.

Just before my near-death experience in 2010, a force like the one that led me to purchase property on the Broad River, also led us to the Granby land purchase. Immediately after buying each property, I found myself questioning the rationale behind the decision to buy. For Granby, our historical research indicates the odds of finding a Granby home site on our ⅓-acre lot was only one in five, based on the 1⅝ - acre size of the original Granby lots. That, in itself, is not miraculous, but when you factor in the odds of finding the Thomas Brown site, an 800-square foot site on a 100-acre colonial lot, you now have a one-in-5,445 chance. Finding the Granby and Brown home sites at the same location becomes a 1-in-27,255 chance. These are real numbers. The odds against these historical finds cannot be ignored. It is miraculous.

Our five years of discoveries in Granby now allow us to bring this lost village back to life.

> *"My encounter with Bernadette (at Lourdes) didn't convert me, but it gave me the hope of finding faith, it made me a free man. I learned that a scientist cannot fear the truth, that God does not deny science and science does not exclude God. I embraced the mystery.[51]"*

---

[51] Lourdes: A Story of Faith, Science and Miracles

Chapter 11 – A Story of Granby

Looking at Charleston newspapers from the late 1700s, one other South Carolina town stands out with Charleston. It's a place most South Carolinians today have never even heard of. Every day through the Colonial period, goods were being moved back and forth from Charleston up the Cooper, Santee, and Congaree rivers to as far as the boats could go. That place was the village of Granby, and it thrived for 70 years before floods and the next-door development of the capital city of Columbia drove the people away. A few families stayed in Granby for another 30 years before all the land was converted to farmland. In 1891, South Carolina Governor and former Confederate General Wade Hampton III made the following comments about Granby at Columbia's Centennial Address:

"Failing to put our capital city at Granby, the present site was selected and the land on which it stands, bought from Colonel Thomas Taylor, distinguished soldier and patriot of the Revolution. Though our city is not at Granby, that old city has many historical incidents connected with it, which should make us regard it with respect and affection."

The story of Granby will be told in a unique way in this book. The more than 16,500 archaeological artifacts found in our Finding Granby project by over 120 volunteers will guide us through this story. We will cover a range from prehistoric artifacts to a couple of relics left by General William T. Sherman and the Union Army when they camped at Old Granby just before the invasion of Columbia in February of 1865.

First, let's go over the basics of our digging in Granby. In this project, we dug one hole, called a pit, at a time. Each one-square-meter pit was carefully measured and marked before the digging started. It only took us a few pits to observe that the Granby-related artifacts from about 1750 to 1830 were all found in the top 50 centimeters, about 20 inches, of the pit.

Like with other archaeological sites, daily human activity in an area leaves behind a rich and dark soil. We also noticed that no matter the depth, when the soil changed from dark to light, no more Granby artifacts would be found.

We quickly developed the three-level method. Level one would go from the surface down to 17 centimeters, level two from 17 centimeters to 34, level three from 34 centimeters to 50 centimeters. At the bottom of each level, we would use trowels to level and clean the bottom and look for archaeological features like post holes. You can think of these features as a stain in the ground. Digging into an archaeological feature destroys it, and much care must be taken to detect a feature and record it. The different levels also allowed us to get a relative age on the artifacts within the pit and within all the pits of the dig.

I recorded all the data, artifacts, and features after every pit. I also generated new statistics and charts after each pit, and I even maintained a pit power rating. This allowed us to center on the richest archaeological area of the dig site. Posting this data and photographs of the finds to our website was also exciting to the diggers involved, and it led to new volunteers for the project. All you had to do was call up our website to see what was going on and what had been found.

On May 26, 2015, Granby lead historian Dean Hunt, lead archaeologist DC Locke, and archaeologist Michael Robichaud were among the diggers when we made a special discovery in pit #80. When we got to the bottom of level two, we found a piece of Brown Salt Glazed Stoneware. This easy-to-identify stoneware type was made in England from 1690 to 1775 and in America starting in 1730. This is a unique item because it could cover the early Granby period or even earlier.

Figure 54: English Brown Salt Glazed stoneware.

Shortly after the stoneware find, we came across a Native American pottery piece. Mixed in with all the items were some obvious Granby artifacts, including English imported window glass. In the late 1780s and 1790s, window glass was not made in the area and had to be imported.

Level three of pit #80 gave us several artifacts that dated to the mid to early period of Granby. After only a few centimeters into the level, the soil made a change to a light sandy yellow color. As expected, the discovery of artifacts stopped. There was the temptation to close the pit at this point, but we had plenty of rested diggers and needed to be disciplined and follow our standard procedure of a 50-centimeter depth.

We leveled the pit at 50 centimeters and could not see any archaeological features on the bottom. That's when I went into the hole to clear the last bit of loose dirt for the final pit picture. Making a last sweep with the trowel, I heard the sound of a miracle. With a "ching," out popped a perfect arrowhead. DC Locke quickly identified it as a Dalton point and Michael Robichaud estimated it to be 10,000 years old.

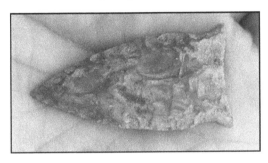

Figure 55: The Pit #80 Dalton Point.

We had found two other points in Granby, but not at this depth. The 14 centimeters of dirt above this find was void of any artifacts, which also showed a significant time difference between this Dalton point and Granby. But was this really a surprise?

It should not have been. In one three-mile-long, ¼-mile-wide area in the United States, man-made artifacts have been found for a span of 12,000 years. No other place in the country has shown evidence of continuous human habitation for as long. That beats the 11,400-year span that England claims around Stonehenge. Where is this special place in the United States? It's in Cayce, South Carolina, along the Congaree River. Our Granby dig site is in the northern portion of it.

Of course, 97% of this 12,000 years is Native American habitation, but the other 3% does include significant historical events. These range from the first European traders and back-country settlement to the first British forts and the significant American Revolutionary War and Civil War events. It also covers when Columbia was an inland port city, moving goods to

Charleston using LST ships from the D-Day invasion of Normandy. It's a mind-boggling 12,000 years of history.

There's no sign of it on the surface. You would have never known about it if not for passionate history lovers. Fortunately, thanks to the additional support of the National Park Service, Cayce Mayor Elise Partin, corporate sponsor SCANA Corporation, and the River Alliance, resources are being applied to create a 12,000-Year History Park so that all can learn and experience this incredible American history.

Figure 56: DC Locke: Historian and Lead Archaeologist for the Granby dig and historical interpreter specializing in Native American.

In 1492, Columbus landed in the Americas and reported the discovery of tobacco being used by the Native Americans. The Spanish would later introduce tobacco to Europeans in about 1528, and Sir Walter Raleigh in 1578 brought the first Virginia tobacco to Europe. Although we had found many European-made ceramic pipe pieces in Granby, we never expected to find ancient tobacco plant remains.

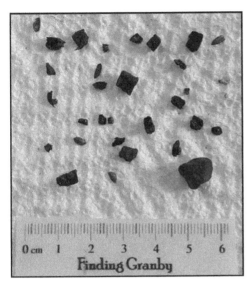

Finding Granby

Figure 57: Ancient Tobacco seed in charcoal.

The most significant find of Granby pit #95 would not unfold until the day after the dig, as we processed the artifacts. While digging the pit, not much notice was given to a small charcoal deposit at the bottom of level three, but nevertheless, it was carefully excavated. During delicate care in the cleaning, tiny seed-like pieces were found in the charcoal. Microscopic examination and expert evaluation indicated the items were tiny burned seed pods. Much time was spent researching this, and the best guess is that this was the very young flower seed pod of a tobacco plant. The amount of charcoal we found was just about what you would expect to come out of a smoking pipe. Europeans only used the tobacco leaves for smoking, but Native Americans were known to smoke these flower seed pods in ceremonies.

In 1917, anthropologist Gilbert Livingstone Wilson, Ph.D. interviewed Maxi'diwiac (Buffalo Bird Woman) of the Hidatsa Indian Tribe (1839 – 1932). The goal was to document, in the publication "Buffalo Bird Woman's Garden", old Native American traditions related to Agriculture. Maxi'diwiac detailed the harvesting of tobacco blossoms: "Tobacco plants began to blossom about the middle of June; and picking then began. Tobacco was gathered in two harvests. The first harvest was of these blossoms, which we reckoned the best part of the plant for smoking. Blossoms were picked regularly every fourth day after the season set in. If we neglected to pick them until the fifth day, the blossoms would begin to seed. These I would pluck from the plants, pinching them off with my thumb nail. Picking blossoms was tedious work. The tobacco got into one's eyes and made them smart just as white men's onions do to-day."

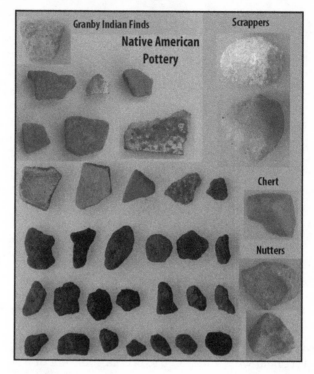

Figure 58: Native American pottery and tools found in Granby.

Further analysis of the charcoal with these tobacco seeds could, through radiocarbon dating, give us a date for this Native American event. The depth at which it was found places this tobacco smoking event most likely before the development of Granby.

The story of Granby will continue with more Native American finds because we know early European trading with the Natives ultimately led to the development of this Colonial village. We need to understand the overlap that occurred between the European settlers and the Native Americans as Granby formed.

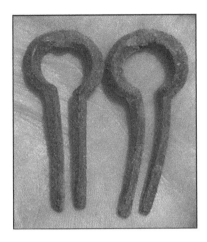

Figure 59: A Jew's Harp (or Jaw Harp) was the most popular trade item for Thomas Brown with the Native Americans.

Native American artifacts represent about 3% of the artifact total in the Granby dig. The 270-year period from Granby until present day is very short compared to the time Native Americans had been here. So why don't we find more items from the Natives? There are a couple of good reasons. This was probably never a long-term settlement for the Natives, and things we find may have been dropped while moving through the area. We would also find more Native items if we dug deeper, since older items are buried over time because of the cycles of plant life that die and turn to dirt. In this area, ants are also responsible for moving dirt up and covering items on the surface.

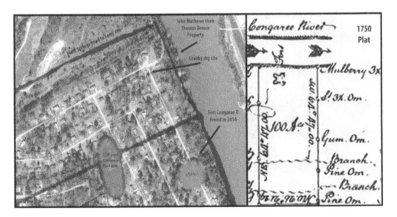

Figure 60: Thomas Brown plat aligned with 2014 pond feature.

Of the Native American items we find, pottery is the most common, followed by tools. A musical piece found in Pits #51 and #67 helped us determine the overlap period of the Native Americans and Europeans.

We had already learned that the area's first European trader, Thomas Brown, had been trading Jew's harps with the Native Americans. Jew's harps feature a metal frame and a flexible resonator. The frame is pressed against the lips or teeth, and the resonator plucked. The vibrations in the mouth cavity create distinctive sounds, thus Jew's harps also are called mouth harps. Both harps we found had the shape and size unique to Jew's harps from 1700-1760. This coupled with Native American pottery and a 1680-1720 dated pipe stem, all found in pit #51, took our dig to another historical period and might connect the site to Thomas Brown's homesite.

Brown was originally from Ireland and probably arrived in this area shortly after the building of Fort Congaree I in 1718. He became the most well-known of traders in the area and married a young Catawba woman. Brown mixed in well with the Native American population, probably because of his wife. In 1740, he purchased the 100 acres that would eventually become the village of Granby. Brown died in 1747, and the land was bought by Martin Fridig (later anglicized to Friday), who would see it developed into Granby.[52]

According to the book "The Expansion of South Carolina," Brown at his death left an inventory of Jew's harps. These harps were very popular with the Native Americans and were often used in bartering and even in land purchases. A Jew's harp was useless if the vibrating tongue was broken off. The harp we found in pit #67 was mixed with charcoal and, at the same level, Native American pottery. Maybe Brown was playing his harp for his Catawba wife by the fire when the instrument was broken and, thus, thrown into the fire. The charcoal material excavated with the harp may tell us, through radiocarbon dating, the age of this event.

Based on archival research and the type of building materials found in the Granby dig, especially the imported window glass and bricks, we concluded the main Granby house had a brick foundation. The discovery of post holes in pits #5, #72, #76, and #79, which overlapped the Granby

---

[52]The Genealogy and History of the Friday Families from Switzerland, Colonial and Southern America (1535-2003).

house, fit with a simple wood structure like Thomas Brown would have owned.

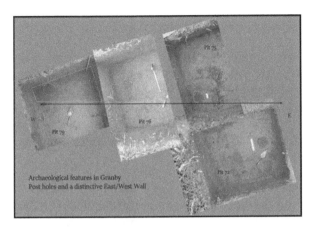

Figure 61: Post holes now believed to have been from the Thomas Brown home site.

Figure 62: Riverland Park neighborhood as it began flooding.

The Jew's harps we found would have been just outside of the structure from these post holes. Once again, things were pointing to the late-1780s Granby house being built on top of the site of Thomas Brown's 1720s-1740s house.

A last piece of evidence for the Thomas Brown site came with the flood of 2015.

When we bought our Granby dig lot in 2010, I knew it was in the floodplain. At the time, the government had run out of funds for flood insurance, and I just had to take a chance. Odess and I spent a lot of time and money repairing the property's house, and we had turned it into a Granby museum by 2015. In the meantime, I had failed to pick up flood insurance when it became available. I was really sweating it out as the October 2015 flooding rains continued and the river approached crest. I finally abandoned things when water geysers started breaking through the ground, flooding the middle of the neighborhood.

Out of more than 250 homes in the neighborhood, only a few properties, including ours, did not file flood damage requests with the Federal Emergency Management Agency. Even with our lot being across from the point where the river broke over the bank into the neighborhood, the water only swept across the front corner of our lot in the road easement area. Not a drop came onto our lot. If that was not a miracle, what happened to that corner in the easement area was.

Just before the flood, a careless heavy equipment operator had damaged and removed all the grass on the corner of our lot. The heavy rains and floodwater exposed almost 600 historical artifacts in this area. Among those were 443 pieces of Granby and pre-Granby pottery, 13 pipe stems, 12 pipe bowl pieces, and 17 Native American artifacts. Just feet away from where the Jew's harps were found, an almost complete ceramic pipe bowl was seen peeking through the ground's surface. Miraculously, the pipe artifact had four maker marks on it, which narrowed the date of the pipe's creation to 1740 to 1750. This was pre-Granby and must have belonged to Thomas Brown who died in 1747.

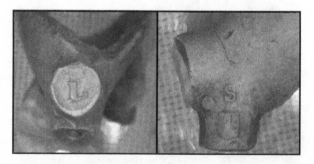

Figure 63: Thomas Brown's Pipe was made between
1740 and 1747 in Gouda, Holland.

After Thomas Brown's death, many important things started occurring. Relations with the Native Americans began to deteriorate to the point where Natives were kidnapping and murdering European settlers. This led to the building of Fort Congaree II as a means to provide protection for the settlers and friendly Natives like the Catawbas. With activity picking up around the fort, people needed an easier way to get across the Congaree River. Martin Friday, who owned a large tract of land about 1/4-mile north of the fort, was able to acquire the Thomas Brown tract adjacent to the Fort Congaree II tract.

Martin Friday and his family had arrived at Charles Town in February of 1735. Martin was 46 years old and from Frutigen, Switzerland. He was one of the original Saxe-Gotha landowners, part of the first push of Europeans into the backcountry of South Carolina. Martin saw the business opportunity of a ferry and started Friday's Ferry soon after getting the Thomas Brown property. Martin was also a miller and tanner. Apparently, he did quite well financially, as his home in 1758 had windows in it. Most backcountry residents had simple wood cabins at that time. We know Martin had windows because a record exists showing a tax assessment on his house and another assessment on the windows.[53]

The town of Granby soon began to form around Friday's Ferry. In the 1760s, activity in the area picked up with the training of men at Fort Congaree II to fight the Cherokee in the French and Indian War. Then the British operated Fort Granby during the Revolution, with sieges of the fort recognized as the most significant Revolutionary War events of Lexington and Richland counties. After the city of Columbia was formed across the river, President George Washington crossed at Friday's Ferry in 1791 on his way to the new capital city. Granby's Wade Hampton would invest heavily in Columbia, and he built three bridges at Friday's Ferry in the 1790s.

As historic as it was, the exact site of Friday's Ferry wasn't marked on the river's banks until two centuries later. In 2007, as part of his Congaree River Historic Mapping Project, land surveyor William J. Schumpert decided to check out a location on the Congaree River where his research pointed to the possible site of Friday's Ferry. As Schumpert paddled around, he noticed a mostly buried wooden structure in the west bank of the Congaree River. Schumpert filed a site report with the South Carolina Institute of Archaeology and Anthropology. A team of archaeologists soon arrived, and they not only verified the structure was Granby period but also found the old roadbed leading to the location.

---

[53] The Genealogy and History of the Friday Families from Switzerland, Colonial and Southern America. 1535-2003

Figure 64: Part of Wade Hampton's 1796 bridge at the
site of Friday's Ferry. Photo by DC Locke.

In September of 2013, the Granby dig team completed a survey of the river around Friday's Ferry landing. A second similar wooden structure was found downstream. This led us to believe the structures may have been parts of the wooden Wade Hampton bridges, which were destroyed or washed away by floods. Hampton built all his bridges at the site of Friday's Ferry.

Martin Friday died in 1758, and his sons John Friday and David Friday would continue their father's businesses, including the ferry. At this period, the village did not have a name, and the general area was referred to as the Congarees. Soon, an event thousands of miles away would decide the name of the village. In what is modern day Germany, the Battle of Warburg raged between the British and French in the Seven Years' War (also known as the French and Indian War in the American colonies.) On July 31, 1760, British General John Manners, the Marquis of Granby, headed a heroic charge that overwhelmed the French in a decisive victory for the British. Manners became an instant hero around the world, spawning the name of several towns in the colonies. By 1761, the village of Granby, South Carolina was officially named after the Marquis of Granby.

The connection of today's City of Cayce and the village of Granby has been confusing for people through the years. It is important that this be clarified. I looked at several sources, including genealogy and the 1860 edition of "The Pictorial Field-book of the Revolution" by Benson John Lossing. Lossing interviewed James William Cayce (b. 1786), whose name he spelled as Cacey. James William Cayce was first married to Ann Friday, who was the great-granddaughter of Martin Friday. The father-in-law that Cayce refers to in the interview is Ann's father, John Jacob Friday. The Tory uncle referred to is David Friday. A Tory was an American colonist who remained loyal to the British during the Revolutionary War. James William Cayce was interviewed by Lossing because he was living in "The Cayce House," which was the former Fort Granby and was considered the most significant Revolutionary War structure in the county.

Figure 65: Ann Friday Cayce's grave is one of the oldest
in the Granby Cemetery. Photo by DC Locke.

Before the war started, the structure was a store, built in 1770 and owned by Chestnut and Kershaw. It appears the Mr. Friday in this interview was operating a store that replaced the Chestnut and Kershaw store when the British converted it to a fort in 1781 following the fall of Charles Town in 1780. James William Cayce's second wife, Elizabeth Rea, inherited The Cayce House from her mother, Ann Geiger. Mrs. Geiger had acquired the house in her first marriage to Major Daniel Tateman, who bought the building from Chestnut and Kershaw at the end of the Revolutionary War.[54]

Although James William Cayce had connections through his two wives to the key founding families of Granby, the city of Cayce was named for his grandson William James "Billy" Cayce. Around 1900, Billy Cayce opened a store at a railroad crossing near the Congaree River, and that area blossomed into today's City of Cayce.

The elder James William Cayce spoke with Lossing shortly before his death in 1849, leading to this reference in Lossing's later publication:

> Mr. Friday, the father-in-law of Mr. Cacey, and his brother, were the only Whigs[55] of that name in the state, and often suffered insults from their Tory kinsman. Mr. Friday owned mills at Granby, and also a ferry called by his name; and when the British fortified that post, the garrison supplied themselves with flour from his establishment. He gave the British the credit of dealing honorably, paying him liberally for everything they took from him – flour, poultry, cattle, &c. On one occasion, when called to the fort to receive his pay, Major Maxwell, the commandant of the garrison, said to him, "Mr. Friday, I hope you are as clever a fellow as those of your name who are with us." "No!" shouted his Tory uncle, who was standing near, "he's a damned rebel, and I'll split him down!" at the same time rushing forward to execute his brutal purpose. Colonel Maxwell protected the patriot, but dared not rebuke the savage, for fear of offending his Tory comrades. After the battle at Eutaw, Colonel Maxwell, and two or three other officers, passing through Granby, stopped one night at Mr. Friday's. Early in the morning, Maxwell said to Mr. Friday, "You Dutchmen are

---

[54] THE COLUMBIA RECORD: March 21, 1936: Trading Post Established by Early Settler
[55] Whigs were Patriots in the American Revolutionary War. They were also known as Revolutionaries, Continentals, and Rebels.

celebrated for fine gardens; let us go and look at yours." When at a little distance from the other officers, the colonel remarked, "Mr. Friday, you are a friend to your country. Remain so. We have not conquered it yet, and never will, and your name will yet be honored, while those of your countrymen who are with us will be despised."

Maxwell's words were prophetic. David Friday, the Tory uncle, was charged with treason against the State of South Carolina. In 1781, the General Assembly passed the Confiscation Acts, and David Friday lost all his property and was banished from South Carolina. He died in 1784, about the time the Confiscation Act was rescinded.

A little Revolutionary War background is necessary before we go into the war action at Granby. On March 26, 1776, South Carolina adopted a new constitution, and John Rutledge, who served in the First Continental Congress and the Second Continental Congress, was elected President of South Carolina. Rutledge began strengthening the state's defenses in preparation for war with the British. Another constitution adopted in 1779 renamed the state's political leader from president to governor. In the spring of 1780, the British took Charles Town. Defeated in their primary role, the State Troops scattered.

Over the next troubled months, the British converted the Chestnut and Kershaw store in Granby into a fort and built a ditch (moat), mound, and wood wall around the building thus fortifying the store. The fort was run by British Major Andrew Maxwell and had a garrison of 300 men. Granby's Wade Hampton and the Friday family owned stores in Granby, and they were required to provide supplies to the fort.

Almost a year after the fall of Charles Town, Governor Rutledge authorized five new regiments of State Troops to be assembled by Brigadier General Thomas Sumter. Granby's Colonel Wade Hampton would, eventually, lead one of these regiments. Later in the year, more regiments were assembled, to be led by men such as Andrew Pickens and Francis Marion.

While the new regiments were coming together, Wade Hampton, based on observations from his store operations, informed General Sumter that Fort Granby was running low on supplies. On February 19, 1781, with almost 300 men but few big weapons, Sumter attempted to take Fort Granby. Sumter's men "would be strange figures beside our trim khaki-clad soldiers, for they wore woolen hunting shirts made by the women of their families, breeches of deerskin, Indian moccasins on their feet, and caps were decorated with the tail of a raccoon. They carried any weapons they could find from a pitchfork to a hunting knife. Sumter was their idol. He exacted the utmost obedience from them."[56]

The first siege of Fort Granby began with Sumter attempting to fool Maxwell with a show of fake cannons. Maxwell did not fall for it, and Sumter could only temporarily lay siege on the fort with rifle fire. Marion was not able to provide Sumter with reinforcements, and Sumter's strategy switched to the destruction of nearby supplies that could be used by the British. The first siege of Fort Granby ended on its third day on February 21, 1781.

Side note: The Fort Granby building, later known as the Cayce House, was purchased by the Weston-Brooker Quarry company in 1923. The owners promised to preserve the structure, but it fell into disrepair during the Great Depression and WWII.[57] It collapsed, and the land it once stood on now is a 400-foot-deep granite quarry hole -- not the proper outcome for the most important historical structure in Lexington and Richland counties. The failure to save this history and the Fort Congaree II site, as was recommended by Dr. Edwin Green in the 1930s, points to a dark time in local historic preservation. We need to learn lessons from this. We should start with efforts to preserve the Granby cemetery and what's left of the old Granby site.

While I was finishing this book, Granby digger Tim Bradshaw brought the Cayce house back to life when he found a set of 1899 pictures of it at the South Caroliniana Library.

---

[56] From William Gilmore Simms story on the first siege of Fort Granby: The State Newspaper April 28, 1930.
[57] The State Newspaper, August 31, 1923: "Historic Old House goes to new hands".

Figure 66: "The Casey House, Lord Cornwallis' Headquarters and afterwards Gen. Nathaniel Greene's," taken by Harry M King, circa January 1899 (Photographs 12050.11.) Courtesy of the South Caroliniana Library.

The 1899 photo shows William James "Billy" Cayce and his wife Louise Elora "Lula" Broughton on the front porch of the Cayce house. Billy and Lula had eight children between 1895 and 1913. The baby in the photo might be Carrie Elizabeth Rea Cayce, who was born in 1897.

The northern half of the town of Granby is also in the quarry hole or under a 275-foot-tall quarry slag pile. The company that now operates the quarry, Martin Marietta, is buying residential property today in the Riverland Park neighborhood. Some of the sold houses are being moved, a sign the property could be used as a quarry and the remaining portion of the old Granby site could be destroyed. Our work to erect historical markers and enact a historic district could prevent this from happening.

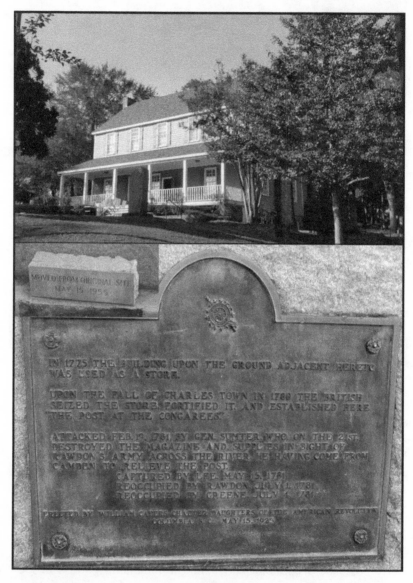

Figure 67: Today's Cayce Historical Museum which is a replica of Fort Granby (The Cayce House).

For now, there is a piece of Granby still intact that provides a tangible connection to the Revolutionary War -- Friday's Ferry.

That leads us to the bloodiest event in Granby's history. On May 1, 1781, South Carolina Lieutenant Colonel Henry Hampton and his newly upgraded Regiment of Light Dragoons quietly moved off State Road as they approached the guarded road to Friday's Ferry in Granby. When Hampton's men assisted in the first siege of Fort Granby, his group was a new militia. They were now better equipped and were official State Troops.

The British, however, had reinforced the fort with additional troops, and the conflict was a daring move by Hampton and his men. They opened fire on a group of the Prince of Wales American Volunteers, who were guarding Friday's Ferry on the west side of the Congaree River. Hampton's men killed 13 of the guards. Another group of British troops made a run for the fort, and Hampton's men were able to chase down and kill five of those men.

Based on the location of Fort Granby and Friday's Ferry and descriptions of Hampton's attack, it should not be surprising that we found 19 musket and shot balls in our lot. A few of those lead balls had impact dents. Could these have been part of the deadly skirmish at Friday's Ferry on May 1, 1781?

Figure 68: Aerial of Granby dig site showing the 19 pits where 21 Revolutionary War era musket balls and shots were found in line with Friday's ferry.

Two weeks later, on May 14, 1781, the bloody attack against the British ferry guards must have been on the mind of Major Maxwell when he woke up to find Patriot Lieutenant Colonel Henry Lee and company with a real six-pounder cannon pointed at the fort from across the Congaree River. Lee, the future father of Confederate General Robert E. Lee, was well known and had won the Congressional Gold Medal for his bravery during the battle at Paulus Hook, where he led his men to victory against the British. When the fog lifted over Fort Granby, Lee's supporting troops moved forward and unleashed a volley of muskets. The show of force was so impressive that Maxwell chose to talk surrender before there was bloodshed.

Maxwell and Lee agreed on terms of the surrender. Maxwell insisted that his men be allowed to walk away with items they had gathered during the war. Maxwell and his men took their substantial plunder and were exchanged in Charles Town for Patriot prisoners. The second siege of Fort Granby was over and the Patriots won a fort loaded with guns and ammunition. Lee and his men tore down the Fort Granby fortifications. The earthworks would be removed years later by a Cayce family member.

Figure 69: Alfred Richardson Simson depicts the May 1-15, 1781 siege of the British post by the combined forces of SC militia General Thomas Sumter and Continental Lt. Colonel Henry "Light Horse Harry" Lee. A 263-man Loyalist force commanded by Maj. Andrew Maxwell defends the fortified frame house. Maxwell agreed to surrender provided he was allowed to maintain possession of his plunder. The green-jacketed Lt. Colonel Lee, depicted to the left, watches his cannon engage the fort from the east side of the Congaree River as General Sumter's and Colonel Thomas Taylor's troops attack. Used by permission of The Cayce Historical Museum, 1800 12th Street, Cayce, SC where the original hangs.

The final event of the Revolution that involved Granby started taking shape on June 19, 1781, when General Nathaniel Greene, commander of the American Continental Army in the South, abandoned his siege of the British outpost at Ninety Six, South Carolina. The small town of Ninety Six, 70 miles north-northwest of Granby, had always been made up mostly of Loyalists, and in 1780 it was fortified by the British. Leading the British forces at Ninety Six was British Lord Francis Rawdon.

Two days later, on June 21, 1781, the Ninety Six fort received 2,000 British and Tory reinforcements from Charles Town, and a number of these men took on the pursuit of Greene. The men would soon turn back as they determined that Greene was too far ahead of them. Greene, however, sent Lee to follow the British forces back and determine their plans. Lee was successful, learning that Rawdon was planning to abandon the Ninety Six fort and split his forces. Half of them were going to Orangeburg under the command of Lieutenant Colonel John H. Cruger. Militia Commander Colonel Andrew Pickens would pursue this group after passing The Indian Head[58] at Goodland Swamp between the forks of the Edisto River. The other half of Rawdon's forces headed to Friday's Ferry, where they would meet British troops of Lieutenant Colonel Stewart coming up from Charles Town.

But Sumter had intercepted a British courier with information that Stewart and his reinforcements had been recalled and would not be able to meet Rawdon's forces at Friday's Ferry. Sumter informed Greene of this. Greene decided they could catch Rawdon by surprise at Friday's Ferry. Rawdon would still be expecting Stewart's men at the ferry, and his limited force would not be strong enough to overcome the combined forces of Generals Lee, Sumter, and Marion. The only problem for Greene now would be to communicate his plan to all the needed forces. He wrote a letter containing the vital information.

This is where the legend of Revolutionary War heroine Emily Geiger comes in. Emily was a descendant of the original Geigers who came to the first backcountry settlement of South Carolina at Saxe-Gotha. Ann Geiger, who would own the Fort Granby house after the war, and Abraham Geiger, who would be a longtime resident of Granby, are believed to be her first cousins.

---

[58] Indian Head: http://orangeburghplats.com/an-indian-head-timeline/

In his 1860 book, Lossing gives his researched interpretation of the story of
Emily Geiger.

> He (Greene) prepared a letter to Sumter, but none of his men
> appeared willing to attempt the hazardous service, for the Tories
> were on the alert, as Rawdon was approaching the Congaree.
> Greene was delighted by the boldness of a young girl, not more
> than eighteen years of age, who came forward and volunteered to
> carry the letter to Sumter. With his usual caution, he communicated
> the contents of the letter to Emily, fearing she might lose it on the
> way. The maiden mounted a fleet horse, and crossing the Wateree
> at the Camden Ferry, pressed on toward Sumter's camp. Passing
> through a dry swamp on the second day of her journey, she was
> intercepted by some Tory scouts. Coming from the direction of
> Greene's army, she was an object of suspicion, and was taken to a
> house on the edge of the swamp and confined in a room. With
> proper delicacy, they sent for a woman to search her person. No
> sooner was she left alone, than she ate up Greene's letter piece by
> piece. After a while, the matron arrived, made a careful search, but
> discovered nothing. With many apologies, Emily was allowed to
> pursue her journey. She reached Sumter's camp, and communicated
> Greene's message.

Figure 70: The Arrest of Emily Geiger: From "The Pictorial Field-book of the Revolution," by Benson J. Lossing, copied from the original painting by Flagg.

The story of Emily Geiger's heroism usually ends here, but what happened after the message was delivered? Lossing completes the story with:

> It is said that Greene's message to Sumter was delivered by Emily Geiger, a young woman of the Fairfield district. On June 25, Greene sent a dispatch to Lee that Sumter and Marion had been contacted, and were mustering their forces in order to come to Granby and help stop Rawdon. However, neither Sumter nor Marion arrived at Friday's Ferry in time to reinforce Lee's troops: General Rawdon was able to push past the American forces on July 3rd and march south to Orangeburg.

The most important aspect of the Emily Geiger story is that South Carolinians were coming out of the woodwork to help the Patriot cause. At Fort Granby and Friday's Ferry, the British were having to make escapes and run away.

In September of 1780, the British seemed well on their way to ending the Revolution after they took Savannah, Charles Town, and Camden. But the people of South Carolina turned the tables with vigilante packs and guerrilla warfare led by Thomas "The Gamecock" Sumter and Francis "The Swamp Fox" Marion.

A one-two South Carolina punch would come in October of 1780 when American Colonel Isaac Shelby and his group of North Carolinians and South Carolinians crushed British Major Patrick Ferguson and his body of American loyalists at Kings Mountain. At Cowpens, backed against the Broad River, Patriot forces under Brigadier General Daniel Morgan managed to disorganize British forces under Sir Banastre Tarleton, and soon Tarleton's forces were wiped out.

By the summer of 1781, the British had lost control of South Carolina and were running for their lives. Although British General Charles Cornwallis had a small victory over Greene in North Carolina, the British cause soon came to an end in his defeat at the Battle of Yorktown in Virginia at the hands of the American Continental Army troops led by General George Washington and French Army troops led by the Comte de Rochambeau. The American Revolution was over.

Figuring out what life was like in Granby just after the Revolution was a difficult task for the Finding Granby team, and it came down to one source that miraculously survived the centuries. In the 1990s, an account book of the Congarees store showed up in a local auction. The book documents items sold in this Granby store from 1784 through 1786. Leo Redmond was able to acquire the book for the Cayce Historical Museum, and the University of South Carolina preserved it and completed a digital scan of it. In 2016, Granby researcher Kathy Keenan, as part of her Masters Theses on Granby, recorded all the entries of the account book into a spreadsheet for further analysis. Some of the entries and analyzed data help reveal the post-Revolutionary War story of Granby.

The account book revealed the list of customers who shopped at the store. It was no surprise that the area's most successful men, the Hampton brothers, and Taylor brothers, were at the top of the list in the total number of store visits. John Compty, the third major area landowner, was also in the top 50 customers.

The most frequent customers of the Congarees store (1784-1786):

Customer name		Visits		Customer name		Visits
Hampton	Richard	139		Slappy	George	6
Sharp	Richard	42		Theus	Christian	6
Hampton	Wade	32		Trair	John	6
Boyd	John	31		Williams	John	6
Seibels,Graff, Braselman		31		Williams	Gardner	6
Taylor	James	28		Curry	Stephen	5
Taylors & Rea		28		Howell	estate of Wm.	5
Arthur	Hardgrove	27		Kelsey	Mr.	5
Brooks	John	27		Stuart	James	5
Goodwin	John	24		Tyler	John	5
Taylor	Thomas	24		Webber	Mr.	5
Stewart	James	23		Bishop		4
Ellis	Charles	19		Butler	William	4
Rilia	Richard	19		Clark	Benjamin	4
Arthur	Ambrose	16		Crawford	Arthur	4
Osman	Paintere	16		Gibson	Joseph	4
Williams	Thomas	16		Gregory	Henry	4
Strange	Henry	15		Hays	James	4
Roden	Thomas	14		Howell	William	4
Wade	George	12		Morrice	Henry	4
Boykin	Samuel	11		Mortimer	William	4
Gillum	Mason	11		Riley	Mr.	4
Foust	Jacob	10		Surgeoner	John	4
Gray	Benjamin	10		Theus	Parson	4
Martin	Dr. James	10		Wells	William	4
McGrew	Alexander	10		Archer	Roderick	3
Brooks	William	9		Archer	Frederick	3
Dorch	William	9		Brown	Thomas	3
Felps	Moses	9		Cunnington	William	3
Howard	John	9		Geiger	Jacob	3
Archer	Wodnick	8		Gozzard	Isaac	3
Emery	Stephen	8		Guigger	Jacob	3

McGowan	William	8		Hogabook	John	3
Roaden	Thomas	8		Kelly	James	3
Roads	Ann	8		Lyle	Robert	3
Beard	Jonas	7		McPherson	James	3
Howell	Thomas	7		Morrisse	Henry	3
Libecap	Mathias	7		Pearson	Thomas	3
Webber	James	7		Ragsdale	Gabriel	3
Allen	Nancy	6		Richmond	Doctor	3
Compty	John	6		Roaf	John	3
Lafloar	Charles	6		Sharp	William	3
Legran	Oliver	6		Thomas	Absolam	3
Miller	Thomas	6		Trayer	John	3

The next statistic is a list of the most popular store products. Given that most people were self-sufficient as far as the basic foods, it was not surprising to see alcohol at the top of the list, with 25% of all sales. Beer was never sold, probably because the people were making beer themselves. One surprisingly low-ranking item was tobacco. Maybe people were growing this within the community and trading with it. Looking closer at the details of the tobacco sales shows the store bought almost 10,000 pounds of tobacco while selling only a few pounds. The Congarees store may have been selling most of the tobacco at wholesale to other stores around the state, and maybe there was another account book for those transactions.

The most popular products sold at the Congarees store (1784-1786):

rum	19.80%	gloves	1.30%
sugar	10.00%	play cards	1.30%
salt	6.40%	tacks	1.30%
thread	5.50%	gun shot	1.30%
shoes	5.40%	locks	1.30%
hats	5.00%	tea	1.30%
buttons	4.50%	oil	1.30%
coffee	4.20%	hinges	1.00%
nails	3.90%	cups saucers	0.90%

silk	3.70%	glasses	0.90%
linen	3.60%	gin	0.90%
wine	3.20%	tobacco	0.90%
paper	3.10%	shirts	0.80%
handkerchief	3.10%	needles	0.70%
gun powder	3.00%	lead	0.60%
knives	2.80%	pans	0.60%
bottles	2.70%	bacon	0.50%
cloth	2.10%	hammers	0.40%
soap	2.10%	butter	0.40%
blankets	1.80%	bowls	0.40%
pepper	1.80%	axe	0.40%
stockings	1.70%	gun flint	0.30%
pots	1.70%	nutmeg	0.20%
spirits	1.60%	cheese	0.10%
buckles	1.40%	spice	0.10%

The products list show many items found at our modern Granby lot. Pit #37 gave us an unusual item which took several months to identify. The breakthrough came one day as I was casually skimming through the book "A Guide to the Artifacts of Colonial America" by Ivor Noël Hume. There on a page was an illustration of the components of an English-made, nine-inch stock lock. This was the kind of lock put on the front door of a house. In the illustration was a lock tumbler that looked identical to our pit #37 artifact. A quick measurement proved they were one and the same. It would probably be another few months before I stumbled across the same nine-inch stock lock in the Congarees store account book. Jacob Geiger purchased it. I began to wonder if we were digging the remains of Geiger's house.

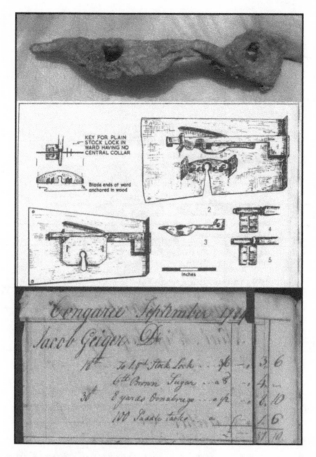

Figure 71: Granby lock tumbler found in the account book. Credit Cayce Historical Museum and A Guide to Artifacts of Colonial America by Ivor Noël Hume.

Many of the artifacts we were finding in Granby were from the 1780s. The stock lock artifact was one of those. It would seem from all the evidence that the house we had found was built about 1784 when Jacob Geiger bought the stock lock.

Another very fascinating statistic in the Congarees store account book involved the pattern of sales from 1784 to 1786. It points to a major change in Granby and the end of the Congarees store.

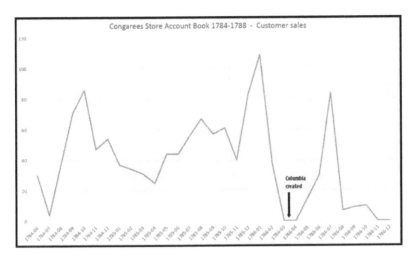

Figure 72: Congarees Store sales

Sales in the store picked up in 1785, probably because that was when Granby was made the seat of Lexington County. At that time, Granby resident Nicholas Hane provided the county with an acre of his Granby land on State Road for a courthouse and jail. This fact would have been lost to time except that the county failed to pay Hane for the land. We discovered Hane's petitions to the General Assembly for compensation of the land. The Granby courthouse was dismantled and rebuilt in Columbia in 1825, and it held the title of the oldest building in Columbia until it was demolished in 1940.

Figure 73: The old Granby courthouse after it was moved to Columbia on the
grounds of the First Presbyterian Church. Historic
photo: Public Domain.

Figure 74: A late 18th century Law Office of Granby now sitting on the grounds of
the Lexington Museum.

Along with the courthouse, Granby also added new buildings for lawyers. One of those law offices is Granby's only surviving building. It was rolled on logs to Lexington, where it became that new town's Post Office.

Back in 1785, things were looking good for Granby. By the end of February of 1786, Wade Hampton had made vast land buys around where he thought the City of Columbia would be formed. He apparently had inside information that the state capital of South Carolina would not be placed in Granby. On March 4, 1786, Hampton's friend Senator John Lewis Gervais introduced a bill to move the state capital from Charleston to a location "near Friday's Ferry." Gervais' plans, no doubt involving the Hamptons and Taylors, would soon target the area of Taylor's Hill, two miles north of Granby on the other side of the Congaree River. As can be seen in the Congarees store account book, the Hamptons and Taylors were the biggest customers of the Granby store. The Hampton brothers purchased Friday's Ferry in Granby in 1785. It seems clear these men saw a great opportunity to make money on a land resale and could influence Senator Gervais into selecting their desired site.

On March 26, 1786, Gervais succeeded in having the City of Columbia created in the middle of the Hampton and Taylor properties on the east side of the Congaree River. This must have been a very anxious and exciting time in Granby. On the last entry in the Congarees store account book, before the store's temporarily closing in March of 1786, the bottom of the page has the word: "AMEN."

In April of 1786, the State of South Carolina purchased over 1,500 acres from the Taylor and Hampton brothers for the main grid of the new capital city. On May 1, 1786, the Charleston Morning Post reported that the area around the new Columbia was buzzing with activity, with sawmills being built on every stream. The Congarees store re-opened toward the end of May. Business was slow in June and picked up in July, only to decline to nothing by the end of October. That was the last time we hear about the Congarees store.

The next Granby timeline artifact is probably the coolest find of the dig. On October 27, 2013, the 3Ds -- Dean Hunt, DC Locke, and I -- were digging pit #52. As I was straightening the north-west corner of the pit with a trowel, a chunk of dirt popped out and fell to the bottom of the pit. A thin round silver edge was sticking out of the dirt chunk. I knew what it was, and I immediately broke away the dirt to reveal a Mexican minted silver half reale.

During the prime of Granby, the American Colony did not have its own coins. The Mexican reale was one of the many imported coins. In the Congarees store, a coin like this would have been converted to the equivalent value of British pounds, shillings, and pence. There were 240 pence in a pound, 12 pence in a shilling, 20 shillings in a pound. The coin we found was about the size of a dime and, at the equivalent of 3.4 pence, it would have paid only for a single shoe at the Congarees store.

As we further cleaned the coin, the date emerged, and the artifact became priceless. It was 1786, the year Granby could have become the capital city of South Carolina. Instead, Columbia would be born, and Granby would be largely forgotten. This was the only coin we found among the over 16,000 artifacts of Granby. It was the miracle silver lining of pit #52.

Figure 75: A Mexican silver coin found in the Granby dig.

As the Hamptons cashed in on their Columbia land deals, a Charleston newspaper, in December of 1787, recorded an advertisement for the sale of their Granby store and property. The Taylor family also tried to divide and sell a proposed addition to Granby in a large tract of land just to the south. The Taylors acted too late, as people were more attracted to property in Columbia. For me, this would be a blessing because that Taylor tract of land was where Fort Congaree II had stood. The fort, and its few remnants would be allowed to survive another 225 years, waiting for a Miracle to Yesterday (see chapter 14).

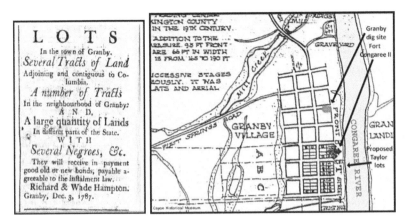

Figure 76: The Hamptons sell their Granby property and the Taylors attempt to do the same as shown in the 20th century "Addition to Granby" drawing in the Cayce Historical Museum.

Advertisements in newspapers during the late 1780s give us insight on the goods that were moving between Charleston and Granby. The moving of these products, the county seat move to Granby, and the influx of people to Columbia were still fueling the Granby economy.

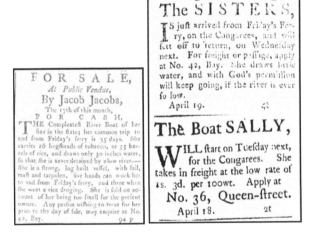

Figure 77: Charleston/Granby boats: Columbian Herald: July 5, 1787 and City Gazette: Charleston: April 1788.

As a new decade began in 1790, the State House building in Columbia was under construction. Newspaper advertisements show lots and homes for sale in Granby, as many people were leaving for Columbia. Wade Hampton, even though he had broken ties to Granby, was beginning to see major problems with getting people across the Congaree River to Columbia. He decided to turn his investment in Friday's Ferry, which he bought five years earlier, into a toll bridge to move people into Columbia faster.

By the end of 1790, the State House was opened, and the first legislative session was held. Among the items approved were Wade Hampton's bridge at Granby and a special provision to allow President George Washington to cross the river without having to pay the toll.

Figure 78: Alfred Richardson Simson's painting "Washington's First View of Columbia – 1791." Used by permission of The Cayce Historical Museum, 1800 12th Street, Cayce, SC, where the original hangs. On May 22, 1791, President George Washington, escorted by Colonel Wade Hampton and Colonel Thomas Taylor, arrived at Granby on the west bank of the Congaree River. Across the river is Columbia, the new Capital of South Carolina.

President Washington, on his Southern Tour, was brought into Granby in May of 1791, but Wade Hampton's bridge was not yet finished. The president had to take the ferry across the Congaree River. Former South

Carolina State Historian A.S. Salley wrote the following description of Washington's visit based on the president's diary:

> Washington left US Hwy. 1 and passed through the town of Granby. At sunset, Washington crossed the Congaree River at Fridig's Landing located south of Granby. Wade Hampton and his brothers had acquired the franchise for the ferry crossing and named it Hampton's Ferry. They had equipped it with a rope and three flat-bottomed boats enabling Washington and his entourage to have a safe and speedy trip across the river to Columbia. Records indicate that crowds lined the Congaree River on both sides anxiously awaiting the President's arrival.
>
> A procession formed as President George Washington mounted his white charger followed by his cream-colored coach drawn by four bay horses. The coachman and footmen were all formally dressed in blanket coats, white and orange liveries, jockey caps, buckskins, and boots. The baggage wagon followed this procession to the State House. From there Washington was taken to a house prepared for his arrival.
>
> Washington dressed in black-velvet formal wear to greet the guests. Sixteen after-dinner toasts were made identifying hopes for the future and concerns of the times. Topics of some of these toasts were: A speedy establishment of a central federal city; The federal legislature -- may their virtues and abilities be as much admired abroad, as they are respected at home; Sufficient means and speedy measures for opening the inland navigation of America.

It is said that the President stayed overnight at the newly completed Rives Tavern and Inn, which was just across the street from the State House.

Moving into the 1790s, a newspaper article that caught our attention described a ½-acre lot with a house and storehouse in Granby. Could this be what we were digging on our lot?

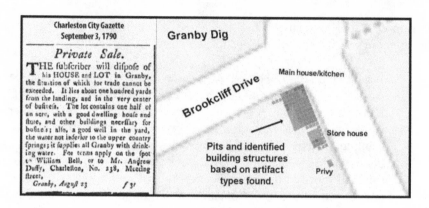

Figure 79: Granby lot for sale and Granby dig site.

After digging 100 pits in Granby, the signs of a house and storehouse became obvious. As part of the statistics I generated after every pit, I had graphs plotted to show the distribution of different artifact categories across the pits -- Kitchen Pottery, Stoneware Pottery, Kitchen Glass, Window Glass, Nails, Brick, Arms, Coins and Jewelry, Activity, Native American, Clothing, Features, and Pipes. What stood out the most was a rectangular area that had, especially around the outside walls, higher concentrations of architecture-type artifacts like brick, nails, and window glass. Within this rectangular area were higher concentrations of kitchen pottery and kitchen glass. This all spelled "Main house" as the building. We then found another rectangular area that was similar, except it had less window glass and higher concentrations of storage-item artifacts like stoneware pottery. This was the "Storehouse."

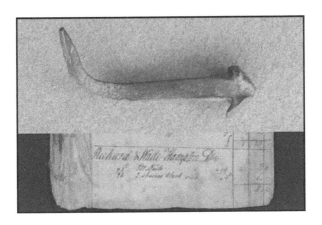

Figure 80: A Granby handmade nail and a large order of nails at the Congarees store by Richard and Wade Hampton. Credit Cayce Historical Museum.

Comparing our finds with a known 18th Century main house and storehouse lends more verification to our theory.[59] Storage buildings in the 18th century often had a cellar lined in clay. Pit #45, just 4-5 meters south of the pits showing the store house finds, had a large quantity of man-formed clay pieces. Artifacts, including stoneware, were found much deeper there than in any other pit. We thought this could indicate the extension of the storage building south and the deeper area of a cellar.

A distinct line was emerging after pit #81, which showed a drop in artifacts that could indicate the south-west wall of the storage room. If so, this makes the storage building smaller and means it would not span to the area of the clay found in pit #45. Another explanation for the pit #45 clay find may be that this is a third building, maybe a privy (toilet). A privy was sometimes capped with clay to contain the odor.

But the question remained, who lived on this homesite? Unfortunately, the newspaper ad did not show who had formerly owned the house, nor who would be the next owner.

As we started to think more about who lived in Granby, a specific artifact type began to draw us to another conclusion. The kitchen pottery we were finding was imported from England and was not something an average

---

[59] Thomas Daniels Archaeological Site:
http://www.ct.gov/dot/cwp/view.asp?a=3873&q=454096

family would have. Granby residents had the signature of wealth, as confirmed in the period documentation.

Figure 81: Pearlware and Wedgewood pottery found.

Among the pottery pieces, the easiest to identify is the Pearlware type. It is very common in our finds, as can be seen in the above picture from pit #22. The Pearlware stands out with its unique bluish tint. Pearlware like this was made only from 1775-1840, which covers the Granby period.

Sometimes we can find a critical part of a bottle, allowing us to identify the item and its age. A bottle top from pit #62 had just the right shape and size to match a documented green bottle from 1800. The combination of a bottle top found in pit #8 and a bottom piece found in pit #46 made it possible to confidently date the bottle type to about five to ten years. The shape of our pit #46 bottom piece was similar to several bottles made between the years of 1761 and 1809, but when you look at the bottle top (same type of green glass), it narrows it down to just the 1804 bottle. The mouth design and size (outside diameter of 1.5") are the same. The neck is maybe even more distinct. The neck is not curved like most bottles, and the angle it takes is just like the 1804 bottle. Furthermore, the 1804 bottle was one of the few wide bottles shown in the artifact drawings.

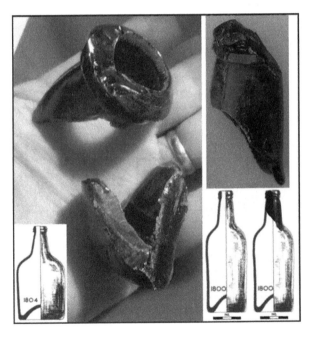

Figure 82: Bottle identification. Credit A Guide to Artifacts of Colonial America by Ivor Noël Hume.

Ceramic types and ages can be identified from a single small piece but determining what the whole item was, whether a bowl, plate or cup, is much more difficult. In Pit #97, however, we got lucky with a rare ceramic piece that had a unique design on it. This Black Basalt Wedgwood piece was almost certainly a specific coffee/teapot made by Josiah Wedgwood in England around 1790. A pot like this was very expensive, which again pointed to wealthy people living in Granby.

Debbie Bloom, a Granby digger and manager of local history at the Richland Library, found a separate section of the 1800 Census that listed only the Granby residents. We finally got a snapshot of the people and possibly the relative positions of the neighbors if the census was taken by going door-to-door.

Granby Residents (1800 Census) Name	FWM under 10	FWM 10-15	FWM 16-25	FWM 26-44	FWM 45+	FWF under 10	FWF 10-15	FWF 16-25	FWF 26-44	FWF 45+	Slaves
Bell, Alexander	2	2	1	1		2		2	1		21
Benson, James K.		1									1
Shaw, James		2	1								
Branham, Peter			1	1							21
Rogers, James			1			1		1	1		2
Seibels, Jacob	2	2	1		1	1	1		1		6
Smith, Joseph					1						2
Sanders, Reuben			1	1					2	1	14
Means, John	1		1	1	2				1		9
Friday, Daniel			1								
Arthur, Hargrove	4			1	1	4		1			30
Johnston, Samuel	1	1		2			3		1		10
Johnston, Henry		1	2	1	1	1		1	1		
McGowen, James	5			1				1	1		
Hane, Nicholas	2		2		1	1			1		7
Pluet, Peter A.			1								
Pelham, Gilbert		1		1					1		
Berck, Gerard			1		1						
Martin, John J.			1		2	1	2	1	1		8
Friday, John	2	1			1	4	2	3		1	6
Friday, Gabriel			1	1			1	1	1		8

Friplin, Benjamin	1			1					1	1
Conyer, Edward			1			2			1	1	
Evans, Lou	2				1				1		
Bynum, John			2	1		2			1		9
Stark, Robert	4		2	1	1	4	1		1		8
Arthur, Jesse	1		3	2	1	1	2		1		4
Rion, Elizabeth		1	1							1	3
	27	11	23	17	14	24	12	13	16	5	170
total inhabitants	332 (162 whites)										

Figure 83: Nicholas Hane's Runaway Slave.

Looking at this census, the statistics indicate Granbyans were wealthy. The people of Granby represented 40% of the population in Lexington County, but they owned more than 60% of the slaves. More than half of the people of Granby were slaves. A May 29, 1826, ad in the Charleston Courier shows just how valuable a slave in Granby was. Longtime Granby resident Nicholas Hane is offering a huge $50 reward for the return of his missing slave Billy. The high standard of clothing Billy is wearing also suggests his master was very well off.

The 1800 Census also narrows down our list of the people and gets us one step closer to identifying who lived in the house at our Granby dig site.

As you can see, the Finding Granby project was not just about digging in the ground. Some of our best finds were dug up in the library. One item that had eluded me for two years was a period drawing of Granby that I had found mentioned in an old book and a newspaper article. This brings us to

205

my personal Granby heroine, Sarah Friday, who was born in Granby in 1795.

If there was a single founder of Granby, it would probably be Martin Friday, whose ferry seemed to attract the development of the town. Martin also acquired much of the property that would make up Granby. It would not be until after his death, however, that the town would take on the name Granby. Martin Friday (1689-1758) would leave some of his property to his son, John Jacob Friday Sr. (1719-1779), who would pass much of it to his son, John Jacob Friday Jr. (1743-1821). This included the house that would be taken and converted to Fort Granby during the Revolution.

Sarah was the daughter of John Jacob Friday Jr. and grew up in Friday's Entertainment house. She probably spent time in the Fort Granby House, where her sister Ann lived with husband James Cayce. After Ann's death in 1814, her children remained in the house, which became known as the Cayce House.

Sarah married John Bryce in 1815, and they had one son in 1818, the future Senator James Edward Bryce. John Bryce's 1850 will indicates he was a very wealthy man. He owned much of the old Granby land, including the land James Cayce lived on. We believe that just before her marriage to John Bryce, Sarah created the only known drawing of Granby. The Granby dig team had been searching for this lost drawing for two years when it was finally found in the South Caroliniana Library on July 19, 2014, by local historian John Allison. The drawing is a priceless artifact, and it provides us with more information than any of the other thousands of dig artifacts. We now had a view of the town and the names of businesses and the people who lived there.

When I applied my overlay process to Sarah's drawing, it only took a couple of extensions on the old State Road and a turn, which Sarah had marked as "Hane's Corner," to make the overlay line up precisely with a 1939 aerial photo. That photo included several familiar landmarks: The Cayce House, the Mill, the Old State Road, and a lone tree at the spot where the old Court House had stood 120 years earlier. Almost 200 years later, we can see how this old drawing falls on today's aerial view. The now known location of Friday's Ferry, owned by Sarah's great-grandfather, lines up exactly with the Ferry Road on Sarah's overlay. And there's no mistake about what our dig site is - the home site of Samuel Johnston from the

1790s until the 1820s. Before that, it was probably the Jacob Gieger house. A large number of metal detector hits across the street from our dig property arises from nails of the old Tobacco Inspection and warehouse buildings.

We owe a debt to Sarah Friday for taking the interest and time to record this image of our lost Granby, but it took more than just her for this to survive for 200 years. In 1905, The State newspaper printed a story about the town of Granby. The following response to this article was by a woman who had found the old drawing among dozens of insignificant documents left in a house she had purchased. She recognized its historical importance and reached out to the readers of The State with the following January 20, 1905, article on Old Granby:

> A Former Columbian Tells of the Old Cayce Fort to the Editor of The State: This is an old Columbian, who spent the "thirties" and the "forties" in your beautiful city. I am always looking to The State to give me items of interest. Yesterday my attention was drawn to that romantic case, Bryce against Cayce. I have a map of the old town of Granby, drawn by the Miss F., whose beauty attracted Mr. John Bryce. In my childhood our plentes were held there, and my many questions to her about this place were hugely answered by this map -- a rough pencil sketch representing every residence and store in the town and also the court house. I have heard persons ask was it ever a town, so this information is historic. (Mrs.) S. A. Caston, Cheraw, SC Jan 18th

Caston's miracle find, documented in the newspaper, was read by a local history lover and collector. Columbia's John M. Bateman acquired the drawing from Caston and added it to his huge collection of historical documents. In 1915, Bateman published his book, "A Columbia Scrapbook," which included a reference to the Granby Drawing. I bought a copy of Bateman's book, and the hunt was on. John Bateman died in 1940, but he had already made plans to donate his collection to the South Caroliniana Library. In 1942, the library took possession and care of the Bateman collection. Although the library's electronic index did not include the Granby drawing, Granby dig team member John Allison worked with the library staff to locate it.

As you can see, it took the care and work of multiple people and a historic institution to preserve what is probably the only surviving view of Granby. So, look (below) at Granby as it was 200 years ago, on top of modern day aerial photos.

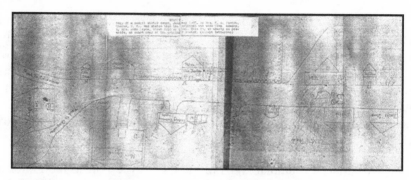

Figure 84: Northern half of Sarah Friday's drawing. "Granby: Copy of a pencil sketch owned, January 1905, by Mrs. S.A. Caston, Cheraw, S.C., who states that the original was made from memory, by Mrs. John Bryce, about 1830 or 1840. This is, as nearly as possibly, an exact copy of the original sketch (except lettering) (Manuscripts Misc. Bateman, John M.) Courtesy of the South Caroliniana Library.

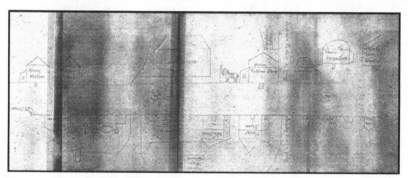

Figure 85: Southern half of Sarah Friday's drawing. Courtesy of the South Caroliniana Library.

Figure 86: Overlay of Sarah Friday's drawing on 1939 and 2013
aerial photos. Credit South Caroliniana Library.

Figure 87: Overlay on 1939 and today's Riverland Park
neighborhood layout. Credit South Caroliniana Library.

We now return to the 1790 newspaper ad about the Granby lot that we
thought might be our dig site. As it turns out, Samuel Johnston had just
married Catherine Harrison when this ad appeared. Samuel was looking to
get into politics and wanted to be close to the new capital city of Columbia.
There is little doubt this ad was for the property of our dig site, and it adds
proof to the accuracy of Sarah Friday's drawing and my overlay. Another
little miracle.

Figure 88: The Granby dig site on top of the Samuel
Johnston home site of 1791-1815.

The decline of Granby:

Although the creation of Columbia on the other side of the river had been a
boon for Granby into the 1790s, the 1800 census and Sarah Friday's 1810
drawing show a rapid decline. Sarah's drawing shows Granby losing as
much as 70% of its population in just 13 years. The Columbia Telescope,
May 14, 1816, gives us a description of Granby in its wane:

> Granby, like London, is divided by a river, over which there was
> formerly a bridge connecting the two towns, which are
> distinguished by the names of East and West Granby, situated two
> miles S. W. from Columbia, the latter of which will only employ
> the attention of the reader, the other merely serving as a landing
> place for Columbia. This town once bid fair to rival Columbia in
> trade, but is at present in its wane. The people hereabouts are
> chiefly Germans or their descendants. It has a Church, but it
> appears now only through the tops of the corn, being situated in the
> middle of a field near the river; the building is low, having no spire,
> except a pine pole 4 feet long, on way of which the inhabitants
> have placed, by way of ornament, a small house for the
> peregrinating swallows, emblematical of their hospitality to
> strangers - in beholding this church we may with Isaiah "there shall
> the great Owl, make her nest, and lay and hatch, and gather under

her shadow; there shall the Vultures be gathered every one with her mate." The Granbyans are great smokers, and have a fondness for their town, few ever leaving it but for another world; they are great observers of Easter Sunday. There is a Crout Factory, established by that enterprising citizen Snyder Scoffle, an inspector of which commodity, is employed, and according to the usage of the people, ex-officio mayor of the town.

Ever since talk of moving the state capital to Granby in 1786, the term "unhealthy" plagued the village. Granby lost its bid to be the capital because of this. We know Granby also suffered many floods through the 1790s, as several of these events washed away Wade Hampton's bridges in Granby. But the historical health statistics of the area reveal that it was a different monster that ultimately killed Granby:

South Carolina Epidemics:

1790 - Influenza; 1792 - Yellow Fever; 1794 - Yellow Fever; 1795 - Yellow Fever; 1796 - Yellow Fever; 1797 - Yellow Fever; 1799 - Yellow Fever; 1800 - Yellow Fever; 1807 - Influenza; 1809 - Yellow Fever and Whooping Cough; 1814 - Diphtheria; 1815 - Influenza; 1816 - Influenza and Smallpox; 1817 - Yellow Fever; 1819 - Yellow Fever.

A newspaper article from the Telescope on April 9, 1816, points out one of these epidemics that hit Granby "where the mortality has been almost unparalleled." The author appears to be a medical doctor. The subject is a particularly unusual strain of influenza that has been moving across the country at the slow rate of 150 miles per year. Men are ten times more susceptible to it than are women. The article also points out that "drunkards" are the most likely to get it, which probably also explains the difference in susceptibility between men and women. People living or working in damp places or near a river were much more likely to get it.

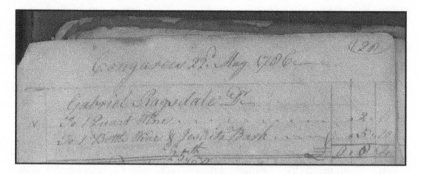

Figure 89: One of many Congarees store purchases of Jesuits' Bark (a Malaria cure). Credit Cayce Historical Museum.

Did the people of this time have any idea that mosquitoes were spreading many of these illnesses? They thought that this flu was somehow traveling through the trees, and many towns clear-cut forests to try to stop the spread of the illness.

An artifact discovery in the Granby dig also points to the mosquito. Finding cloth deep in level 3 of pit #43 was a big surprise. All the other artifacts from the level were Granby and Native American period. It is possible, however, for cloth to survive in the ground for hundreds of years. The cloth artifacts had the color of indigo (blue), which was very common in Granby. In 1968, Gladys N. Chambers wrote the book: "The History of Cayce, South Carolina" and noted the following about Granby indigo:

> The indigo plant had been first brought to North America into South Carolina in 1742 by Elizabeth Lucas Pinckney, and had become one of the main home industries of this area. Millions of pounds were also shipped to the dye plants in Europe. Sometimes the plant grew wild, but as a chief source of income it was cultivated. The ground was plowed near the end of the year, and some mulching done. In the following spring the seeds were sown. The plants were cut two times each year, once in the early or midsummer, and the second time about two months later. The dark blue dye was used in calico printing and dyeing, also for other materials.

> The last record found of Granby as one of the LEADING TOWNS of South Carolina was in 1815. Rumors of mosquitoes and a low,

sandy place were circulated when the talk of changing the Capital from Charles Town to some central place was in progress (in 1786). This had its effect on the popularity of the town. Many of the Granby people who grew indigo plants were building summer homes in other places, because of the many mosquitoes. The water used in making the dye for home use became stagnant and thus bred millions of mosquitoes.

Figure 90: Indigo Blue from Granby.

In the end, what really killed Granby was people living in a low-lying and mosquito-infested area.

Our archaeology work in Granby does give us one interesting, but not yet proven, connection to the 1816 influenza story. In the article, one Granby man successfully protected his family from the illness by burning tar around his property and house. Could this man have been our Samuel Johnston? Many of the Granby pits around the outside of the house structure have produced a dried black substance that floats. This is different than most of the asphalt pieces we find that are related to 1960s road construction. Could this strange material be a by-product of some modern-day asphalt processing, or was this Samuel Johnston's 1816 successful attempt at protecting his family from the epidemic?

Reports of flooding and poor conditions in the Granby courthouse and jail led the county to create the new town of Lexington, and in 1820 the county seat was moved from Granby to Lexington. Many historians mark this as the end of Granby.

Samuel Johnston and his family left Granby about this time, but a handful of families would remain. As referenced in the 1816 article, these people were the "few ever leaving it (Granby) but for another world." Nicholas Hane was probably the last of the Granby old-timers to leave for the other world when he passed away in his Granby home in 1829.

In his book, Lossing reports visiting the Cayce house (Fort Granby). The year would have been about 1849. Lossing remarks about Fort Granby: "It overlooks ancient Granby and the country around. Several houses of the old village are there, but the solitude of desolation prevails, for not a single family remains."

By February of 1865, all the buildings of Granby had collapsed or been moved. On his way to burning Columbia, General William Sherman mentioned camping in "Old Granby" shortly after the Battle of Congaree Creek on February 15, 1865. A handful of artifacts from the Granby dig attest to this. The following appeared in a 1966 State Newspaper article. It raises the possibility that some of the lead balls we have found in the Granby dig could be from this 14-year-old Confederate Granby sniper.

> One often overlooked anecdote reported in an old newspaper centered around the experience of a company of Yankee troops bivouacked near old Granby in Cayce. Periodically a Yankee soldier would plop over dead with a rifle ball through his head. Scouts determined the firing as coming from a wooded area on the Columbia side of the river. The commandant became alarmed, especially because the accuracy of the rifle fire was almost unbelievable. Cannon were brought to bear, the report said, and a barrage practically leveled the source of the firing. The bombardment appeared successful as firing from the area ceased. Cautiously, a Yankee patrol paddled across the Congaree River and scouted the area to find only the body of a 14-year-old boy lying beside his muzzle-loader rifle. As it turned out the boy was the only defender of Columbia at that site and the Yankee commandant was said to have sorrowed at the report but credited the youth with valor as well as "being a darned good shot with that gun."

This young boy may well have killed more Union soldiers in Granby than all the other Confederates defending Columbia. Keep in mind that, in the

1800s, "Granby Landing" was the old site of Friday's Ferry. It was not the site of today's Granby Landing, which is one mile south.

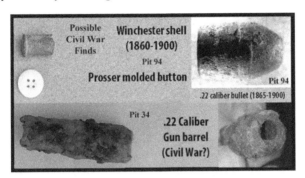

Figure 91: Civil War era artifacts found in the Granby dig.

On Halloween in 1978, vandals burned one of the two surviving Granby structures near the remains of the Saluda Factory. Today, the only Granby building left is on the grounds of the Lexington County Museum in Lexington. It's not surprising this last structure is the finest looking one among the others on the museum property despite being one of the oldest.

Once a vibrant center of commerce and wealth, and considered as a likely site for the new state capital, Granby faded away and disappeared. Its name would appear on dozens of streets and buildings miles away from the original site of the village. The land it stood on would be farmed for 100 years, with the plows breaking remnants of Granby into small pieces. A quarry would then destroy a third of the land of Granby while burying another third under a slag pile. The other third would have a modern-day neighborhood built on top of it. There, small buried pieces of Granby would wait another 50 years for a Miracle to Yesterday.

Figure 92: Odess Brinkman at the Finding Granby display during "Christmas in Cayce" at the Cayce Historical Museum.

Chapter 12 – The King is Found

Figure 93: Wales Cardiff Castle Stained Glass window showing King Richard III and Queen Consort Anne Neville. Photo licensed through Alamy Limited.

This chapter is here for several reasons. It introduces you to my unexpected and stunning connection with King Richard III, which will be covered in the next chapter. It tells the story of the miraculous discovery of King Richard III's bones. And, finally, it shows a classic example of the simplistic mindset of so many scientists. The excavation of the king and basic scientific proof of the bones could only have been done by trained scientists. These scientists on their own, however, never would have suggested looking for Richard III much less have found him. These scientists simply went through a bunch of scientific steps in the excavation and analysis of the bones. What I have done in this chapter is to summarize the discovery based on interviews and the day-by-day work documented in the book "The King's Grave" by Philippa Langley and Michael Jones.

On August 25, 2012, a small volunteer archaeological dig team (DC Locke, Jocelyn Locke, Odess, and I) was beginning pit #12 in our Granby dig. DC, with a degree History, Art, and Archaeology, was the lead archaeologist for the Granby project. DC and I had met through our mutual friend, Dean

Hunt, who was the official historian for the Granby project. At this early point in the Granby dig, we had found 750 Colonial period artifacts.

On that same day, the bones of King Richard III were being discovered in Leicester, England, 527 years after he had been killed by Henry Tudor's men in the Battle of Bosworth. The king had been interred in the Greyfriars Church in Leicester (also on August 25), though his grave site had been lost to history and there had long been heated debate on the fate of his bones.[60] The discovery of Richard's bones in 2012 was the international archaeological find of the year and, so far, the century.

Most historians had accepted a second story on the fate of the king's bones, that his body had been thrown off a bridge into a river, never to be found. This 2012 finding was not something a scholarly historian or archaeologist could take credit for, which made the discovery even more interesting to our "wet behind the ears" Granby diggers.

You could say that the story behind the discovery of the king's bones dates back to 1924 when a group of amateur historians formed the Richard III Society in England. These men were disturbed by the lack of historical evidence behind the myths about King Richard III. It seemed these were lies created by the Tudor dynasty, and their puppet William Shakespeare, to distract people away from the questionable claim Henry Tudor had to the throne.

Shakespeare's play on Richard III was written over 100 years after the death of the king and was based on a writing of Thomas More (the Saint) when he was only 20 years-old. Thomas More was not a historian and would have just been a young child when Richard III was killed. One theory is that More was simply making a copy of someone else's work. Another theory is that More, known to be an "intellectual joker", was just writing a parody of history. [61] One thing for sure is that More had no intention of having the writing published. Nevertheless, many years later, More's work was acquired and published after he was executed by his dear friend, and son of Henry Tudor, King Henry VIII. Closer study of More's piece also shows More never finished it and that the piece had multiple

---

[60] Ricardian Bulletin Spring 2009: Some Final Thoughts
[61] http://www.r3.org/links/to-prove-a-villain-the-real-richard-iii/these-supposed-crimes/thomas-more/

writers and may have been modified after More's death.[62] Thomas More was a supporter and friend of the Greyfriars. This is the same Order of men who so respected King Richard III that they bravely gave the devout Catholic king a burial in their church in Leicester in 1485. When More and these Franciscans later challenged the divorce of King Henry VIII, and the legitimacy of the Church of England, many of them were put to death, including Thomas More.

The tragic misuse of Thomas More's Richard III writing, and the Shakespearean fiction are just a couple of the areas of research undertaken by the Richard III Society. Over the decades, the society's membership has grown into the thousands. The members are known as Ricardians, and their research has dispelled many of the myths and shown that Richard III might have been a very good man and king.

The most excellent accomplishment of the society has been through their Scottish member Philippa Langley, who single-handedly drove the project to find Richard III's body. As Langley said herself, "I'm not a historian. I'm not a scientist and not an academic."[63] Langley's motivation, research, and fundraising in the society made the find possible, and the discovery itself was nothing short of miraculous.

Langley, a mother of two, started her career in advertising, but after an illness in the early 1990s, she decided to change careers to write a script for a film about King Richard III. Years before, she was drawn toward the tragedy of how Richard's reputation was unjustly destroyed after his death. She became a member of the society, and in 2004 she visited the site of the old Greyfriars monastery in Leicester. She had heard Richard might have been buried in a Franciscan church that stood there in 1485. King Henry VIII had this church demolished in the 16th century when he cut ties with the Catholic Church. Its exact location would be forgotten over the next centuries. The city of Leicester is quite densely developed, and only a couple of open parking lots allowed Langley to walk over where the church may have stood. As she entered the second parking lot, a strong feeling came over her at a specific spot. She somehow knew Richard was under her feet.

---

[62] The Betrayal of Richard III by V.B. Lamb and revised by Peter Hammond (pg. 94,95.)
[63] How One Woman's Secret Discovery Under a Parking Lot Changed 500 Years of History: SNAP JUDGMENT from PRX and NPR.

A year later, she returned, and the same feeling came over her at the same spot. But there was something different this time; someone had painted the faint letter "R" on the asphalt at that exact location. No solid explanation for the letter "R" could be found, although some guessed it might have identified a "Reserved" or "Reverse" parking space. Langley took it as a sign that this is where Richard was and that she must find a way to uncover him. [64]

Langley had a tough task ahead of her, which I could relate to. She had to get top-notched archaeologists involved and somehow get permission from the landowners to do archaeology on the property. This was the same challenge I faced just a few years earlier with the Confederate Bridge site and Sherman's pontoon crossing in Columbia. Just like I had done, Langley pitched the idea to do a television program covering the archaeology dig. I used the Public Broadcasting Service ("History Detectives") in the U.S. while Langley targeted the British public-service Channel 4.

The difference between her project and mine would be the costs. My project was solved by a geophysical survey and did not require digging or the property restoration after a dig. For Langley, the geophysical survey, using ground penetrating radar (GPR), was inconclusive because there had been so much disturbance of the soil just below the asphalt. Her solution was brute-force archaeological digging, which would be expensive.

Langley was very successful at raising funds. Her connection to the Richard III Society paid off, with their members providing over half of the project's budget. With money in the bank, Langley was able to get approval from the Leicester City Council and attract archaeologists with the University of Leicester. The archaeologists' interest was very different than Langley's. They had no hope of finding Richard III but were looking forward to finding evidence of the old church. With £34,000 (about $50,000), the newly formed project team planned to do two trenches in two weeks. The idea was to dig across the parking lots in lines (trenches) which would hopefully intersect a wall of the old church. Langley did not have to push her letter "R" hunch, as the archaeological team just happened to choose the "R" spot as the starting location for the first trench.

---

[64] Philippa Langley: I just felt I was walking on Richard III's grave. I can't explain it: https://www.theguardian.com

The day arrived to start the digging. If the burial myths were correct, August 25, 2012 was also the 527th anniversary of King Richard III's interment in the Greyfriars Church. Langley hoped it would also be the day his bones would be discovered. The archaeologists began excavation, and in just 10 minutes at a depth of three feet, they found a small wall made of medieval stones. Digging further, the wall disappeared, and lead archaeologist Richard Buckley concluded this must have been medieval stone the Victorians used to build an outhouse building. Buckley had done his homework and was expecting to possibly find this outhouse based on an old map. Langley was disappointed and was beginning to feel the pressure. Lots of people had donated money towards this "finding Richard III" project.

At 2:15 p.m.[65], archaeologist Mathew Morris was monitoring the excavator, which was down to five feet deep when suddenly, he motioned the operator to stop. Morris jumped into the trench and looked up to Langley and said, "There's a bone here." Langley got a reference point and realized that the bone was under where the letter "R" had been on the asphalt. Further clearing around the bone revealed it was a human leg bone, and another leg bone was next to it in a position that suggested this was a burial.

A dark storm cloud quickly moved over the dig. The last thing archaeologists want to let happen is to expose old bones to water, which could ruin the ability to complete DNA tests on them. The team frantically worked to cover the area of the bones just in time. The storm went through, and that marked an end to the first dig day. Although told by the archaeologists not to get her hopes up, Langley felt certain they had found Richard.

---

[65] The discovery of King Richard III happened at 9:15 a.m. EST while the Granby dig team (according to timestamps on our photographs) was breaking ground level on pit 12.

Figure 94: DC and Jocelyn Locke break ground on Granby pit #12 at the exact
same time that the bones of King Richard III are found in England.

At the start of the second dig day, Langley was excited about the bones
discovered the day before. Lead archaeologist Richard Buckley, however,
started the day by telling Langley about a possible discovery of another
medieval wall in the second trench. He didn't say anything about the bones
discovered until Langley brought it up. He told her the bones are probably
not significant, and the archaeology work completely shifted to finding the
church. The makeshift rain cover from the day before remained over the
bones, while the team continued digging the rest of the trenches. No
medieval evidence of the church was initially found in the first "R" trench
except for those "reused" stones.

By the end of the sixth dig day, evidence was mounting that the second
trench was in the Greyfriars' precinct. While work was still on hold at the
"R" end of the first trench, the other end of the trench produced interesting
finds, including a piece of stained glass that could have been from the
church. Closer to the "R," a significant wall structure was discovered that
could be the southern wall of the church.

The stained glass was identified as medieval, and a glazed roof tile found on the seventh dig day pointed again to the possibility that this was the church site. Even though Buckley acknowledged that the bones appeared to be within the friar, they were of no interest to him, and he asked Langley what she would like to do with them when they were removed.

By the end of dig day 10, the bones had still not been touched, and a third trench had been dug. Buckley was now convinced they had found the church. He had accomplished his mission.

Finally, on dig day 11, focus returned to the bones. Dr. Turi King of the University of Leicester was the one to carry out any DNA testing on the bones. She also did some of the digging and was ready to go as work began to clear the dirt and debris around the bones. She was assisted by osteologist Dr. Jo Appleby. Meanwhile, Buckley had now discovered a grave in the third trench and had little interest in the "R" bones. By the end of the day, the three women had cleared dirt and removed the leg bones. Not quite enough soil had been removed to reveal more skeleton if it existed.

Dr. King could not take part in dig day 12. How crazy Langley must have felt to be forced to wait until the end of the dig to have an answer on her "R" bones. With the rest of the crew excited and working trench three, Langley and Dr. Appleby began working on the bones in trench one, the "R" trench. To Appleby's surprise, she hit a human skull at a depth higher than the leg bones. Appleby told Langley it must belong to another skeleton. As she continued, a full adult male skeleton, minus the feet apparently cut off in that Victorian construction, started to appear. The body was not lying flat, and the skull was, in fact, part of the same skeleton.

No battle wounds were noticeable, and Appleby guessed it might be a friar burial. Langley was extremely disappointed and made her way over to trench three, only to be stopped by the film crew who wanted to know about her "R" revelation. As the cameras were rolling, Appleby's continued excavation revealed an extreme "S" shaped spine in the skeleton. Appleby then removed the skull, and multiple wounds could be seen. Langley fell to the ground. They had found King Richard III.

Langley was not, however, surprised. For years she believed Richard would be found here. What shocked her was what she interpreted as a hunchback from the "S"-shaped spine. Langley felt the description of King Richard III as a hunchback was a lie made up by Shakespeare to help turn Richard into some kind of monster.

Although the archaeologists were not convinced this was Richard, their cumulative finds seem to show the site of the "R" bones might be in the choir of the church, where only a very important person would have been buried.

All the "R" bones were excavated and placed in a box. The only two people on site who were certain of the find, Langley and fellow Richard III Society member John Ashdown-Hill, draped the box with the banner of King Richard III and ceremoniously placed it in the vehicle that transported the bones to a laboratory for further study.

A few days later on September 8, 2012, a public day was held at the dig site. The team told Langley she couldn't mention the possibility that Richard III's bones had been found until the scientists had done their work. The university would make a formal announcement at the end of the digging, stating that two sets of human remains had been found with the male skeleton showing severe scoliosis and head wounds. To Langley, given the odds, it made common sense this was King Richard III, but science is about taking measurements, and you can't measure common sense. She would have to wait another three months.

In December of 2012, lead archaeologist Richard Buckley met with Langley to go over the carbon dating results. He first explained that the level at which the bones were found was the same level as other medieval artifacts and features found in the dig. The carbon dating showed a 95% probability the skeleton's age was in the date range of 1450 to 1540. That is what it needed to be for Richard III, given his death date of 1485. Buckley for the first time seemed to show a smile of confidence that the bones could be Richard III.

Later that day, Dr. Appleby confirmed the head injuries were battle-inflicted, and one was almost certainly fatal. The scoliosis was also confirmed, and historians accepted that this made sense. But this scoliosis would not have caused a hunchback feature, so the Tudor hunchback lie remained a fabrication that Shakespeare created.

On February 3, 2013, the final significant piece of evidence came in. Dr. Turi King had taken four molars from the skull of the Greyfriars male skeleton and ground them into a fine power. Teeth are the best place to look for DNA in old skeletons. Dr. King divided the sample and sent it to two independent labs for DNA testing.

Some years earlier, Ashdown-Hill had been brought into a project to verify if discovered bones might have been those of King Richard III's sister. Ashdown-Hill completed the genealogy of a maternal line from Richard III's sister to a living descendant.[66] That project, however, never got to the DNA-testing phase, as carbon dating showed that the bones were nowhere near old enough to be Richard's sister. Ashdown-Hill's work on that project was brought back to life because the bones of King Richard III would hold the same maternal DNA (mtDNA) as his sister's.

Ashdown-Hill's earlier research had led to Joy E. Ibsen, but she had passed away by the time of the Richard III dig. However, her son Michael Ibsen carried the same maternal DNA (mtDNA) haplogroup type. Below is the genealogy Ashdown-Hill completed from Michael Ibsen to King Richard III.

Michael Ibsen is Richard III's 15th great-grandnephew

1. Michael Ibsen is the son of Joy E. Ibsen.
2. Joy Ibsen is the daughter of Muriel S. Brown.
3. Muriel Brown is the daughter of Charlotte V. Stokes.
4. Charlotte Stokes is the daughter of Charlotte Vansittart Neale.
5. Charlotte Neale is the daughter of Anne Vansittart Neale.
6. Anne Neale is the daughter of Barbara Spooner.
7. Barbara Spooner is the daughter of Barbara Gough.
8. Barbara Gough is the daughter of Barbara Calthorpe.
9. Barbara Calthorpe is the daughter of Barbara Yelverton.
10. Barbara Yelverton is the daughter of Barbara Talbot.
11. Barbara Talbot is the daughter of Barbara Slingsby.
12. Barbara Slingsby is the daughter of Barbara Belasyse.
13. Barbara Belasyse is the daughter of Margaret Cholmley.
14. Margaret Cholmley is the daughter of Barbara Babthorpe.
15. Barbara Babthorpe is the daughter of Katherine Constable.
16. Katherine Constable is the daughter of Anne Manners.

---

[66] Ricardian Bulletin June 2009: Scottish Branch Report: "Honour My Bones"

17. Anne Manners is the daughter of Anne de St Leger.
18. Anne de St. Leger is the daughter of Cecily Neville, Richard III's mother.
19. Richard, therefore, is the 16th great uncle of Michael Ibsen.

Ibsen's DNA had been tested during the August 2012 dig, and his rare mitochondrial DNA (mtDNA) was an exact match to the bones. Finally, the scientific community concluded what Philippa Langley had known since day one: These were the bones of King Richard III. In a parallel effort, University of Leicester historian Kevin Schurer worked out another maternal line that branched from the Michael Ibsen line almost 500 years ago. One modern-day link to that line was New Zealander Wendy Duldig, whose mtDNA also proved to be a match to King Richard III.

Langley was thrilled at the results, and that the public would finally find out about it in just one more day. It would put her on a stage where she could publicly dispel the lies about King Richard III and show the real man and king that he was.

Throughout the different accounts and interviews I have seen with Langley, her description of the feeling she had standing over that "R" spot ranges from "intuition," "hunch," to "I can't explain it." In dictionaries, you will see different definitions for the words intuition and hunch, but they all come down to something mystic or knowing something without any knowledge. This is three steps away from calling something a miracle. In step one, the intuition or hunch must prove true. In step two, no explanation can be given as to what has happened. In step three, the person feels unworthy of accepting credit for the event and chalks it up to divine power.

Richard Buckley, the lead archaeologist with the University of Leicester, was one of those who had no hope in finding King Richard III and was really there to find the church and add it to the historical documentation of Leicester. After looking at all the evidence and admitting that Richard III had been found, Buckley described himself as being "stunned" and "in disbelief." He said, "In archaeology, you don't go out looking for someone famous and find them. It just doesn't happen." Translation: Miracle.

Even after the initial discovery and announcement of the find of Richard III, continued work in England captured my attention. Scientists looked at different bones in Richard's body to determine his diet during youth and his diet in the few years before his death. Some of our bones hold information on our early life and others reveal things about our later years. The results for Richard III were stunning. In youth, Richard ate well, but his diet improved dramatically in his later years, including lots of fish, exotic foods, and a bottle of wine every day. For the time period, only a king could eat like that.

Another study was done to understand how someone with the degree of scoliosis Richard had could have been such a formidable warrior in battle.[67] To do that, researchers found a man with almost the same scoliosis and put him through the training Richard would have had. The scoliosis did not hamper the man's ability to fight from a horse, but he would have been at a great disadvantage on foot. In all the battles in which Richard fought so hard and so well, it was at Bosworth where he was knocked off his horse. He was immediately swarmed by the enemy and beaten to death.

The evidence was now substantial that the bones were, in fact, King Richard III's, and no one was questioning the conclusions. The results of scoliosis, the carbon dating, the battle wounds, and the diet were things everyone could understand. But for me and many others, the DNA matching was not well-explained. I think we accepted it because DNA has become such a reliable form of evidence in law enforcement and in the courtroom. I wished I could better understand how DNA was used in the case of Richard III. I had no idea how quickly I would learn all about DNA and how personal King Richard III would become to me.

[67] The Telegraph: Richard III, the 'hunchback king', really could have been a formidable warrior . . . and his body double can prove it : https://www.telegraph.co.uk/news/11038600/Richard-III-the-hunchback-king-really-could-have-been-a-formidable-warrior-...-and-his-body-double-can-prove-it.html

Chapter 13 – A King's Match in America

In the fall of 2013, I decided to take a $99 DNA test with the company 23andme. Initially, this was not for ancestry work; I wanted to compare my raw DNA to a set of markers associated with a higher probability of non-Hodgkin's Lymphoma. This is the cancer that killed my father and others on that side of the family.

To do the raw DNA compare, I would need to learn some basic things about DNA. For one thing, there are three types of DNA. Autosomal DNA is what really makes you who you are. There are about 10 million markers, but DNA testing companies only test for what they believe are the most significant markers, fewer than one million. Among these Autosomal DNA markers are ones that might show susceptibility to disorders and diseases like cancer. You could be more prone to a health issue if you have a mutation in a marker, or in other words if the marker has a different value from the reference standard.

You get half of your autosomal DNA from your mother and half from your father. What you get from each is mostly random. For my dad's cancer, medical genetics research had identified five possible marker mutations that could increase your chances of developing the cancer. Unfortunately for me, the 23andme test had a "no call" on two of the markers. Most DNA testing requires a quality assurance of 95% or better, meaning that your test could miss 50,000 of 1,000,000 markers and still be considered a good test. So, three of the possibly dangerous markers were tested and showed no adverse mutations. I would have to submit another DNA test to catch the other two markers.

While waiting on a second test, I decided to take a closer look at the other two types of DNA testing included in the 23andme test.

Y-DNA is the DNA that is passed directly from father to son. Women don't have it. You are given a name for your particular Y-DNA, termed the Y-DNA haplogroup. In my case, it was a very common group and not that interesting.

Recent high-profile testing points out a genealogy issue with Y-DNA, which has been around for as long as people have been around. Who's your daddy? Before blood testing and DNA, no father could be sure if a child was his unless there was a significant and unique physical feature in common. As in the case of King Richard III, Y-DNA showed that more than one of his ancestor grandmothers was unfaithful.

The third type of DNA is mitochondrial DNA (or mtDNA), which is passed from the mother to her children (male and female) but only can be passed on by the daughters. This type of DNA has an advantage over Y-DNA. Every mother knows who her children are. There's no question about that. It makes maternal DNA a great tool when researching maternal line ancestry.

Even with as much as I had kept up with the find of King Richard III, I did not remember the fact that the DNA proof of Richard III's bones was a mitochondrial DNA match with a known maternal line descendant of Richard III's sister. As for my mtDNA, the haplogroup was called J1c2c. That meant nothing to me until I did a Google search that returned numerous pages on King Richard III. I belonged to the same relatively rare haplogroup as the king. I was in a bit of shock over the whole thing.

No one on my mother's side of the family had any idea of a connection like this. What this all meant was that if I followed my maternal line from my mother, to her mother, to her mother, and so on, I would eventually get to King Richard III's sister or to his mother, grandmother, and so on. If not through his sister, how far back could our common grandmother be? Other online documentation showed that scientists had estimated the first J1c2c to be 2,200 to 6,900 years ago. Of course, that's too far back to do any genealogy, but if the relationship were through Richard's sister or his grandmother or great-grandmother, then it would be possible to build the family tree back to Richard III, just like was done for Michael Ibsen and Wendy Duldig.

All I knew at this point was that a lot more work had to done and this was going to turn into another history mystery project. While learning more about mtDNA, I would set up a new website for the project with the hope that other J1c2c matches and mtDNA researchers would find me and join the effort.

Unlike all my projects from before, this was something that hit me in the most personal way. And how appropriate that it was about my mother and all the mothers before her. After being so driven by honoring my father's

WWII experience, now it would shift to my mom. She would have loved taking part in this. How I wished she was here, but her sister, Dorothy Weaver[68], would take her place.

It didn't take long for English family historian and mtDNA expert Dr. Ian Logan to find my new website.[69] Only a handful of living people in the world had been tested to be J1c2c. Dr. Logan informed me that my test and the tests of the others, including Richard III, were partial mtDNA tests. This incomplete testing only looked at a few thousand of the over 16,500 mtDNA markers. He suggested that I have a more expensive full sequence mtDNA test done with the company Family Tree DNA (FTDNA). This test would get every single mtDNA marker. Dr. Logan noted that they had just begun the same type of test, which could take months to complete, on King Richard III's bones.

I wasted no time in doing the full sequence mtDNA test. While waiting on the results, I took some time to look at other DNA and genealogy data. I first noticed my overall DNA data (autosomal) showed I was mostly English and only 5% German. Because of my German last name, I had assumed I was primarily German. In an incredible coincidence, the maternal line down from King Richard III's sister would produce a line of men with the surname "Manners." One of them was the popular English war hero of 1759, John Manners, the Marquis of Granby - the man our lost and found Colonial town of Granby was named after! I was almost overcome with emotion at this revelation.

In the last years of my mother's life, my wife and I took her to England, where she thought she had ancestral roots. While we were there, we visited the tombs of Anne St. Leger and George Manners in St. George's Chapel at Windsor Castle. Anne was the J1c2c niece of King Richard III and possibly an ancestor of my mother, myself, and the Marquis of Granby. Until this revelation, I had wrongly thought this project was distant and disconnected from my previous history projects.

---

[68] Veterans History Project: Dorothy Weaver (Second Class Telegrapher): https://www.youtube.com/watch?v=xqUfjJT18U8
[69] Genetic Connections: King Richard III web site: http://www.historysoft.com/richard3/

Figure 95: (l) David Brinkman and his mother (Roberta) at Windsor Castle in 1996. (r) Standing in front of St. George's Chapel.

My full sequence mtDNA results came through in about two months in February 2014. There was an additional mutation found. Dr. Logan explained to me that this would probably take me away from the immediate family of King Richard III. Dr. Logan created a new haplogroup for the scientific community with my unique mtDNA full sequence. He called it J1c2c3. I was the first J1c2c3 to be recorded.

The first J1c2c3 sequences submitted to Genbank[70]:

David Brinkman - Received 21-FEB-2014[71]
King Richard III - Received 29-SEP-2014[72]
Michael Ibsen - Received 29-SEP-2014[73]
Wendy Duldig - Received 29-SEP-2014 (One new mutation)[74]

At this point, I still did not have a good feel for DNA matching. So, despite some disappointment with this additional mutation, I moved forward and

---

[70] GenBank ® is the NIH genetic sequence database, an annotated collection of all publicly available DNA sequences. GenBank is part of the International Nucleotide Sequence Database Collaboration , which comprises the DNA DataBank of Japan (DDBJ), the European Nucleotide Archive (ENA), and GenBank at NCBI.
[71] David Brinkman sequence: https://www.ncbi.nlm.nih.gov/nuccore/KJ486154
[72] King Richard III sequence: https://www.ncbi.nlm.nih.gov/nuccore/KM676292
[73] Michael Ibsen sequence: https://www.ncbi.nlm.nih.gov/nuccore/KM676293
[74] Wendy Duldig sequence: https://www.ncbi.nlm.nih.gov/nuccore/KM676294

started working on the maternal side of my family tree on Ancestry.com. I was able to work back to my maternal fourth great-grandmother, Polly Sawyer in Pasquotank County, North Carolina. I also received autosomal test results from AncestryDNA. With this, I captured those other two potentially dangerous markers that could show an increased risk for the cancer that killed my father. Fortunately, they did not show mutations. I should have felt relieved that I might have dodged a bullet by inheriting these genes from my mother and not my father. But with cancer, I don't think you can ever really feel safe.

Services like 23andme and AncestryDNA also provide information on other people in their databases that have strings of DNA that match with yours. Based on the length of the matches and the total number of matches, they can make an educated guess at the relation between the two people. For example, when my son and aunt submitted tests, they were identified as my son and aunt even with no additional data to draw that conclusion. Most of the matches you get, however, are distant cousins, and it can be very challenging to figure out the exact genealogy between the two people. AncestryDNA provides an additional feature called DNA hints, which will look into the family trees of each person and, if possible, determine a common relative and relationship between the two people in the DNA match. These match features proved to be very important as the project moved forward.

One month after my full sequence came through, the FTDNA service reported that two more perfect mtDNA matches came in. I contacted both men and gave them the news. We then shared family trees. Unfortunately, they had hit a dead end on their maternal lines in the mid-1800s. All three maternal lines were pointing to the state of Virginia, but we would have to go back many more generations to find our common nth great-grandmother. The 23andme service also provided mtDNA matches, but they were behind on updating their DNA haplogroup definitions, and J1c2c3 matches reported as J1c2c instead of J1c2c3. Although a raw DNA check could be performed on that single marker to distinguish a J1c2c3 from a J1c2c, it was something that was difficult to communicate to the J1c2c matches. As it turned out, all the J1c2c matches I had on 23andme did not have the additional J1c2c3 mutation. A fundamental question became, just how rare is the J1c2c3 haplogroup?

Almost ten months after my full sequence mtDNA results came through, the big news came. In December of 2014, I received an email from Dr. Logan saying "Congratulations! King Richard III's full sequence results show he has the same additional mutation and is also J1c2c3. All 16,569 markers are the same as yours. You are exact matches." I was elated and glad I had not suspended the project. I was now able to start reaching out to other possible matches with the hope that our combined genealogies would build a family tree back to England and King Richard III.

No more J1c2c3 matches had come in over the year. The total number of tested people in the world was holding at five, and my project now accounted for three of the five. I decided to try something new and was also interested in proving my genealogy back to that fourth great-grandmother, Polly Sawyer. Using Ancestry.com, I located the same Polly Sawyer in someone else's family tree, where it was also a dead end for them. It showed a well-developed maternal line coming down from a different daughter of Polly Sawyer. This would be a fifth great aunt to me. As I followed the maternal path down, it came to a living descendant.

By default, and for privacy reasons, Ancestry.com does not show the names of living persons in these public trees. I contacted the owner of the tree. I explained the craziness of the matter, that I was an exact DNA match to King Richard III, and that I was looking for this fifth cousin. As luck would have it, the private person in question was the cousin of the Ancestry.com family tree owner. She also informed me that this cousin was very much into genealogy. She passed on the information, and I soon made contact with my new found J1c2c3 fifth cousin, Ed Abrames in Chesapeake, Virginia.

Ed was very excited that he might also be a match to King Richard III, and he immediately ordered and completed the DNA test. Two months later, Ed became the sixth match in the world. The rare J1c2c3 haplogroup match between us also proved our genealogy through that fourth great-grandmother. Ed and his wife and my family would be in close contact over the next years.

Ed did volunteer work at the Family Research Society of Northeastern North Carolina Library in Elizabeth City, North Carolina. Much of our maternal line lived in this part of North Carolina, and the library proved to be a valuable resource in our research. It was also a good meeting spot for our families. We discovered the oldest house in Elizabeth City, the Grice-Fearing House, and made this excellent bed & breakfast our place to stay.[75]

As the search continued for more J1c2c3 matches, Elaine Campton Gherardi in California saw a public posting I made on 23andme about J1c2c matches. Elaine's son Greg had given her a 23andme DNA test kit for Christmas, and Elaine's results came in as a J1c2c for mtDNA. I took Elaine through the raw data check, which showed she was indeed a J1c2c3 match. Elaine was so excited, and she quickly became a workhorse in the project. She would hunt down J1c2c matches on 23andme and take them through the check for J1c2c3. She also worked her genealogy back to 1800, and once again the maternal line was heading into Virginia.

Sadly, a year after he bought his mother that DNA test kit, Greg Gherardi died unexpectedly. Elaine would continue more than ever working on the journey Greg had started, and by the end of the year, she had made contact with the lead King Richard III DNA and history researchers at Leicester University (Dr. Turi King and Dr. Kevin Schurer). By now, Ed, Elaine, and I were working very closely with Dr. Logan on both DNA matches and our genealogies. It became clear, unfortunately, that Dr. King and Dr. Schurer would not be able to do much for us. We would be on our own.

Through continued work over the next two years, the project located 20 matches, and all these people became active in the project. They all lived in the United States and included a nursery owner from Hawaii; a WWII veteran/retired nurse, a corporate legal secretary, a medical doctor, and an actress/producer/writer from California; a retired national park ranger from Arizona; a Congressional campaign strategist from Texas; a business analyst from Illinois; a software engineer and historian from South Carolina; a North Carolina family with four generations of J1c2c3 women; a retired government contracts manager, a WWII Navy WAV/retired corporate secretary from Virginia; a university assistant dean, and a historian/librarian from New York. All their maternal lines appeared to have come from England. Most of the lines came through the Jamestown settlement area in North Carolina and Virginia. Not a single other match was found outside of our project, leaving the other matches at just Michael Ibsen in Canada and Wendy Duldig in New Zealand.

---

[75] Grice-Fearing House: http://www.gricefearinghouse.com

Dr. Logan, Ed, Elaine, and I kept very busy through this time with the new matches, but most of the new maternal line genealogies were stuck around the year 1800. Ed and I had a major break in 2016 when North Carolina estate papers from the late 18th and earlier 19th centuries showed a matching signature between two different estates. Our Polly Sawyer had died young, and her widower, Lemuel Jennings, followed her four years later. This left one of their children orphaned, and a Joel Sawyer appeared as a representative in Lemuel Jennings' estate. Joel seemed to be representing the late Polly Sawyer. We later found, by matching signatures, that Joel was the executor of his father's estate. Out of the many different Sawyer families in that area, we knew this must be Polly's family. More evidence would show that Joel was Polly's uncle. This allowed us to determine the parents of our fourth great-grandmother Polly Sawyer.

From there many other family trees on Ancestry.com showed three more maternal line generations back. Just like that, we jumped back four generations and 100 years. We were now at the year 1700. Further DNA matches on Ancestry.com proved these new-found great-grandmothers.

On one trip to Elizabeth City, Ed, Odess, and I, had a full day of family research which culminated in finding the house of our seventh great-grandparents, Joel and Miriam Hollowell. Miriam was our most distant proven J1c2c3 great-grandmother. The old Hollowell house, many years before, had been turned into a tin-covered barn. It seems the tin has preserved the old house with much of the original wood still in place and being held together by the original handmade square nails.

Figure 96: J1c2c3 5th cousins, Ed Abrames and David Brinkman locate the 1750 home (now a tin covered barn) of their J1c2c3 7th great-grandparents in Perquimans County, North Carolina.

That day in Elizabeth City was not over yet as another miracle was about to happen which would resolve a forty-year mystery (from Chapter 2: Faith.) I was exhausted and ready for bed when we returned to the Grice-Fearing House. I laid down on the bed and immediately fell into a deep sleep. After about an hour, I was rudely awakened by what seemed to be a vigorous shake. I took a moment to fully awake and concluded that it was probably nothing. Odess and Jeremy were still in another room watching television. Then, in what seemed like a possible practical joke by Jeremy, the heavy blanket of the bed was shook out with the end whipping across my legs. It ended with the feeling of pressure coming down on my legs. Unlike the paranormal experience of forty years earlier, I wasted no time in jumping out of bed and turning on the lights. Once again, nothing was there. I walked into the other room and found Odess and Jeremy asleep in front of the television. I had not yet connected the event with the one from forty years ago, but my first thought was, could it be paranormal? After all, the Grice-Fearing House is the oldest house in Elizabeth City. Is it haunted? As I got back into bed, I realized that, for the first time in many years, I had not prayed before going to sleep that night. It all hit me then. What happened here, what happened when I was 14, the stroke I had at 15, and the hypoglycemia, depression, and amnesia I had at 19....maybe it was God saying "don't you forget me." I quickly completed the evening with a prayer. The next morning, as a scientific follow-up, or maybe it was a little doubting Thomas in me, I asked the owners of the Grice-Fearing House if the old house might be haunted. The answer was "Not that we know of. We've never experienced anything unusual."

While all this was going on, Aunt Dot, my mother's sister, took DNA tests with 23andme and Ancestry.com. The 23andme test showed her, as expected, to be a mtDNA J1c2c3 match. Aunt Dot was so excited about King Richard III. She closely followed all our new finds, but shortly after submitting her second DNA test, she was diagnosed with colon, liver, and lung cancer. We made three trips to visit her in 2016. She was the last relative I had from that Greatest Generation and had served in WWII as a Navy WAV.[76]

Our fourth visit to Richmond that year would be for Aunt Dot's funeral. Just after her death, many autosomal DNA matches to Aunt Dot produced DNA hints on AncestryDNA. Incredibly, they all pointed to and proved another maternal line great-grandmother that took us into the 1600s. What were the odds? That's nine generations back from Aunt Dot and is really pushing the limits of autosomal DNA matches - so much so that only one of the six matches of Aunt Dot also showed as a match for me.

When you go back that many generations, your family tree has 512 grandparents, two to the power of nine. On the maternal line, however, you have only 18 grandparents, two multiplied by nine. If you have a DNA match, there is only an 18-in-512 chance that the match is in the maternal line. But there was a total of six matches that came in for Aunt Dot, and they were all maternal lines to the same eighth great-grandmother. That becomes a 1-in-171 chance. And all the matches came in while we were at Aunt Dot's funeral.

Thanks to Aunt Dot, my J1c2c3 fifth cousin Ed Abrames and I now had another generation back in our tree, which quickly tied into more genealogy, which took us back to the first permanent English settlement in America at Jamestown, Virginia. Continued work has led to possible lines with Plantagenets who came to Jamestown. One of these lines takes us right into the heart of the Plantagenet family and into the area of King Richard III's immediate family. Proving this and the rest of the genealogy will require more DNA tests. We are waiting and looking every day for new matches.

---

[76] Veterans History Project: Dorothy Weaver (Second Class Telegrapher): https://www.youtube.com/watch?v=xqUfjJT18U8

In March of 2017, Dr. Logan and I started putting together all our work and looking at the numbers. The results produced a scientific paper.[77] These all led to the following significant conclusions:

Point 1: An overwhelming piece of evidence for the bones of King Richard III.

Our J1c2c3 research provides an overwhelming piece of evidence that the bones found at Greyfriars are those of King Richard III. When the full sequence mtDNA work was completed on the bones of King Richard III in December of 2014, it was noted in GenBank2 that the evidence for the case was overwhelming merely because they could not find a single match in a database of 9,162. That's not overwhelming in my book. We believe our J1c2c3 research has significantly raised the level of certainty that the bones are those of King Richard III. The initial proof of the bones was based on a partial mtDNA test in 2013 that showed a haplogroup of J1c2c. The full sequence revealed a new mutation, making the real haplogroup to be J1c2c3. Dr. Logan had already created the J1c2c3 haplogroup for the first documented J1c2c3 (David Brinkman) in February of 2014.

Our work over the last four years provided the missing point needed for the statement of "overwhelming" evidence by showing that the new mtDNA haplogroup of J1c2c3 is extremely rare. The initial King Richard III work noted a match probability of one in 9,163 for the mitochondrial DNA. Our work shows that probability is dropping to an overwhelming level of proof. Looking at all the lineages of the known J1c2c3 matches, we have concluded that there are only 300 possible J1c2c3 matches that could come from these lines. Over the world's total population, this makes the probability one in 26,666,667. Given that almost all the matches are in the United States, and none in Europe, we had to consider the fact that European descendants, especially Americans, dominate the world's DNA databases.

Our four years of researching different DNA databases and contacting J1c2c matches show a J1c2c3/J1c2c ratio of three J1c2c3's to 142 J1c2c's. This has been observed in both 23andme and the National

---

Geographic Society's Genographic Project. Given this ratio, we could now apply it to a predicted number of J1c2c people in the world. The mitochondrial genetics community has this number as 3,000,000.

Could we verify this number some way? In another paper "J1c2c3: Discoveries: Points, Details, and their Sources", I did just that by looking at the total number of J1c2c's in the 23andme database and then normalizing this with other 23andme data showing that Europeans make up 80% of the database. Sparing you all the numbers and calculations, the total number of J1c2c's in the world came out to be 3,117,437. This was very close to the predicted 3,000,000. This gave us confidence that the next predicted subclade, or subgroup, of J1c2c was also accurate at 500,000. This subclade, being the first defined subclade of J1c2c, is also called J1c2c. With this, we could apply the ratio from before (3 J1c2c3's to 142 J1c2c's) to the 500,000. This means, if everyone in the world were to be tested, we should find 10,563 J1c2c3 matches with King Richard III. A probability of one in 757,333. This is three magnitudes more significant than the original proof given on the mtDNA work of King Richard III. Our work indeed makes the evidence overwhelming.

Point 2: J1c2c3 may have been born in England in the Plantagenet Family.

Our research also showed that all living J1c2c3 people have maternal lines going straight to England, unlike the J1c2c line, which is scattered over Europe. This may mean the mutation that started J1c2c3 occurred within the Plantagenet family itself, maybe only a few generations from King Richard III. This theory is also based on an interesting population phenomenon that happened in the prime era of the Plantagenet family between the years 1200 and 1500.

This is the only historical period when the world's human population declined. Despite this, however, the well-documented genealogy of the Plantagenet family shows many women having four to 12 children each and most of these children living to adulthood. A considerable population explosion occurred in the family during this time. The mutation that formed J1c2c3 may well have happened here. The low numbers and pure English maternal line ancestry of J1c2c3 people also point to this possibility.

Point 3: Why there are no J1c2c3 matches in Europe.

Despite the pure English maternal line ancestry of the J1c2c3 matches, none of them live in England. Eighteen are in the United States (all found by this project), one is from Canada, and one is from New Zealand. Not a single living J1c2c3 has been found in Europe.

Much of our effort over the last four years had been searching through DNA databases, advertising, and contacting possible matches. To date, only a total of 20 living J1c2c3s have been found in the world. National Geographic Society's Genographic Project database shows a more than four times greater number of J1c2c matches in the United States than in Europe, even though there are more people in Europe. The J1c2c haplogroup originated in Europe over 2,000 years ago. This clearly shows that at least four times, maybe as much as ten times, as many people in the U.S. are doing DNA tests.

With only three of these J1c2c people in National Geographic Society's Genographic Project from England, and the fact that J1c2c3 is relatively young and smaller in numbers, this explains why no J1c2c3s have been found in England. If J1c2c3 developed in another part of Europe, you would expect, even with the four times greater testing in the U.S., at least a few J1c2c3's to show up by now. Again, as stated in Point 2, J1c2c3 probably developed in England, where there has not been enough testing to show J1c2c3 matches. We do expect some to show, in the near future, as more people are tested.

Point 4: All living J1c2c3 people are likely to be related to the immediate family of King Richard III.

This point is covered in our peer-reviewed scientific paper: "King Richard III and his mitochondrial DNA haplogroup J1c2c3."[78] Work continues to complete the genealogy of the different lineages to King Richard III.

---

[78] King Richard III and his mitochondrial DNA haplogroup J1c2c3:
http://www.qualifiedgenealogists.org/ojs/index.php/JGFH/article/view/32

Point 5: The DNA ancestry of the United States is heavily weighted to the Jamestown settlement and the Plantagenets.

Continued genealogy is also showing that the settlement at Jamestown strongly influences the DNA of the United States and that many of the people that came to Jamestown were Plantagenets. This goes along with the extensively studied ancestry of U.S. presidents, which shows all but one had Plantagenet ancestry.

Without the genealogy in place, the American matches did not feel worthy of requesting a place in the family section during the reburial ceremony for King Richard III on March 25, 2015. We do look forward to future family gatherings after we are successful with the continued work. Building a maternal line genealogy bottom-up from today through Colonial America to King Richard III would be one of the greatest genealogical accomplishments since the 77-generation paternal line from Jesus to Adam was completed and documented in the New Testament. Without any physical evidence, that case would be impossible to scientifically prove. This case is different. Between the incredible finds in old North Carolina probate papers, autosomal DNA matches, and the extremely rare J1c2c3 mtDNA haplogroup, we feel it is possible to complete and prove the genealogy.

The finding of King Richard III's bones was a miracle. The genetic connection of Richard III to me is mind-boggling when looking at the numbers. The coincidental connection to Granby, the similarities of the king's archaeological find with our finds of the Confederate Bridge site, Sherman's crossing, and Fort Congaree II (next chapter), and the miracle timings of my Aunt Dot's DNA matches leave no doubt this is all a multi-miracle.

It also takes me back to my dad's WWII shipmates, who gave divine credit to that address mistake in Chapter 6. After the miracle that led to our first property purchase and the discovery of a bridge abutment in the backyard, the City of Columbia informed me that our address was not really 170 Castle Road. It was 154 Castle Road. The old USS Lowndes (APA-154) crewmen suggested that a supernatural force may be pointing my APA-154 historian duties into a new direction. But what would the "Castle" part of the address have to do with it? Now we know.

King Richard III's life and short reign exposed him to almost everything a human can experience. His father and one brother were killed in battle when he was young. He risked his life many times in bloody battles supporting his brother, King Edward IV. Richard, being the youngest of the brothers, was never expected to be king. He was groomed for a position with the church and embraced his religious education. Throughout his life, he was a pious and organized man.

During Edward's reign, their brother Clarence attempted to overthrow Edward. Richard and Edward forgave him in a time when treason was usually punished by a quick and horrible death. Clarence would, again, cause trouble and Edward put him to death. When Edward took ill, he called in Richard. Edward easily placed all his trust in the one person who had always been so loyal to him. Richard promised to protect the young son of Edward and take him to London, where he could be crowned the new king. Richard signed his name on this promise with his lifelong motto: Loyalty Binds Me. Richard completed his promise and left Edward's son in protective custody in London where he would be joined by his younger brother. An attempt to kidnap the brothers (the Princes in the Tower) would later be thwarted. Before their execution, evidence (letters) showed Henry and Jasper Tudor employed the four would-be kidnappers.[79]

With no involvement from Richard, the powers in London found that King Edward IV had not properly terminated his first marriage; thus his heirs were all illegitimate. Edward's sons could not be king. Richard became the king by default. Richard probably reluctantly accepted this, knowing like those before him that his days would be numbered, and he would eventually be overthrown and killed. This was the War of the Roses. Not even one year into Richard's reign, his only child and heir died unexpectedly at the age of ten. Devastated by the loss, Richard's wife Anne declined rapidly from tuberculosis and died less than a year later. Five months later, in a battle for the first time without his brother Edward, and betrayed by a large number of his troops, Richard would lose his own life and the crown that his Plantagenet family had held for centuries. Henry Tudor had eliminated all of those in his way, and he became King Henry VII.

---

[79] Historian Sir George Buck (The first Ricardian)

Richard III was the last King of England to die in battle. But instead of being honored and remembered as a hero, his body was stripped of clothing, violated in horrible ways and dragged through the town for days.[80] The people of his kingdom, who loved him by all historical accounts, were silenced by the threat of death from the new king. His portrait would be modified by the new king to make him look evil. And the campaign of slander would continue for hundreds of years.

Looking at the real historical data and ignoring the misleading accounts of Thomas More, from whom William Shakespeare built his outrageous set of lies, you can see why the movement to correct Richard's reputation has been taken on by thousands of people. It's not hard to see how a higher power would be behind an effort to correct an over 500-year horrific injustice.

My miracles with Richard III have made me a Ricardian with a purpose to correct the history and reputation of a good man who could have been the finest King of England.

---

[80] Ricardian Bulletin Fall 2007: Richard III's Burial: The Saga Continues:
"The despicable treatment of Richard's body is confirmed by the Crowland Chronicle, which reports that 'many insults were offered to King Richard's body after the battle."

Chapter 14 – A Fort is Found

The chapters of this book cover historical discoveries in the chronological order of their discovery. The idea for finding Fort Congaree II actually started while doing work to pinpoint the location of Granby. A map, now thought to have been created by an early 20th century historian, showed Fort Congaree II less than 1,000 feet south of the southern boundary of Granby in what is today, Cayce, SC.

The map's location of the fort probably came from a 1739 survey for the first backcountry settlement of South Carolina inland from Charles Town. This Saxe-Gotha settlement would be an attempt to move European settlers into the central section of South Carolina and push back Native American populations.

European advertisements around 1740 described the Saxe-Gotha district as being beautiful and vast, with bountiful lands and friendly Natives. All you had to do was pay for the voyage, and upon arrival, you would have your own 1/2-acre town lot on the Congaree River and another 100- to 300-acre lot outside of the town. Indentured servants also made the inland voyage, but they would have to work for several years to pay for their trip before they could acquire land. More than 100 Swiss and German families took the chance and made the hard journey to Charles Town and then through the rough backcountry of South Carolina.

By the time they got to the Saxe-Gotha settlement, the area already had several European settlers who had been trading with the Indians for 10 to 20 years. When these traders first arrived, Fort Congaree I was built around 1718 and was garrisoned with men who could handle any problems with the Indians. After several years of peace, the garrison was removed, and the fort was turned into a trading post. By the time the Germans and Swiss arrived, however, problems were developing with the Indians who thought they were being taken advantage of in the many trades and land transactions.

Hostilities began to occur, and some settlers were assaulted or kidnapped even in the Saxe-Gotha town. Living on a large remote lot was very dangerous, and the climate was a shock to the Europeans. Summer months brought almost 100-degree days with extremely high humidity and virtually no cooling wind. Some settlers died within months of arrival from heat or illness.

In response to a series of deadly Indian attacks against these first South Carolina backcountry settlers, the palisaded British outpost Fort Congaree II was built in 1748. Its location was at an established Indian crossing just below the fall line on the Congaree River, probably close to where that place-marker was put on the original Saxe-Gotha survey of 1739. Fort Congaree II would serve its initial purpose of protecting early European settlers, and it became the launching ground for attacks against the Cherokee in the French and Indian War around 1761. During this time, it was also the training ground for young men who would later become heroes of the American Revolution, including Francis Marion, William Moultrie, Isaac Huger, and Andrew Pickens.

As the town of Granby developed slightly north of Fort Congaree II, the fort was shut down in the mid-1760s and mostly lost to history, as the Revolutionary War exploits took precedence. One of the last references to it until recent years appears in a 1935 newspaper article in which South Carolina historian Edwin Green makes a plea for a marker to be placed at the site of the "last signs of the fort." A marker was never placed, but in 1939 the first aerial photos of the area show that several areas near Green's proposed location of the fort appear to be unplowed. Did the farm owner intentionally protect this area because of its historical significance? And just what were the "last signs" of the fort that Green mentioned? Certainly, the wood structure was long gone. Could the ditch around the fort and palisade wall dirt mound still have been visible? Unfortunately, the 1939 aerial photo was poor in quality. We needed something else.

Just as I had done with the 1870 Canal Survey, which solved the Confederate Bridge and Sherman's crossing locations, I applied the overlay process to the 1739 Saxe-Gotha survey to determine where the fort's planned location was marked. I didn't know whether the fort was eventually built at this place or another location, but the survey was the only thing I had to work with.

The overlay of the 1739 survey onto today's aerial photo showed something very convenient. The fort fell on the same modern residential neighborhood as the town of Granby, in particular on two undeveloped lots on the river. Those lots just happened to be for sale. The landowner allowed us to survey the property, but nothing special was noticed. Granby digger Fred Morrison and I discussed purchasing the lots so we could do full archaeology on the site, as I had done in Granby. However, the irrational feeling of urgency that had engulfed me and led me to purchase the Compty bridge abutment site and the Granby lot never came to me. There was just an empty feeling. I would put aside Fort Congaree II for a year and focus instead on the Granby work.

One day in 2013, Granby historian Dean Hunt sent me a copy of a 1750 survey he had come across. It showed a 100-acre lot on the Congaree River with Fort Congaree II drawn on it. There was not enough river frontage on the lot for us to line it up with a feature like a curve in the river, but a pond was shown close to the fort. A creek fed the pond, but that was done away with many years ago. Looking at an aerial photo of the neighborhood and considering that the fort was probably built close to the reserved location in the 1739 survey, I began to wonder if the pond was where today's neighborhood has the most problems with flooding.

In 1960, the Riverland Park neighborhood was built in the floodplain against much opposition. Over the next 57 years, the neighborhood severely flooded five times, with the worst occurring in this low-lying area. When I looked at the elevation map, that low-lying area happened to be the same size, shape, and orientation of the pond shown in the 1750 survey.

I quickly processed the survey and lined the pond up with the elevation map. Using this pond-location logic, the fort would have been about 200 feet north of the Saxe-Gotha survey's reserved location for a fort. That's a significant difference, given that the fort was only about 170 feet square. The fort would have been 200 feet from the Congaree River compared to 100 feet in the Saxe-Gotha survey. 200 feet proved to be a standard distance from the river when compared to other South Carolina forts of that period. Not so convenient for us, based on this overlay, the fort sat on the property of four occupied homes. If we wanted to do archaeology, we would need to convince the owners to allow it.

While all this researching and location estimation was going on, Dr. Dan Tortora of the History Department of Colby College in Maine was doing work at the University of South Carolina. Dr. Tortora had a keen interest in Native American history, and we met him by chance at a local history talk. We took him to the spot where we believed the fort was located, and Dr.

Tortora instantly was inspired. He would spend many hours researching Fort Congaree II, and would turn that research into a scholarly paper - "Fort Congaree II: British Outpost in the South Carolina Midlands, 1748-1756."

I once again approached State Archaeologist Dr. Jonathan Leader about the project, knowing we would need professional archaeologists to complete the work. Finding an old British fort would be a significant accomplishment in American archaeology, and Dr. Leader was intrigued by the idea. After the 1750 fort/pond discovery, Dr. Leader was completely on board. As past and present chairs of the Greater Piedmont Chapter of the Explorers Club, we both saw this as an excellent opportunity to do the project as an official Flag Expedition of the Explorers Club. Explorers Club Flag Expeditions are intended to further the cause of exploration and field science. They have been carried out all over the world, and on the moon, by club members for the past 100 years. I wrote a proposal for the expedition, and the Board of the Explorers Club quickly approved it in New York City.

Using some of Dr. Tortora's findings, I compiled a paper for the neighbors, showing the fort under their homes. Dean Hunt and I targeted three of the most promising properties and gave our sales pitch to the owners. The owners of the home at the center of the fort placement had absolutely no interest and appeared to be quite annoyed by our presentation. The other two owners, however, were open to the idea. Dean and I had to make a decision on which property to focus on. Dean on his own convinced the most northern property owners, Karen Kennedy and Larry Burton, to allow us to excavate their beautiful front yard. I was a little uneasy because we were moving even further away, to the north, from the Saxe-Gotha survey placement of the fort. But I figured if we failed at this location, we could still go back to the neighbor at the south end of the placement. At the time, I had no idea just how difficult digging one location could be. This was not going to be like the Granby dig. This would be painstaking digging with trowels through the entire scorching summer.

With permissions secured, I took up the job of organizing the opening weekend of digging for May 31, 2014. Explorers Club members were coming from as far away as Colorado, in all almost 40 people. But first, Dr. Leader and I met at the site. Just like in the archaeology for King Richard III, Dr. Leader chose to dig a trench in the hope of intersecting with a palisade wall and the fort ditch. Dr. Leader said artifacts would probably be useless, so we had to find something unique to a fort like the archaeological features of a palisade wall and ditch.

When we met at Karen Kennedy and Larry Burton's house, Dr. Leader and I quickly realized our targeted dig area between the south side of the property and the driveway was filled with massive tree roots. Thick roots are difficult to dig through, but more importantly, they destroy archaeological features. Our only option was to move even further north to the other side of the driveway.

I was now really feeling nervous. We just kept moving further north and away from both survey placements. I stepped back and watched Dr. Leader decide where to place the center of the trench. What I saw, and what everyone else saw, was a perfectly flat front yard with nothing unique about any one part of it. Dr. Leader walked back and forth a few times, and then, suddenly, he extended his arms and said: "something is going on here." We made that spot the center of the trench, and we outlined the entire trench for Saturday's dig.

It would not be until a year later that I would first read the details of the King Richard III dig, specifically Philippa Langley's miracle detection of King Richard III under her feet as she stopped at that spot in the parking lot. For now, facing the opening weekend of the Fort Congaree II dig, I had trouble sleeping at night. So many people had put their trust in me and this project. I was afraid we would be looking too far north and would completely miss the fort.

Saturday finally arrived, and we had a huge turnout for the start of the dig. As State Archaeologist, Dr. Leader is the state's expert at certain types of geophysical surveying, and he was called in on this day to do law enforcement work. Dr. Leader put his colleague, archaeologist John Fisher, in charge of the work for Saturday, and we had five other archaeologists to help: Helena Ferguson, Meg Gaillard, DC Locke, Nena Rice, and Erika Shofner. About 30 other Explorer Club members and volunteers also took part.

The trench I marked with Dr. Leader would be seven one-meter square pits in a line. We would simultaneously dig each pit at 10 centimeters (about 4 inches) deep layers. Helena Ferguson took pit #3 in the center of the trench, where Dr. Leader had that "something is going on here" revelation. Period artifacts appeared about eight centimeters (three inches) into the level, including the mouthpiece of a pipe stem.

Europeans became interested in tobacco from the Native Americans, and by 1612 tobacco was the main cash crop for the Jamestown, Virginia settlement. By the early 1700s, ceramic pipes were being mass produced in Europe and imported to Colonial America. For several hundred years, the pipe stems were made longer for two reasons. As the pipe was smoked, saliva and tobacco clogged the end of the stem, and it had to be broken off. The longer the pipe, the longer it could be used. In the case of public sharing of a pipe, the tip of the stem was also broken off for sanitary reasons as it was passed to a different smoker. To keep the stem strong as it was made longer, the borehole in the stem was made smaller. About every 30 to 50 years, the stem's borehole was decreased in diameter by 1/64 of an inch.

When a section of a pipe stem is found today, its borehole can be measured to determine the approximate age. The stem found in pit #3 proved to be from the date range of 1720 to 1750. Just the right range for Fort Congaree II. Dr. Leader would surmise this pipe stem could also have come from the first Indian trader in the area, before Fort Congaree II.

What happened next, however, clarified things. As Helena leveled and cleaned her pit at 10 centimeters, an apparent archaeological feature appeared - a dark rectangular area on the south side of the pit. When wood is left in the ground, it can leave a soil color change or stain. It can also leave an area that is soft relative to the compacted virgin soil around it. This is where you need experienced archaeologists. John Fisher inspected the feature and discovered soft round cylinder areas within the dark feature. This could be a section of the palisade wall.

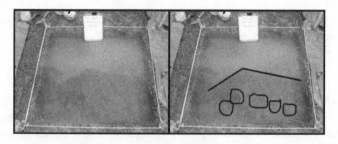

Figure 97: Pit #3 Palisade wall feature.

Dr. Leader and John Fisher, for some time, remained very low key on the find, but they obviously were very interested in it. All work was frozen on pit #3 to preserve the feature. Likewise, to the south of pit #3, pit #4 showed more of the feature so we stopped that pit also at the first level.

Figure 98: Artifacts from level 1 of Pit #3.

The pit on the north side of pit #3 (pit #2) was dug by John Fisher and Nena Rice along with Explorers Club member John Hodge. Level one held a colonial period pipe bowl piece, and level two gave us the first handmade nail, which could also have been from the fort period. Level three of the pit revealed an obviously removed post. When a wood post is removed, the dirt that ends up filling the hole can take on a lighter color, unlike a hole where the post is left to decay in the ground and leave a dark spot. The removal of the post was evident by the rounded "push-pull" areas where the post was pushed sideways to loosen it as it was pulled out. The emerging theory was that this was a support post on the outside of the main palisade wall or a bastion support. Once again, we had to stop after level three to preserve the post feature.

Figure 99: Post hole in Pit #2.

Figure 100: Archaeologist John Fisher (center) working Fort Congaree II.

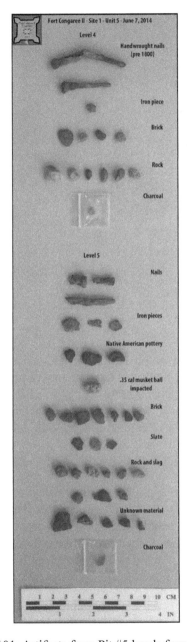

Figure 101: Artifacts from Pit #5 levels four and five.

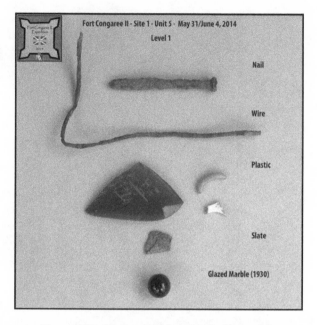

Figure 102: Modern artifacts in Pit #5 level 1.

Back on the south side of pit #3, in pit #5, we had archaeologists Meg Gaillard and DC Locke, Explorers Club members Jim and Linda Alexander, and PBS Nature Scene host Jim Welch, also an Explorers Club member. Adding color commentary was my work friend and Granby digger, Ken Banks. These interesting people would provide exciting results in pit #5. Outside of the palisade wall feature, they could go deeper. Level one showed modern items and a glazed marble that could date to the 1930s.

This made me wonder again about the "signs of the fort" that Green mentioned in the 1930s newspaper article. Maybe the fort location was known at that time, and people of the past took an interest in history. Maybe early 20th century families visited this historic fort site with their children, who passed the time by playing marbles on top of the palisade wall mound.

Next, in pit #5 was something archaeologists love to see. A separation of time periods. Not a single artifact was found in the next two levels. In level four, period handmade nails, small brick fragments, and a piece of charcoal were found. In level five, more of the nails, brick, and charcoal.

Dr. Tortora's Fort Congaree II research prepared us for the next finds. The Catawba Indians were the Natives most friendly and loyal to the Europeans during these early years. Dr. Tortora's research predicted these Catawba people would have camped in and around the fort. In level five, we found Native American pottery pieces. And last but not least, the bottom of pit #5 gave us a .35 caliber musket ball.

The outer pits in the trench did not deliver important artifacts or features. The center pits, Dr. Leader's "something is going on here" location, gave us what we needed to know. Dr. Leader, being the professional scientist he is, would not confirm the find of Fort Congaree II on this day. Like the archaeologists at the King Richard III site, Dr. Leader would force us to work almost every burning hot weekend that summer to extend the trench and complete a second perpendicular trench. Only on that first dig day did we have a large team of workers. We did acquire the services of another archaeologist, Jacob Borchardt, but for the most part, the remaining 14 dig days would be completed by Jacob, Dr. Leader, John Fisher, Jocelyn and DC Locke, Dean Hunt, Alex and Julie Wallace, Jan Ciegler, and Odess and me.

Figure 103: Julie Wallace, Jan Ceigler, and Dr. Jonathan
Leader prepare for geophysical survey work.

Those brutal dig days provided evidence of the documented ditch around the outside of the fort. We had found the only two distinct features that could prove this was a fort. Artifacts from day one supported the find. We still didn't know, however, what the final verdict would be from Dr. Leader. We would have to wait, just like in the archaeological case of King Richard III.

Figure 104: (l to r) John Fisher, David Brinkman, and Dr.
Jonathan Leader continue Fort Congaree II.

By the end of the summer, Karen Kennedy and Larry Burton had had
enough of their dug-up yard. The Greater Piedmont Chapter of the
Explorers club paid for the repair and sodding of the property. Closing out
the summer, Dr. Leader led a non-destructive geophysical resistivity survey
of the backyard. What was he looking for? We were not told.

257

Figure 105: (l to r): Dean Hunt, Dr. Jonathan Leader, and
Jacob Borchardt perform the resistivity survey.

On October 10, 2014, Dean Hunt and I opened a presentation to the
Explorers Club on the Fort Congaree II research. We still had no idea what
Dr. Leader would reveal in the closing archaeological portion of the
presentation. One by one, Dr. Leader detailed archaeological evidence of
the fort. The final piece of data was the geophysical resistivity survey. The
survey, done shortly after a rain, showed a path of low resistivity traveling
in a line through the backyard. The line agreed with the ditch we found in
an archaeological feature in the front yard. The ditch was filled, probably in
the mid-20th century, and the soil density was lower in it compared to the
area outside the ditch. A recent rain deposited more water into this area,
which the resistivity survey had detected. The findings proved a
continuation of the ditch exactly where it should have been for the fort. Dr.
Leader ended the presentation with the conclusion that we had, indeed,
found Fort Congaree II.

Figure 106: Land owners Karen Kennedy and Larry Burton, with David Brinkman (r). Karen Kennedy and Larry Burton holding the Explorers Club Expedition flag at the Explorers Club Fort Congaree II presentation with the Explorers Club members.

In the end, the overlays of both the Saxe-Gotha survey and the 1750 survey proved to be off the mark. Had we dug at the location of the Saxe-Gotha survey, we would have missed the fort by about 200 feet. Had we chosen the two target areas of the 1750 overlay, we would have missed the southern palisade wall by 50 feet and the northern wall by 40 feet. The tree roots at the northern site forced Dr. Leader's last-minute, incredible re-position that made it possible for our limited trench to cross the palisade wall.

What do you call it? A hunch? Intuition? Miracle? It all depends on how much you can think outside the box of science.

Chapter 15 – A Story of Fort Congaree II

Every history project I have been involved in, at some point, took advantage of genealogy resources. The passion people put into researching family histories never ceases to amaze me. Genealogy societies go one step further and spend numerous hours documenting and recording the history of many families in a particular area. We now have services like Ancestry.com that tie these resources together and provide funding to do even more.

Of course, understanding where you came from is essential. As I once heard in a sermon by Father Linsky at our St. Peter's Church:

You must know three things to have a joyful life:

1. Where you are.
2. Where you are going.
3. Where you came from.

The Church of Jesus Christ of Latter-day Saints felt so strongly about this that they invested millions in a goal to have every genealogical document in the world made available on the internet to help people find out where they came from. Maybe finding where we came from, and Who created us, is a fundamental purpose of our lives.

Once again in our search for Fort Congaree II, a vital and unique genealogy resource came to the rescue. Fort Congaree II was built in 1748 by Captain James Campbell. His family did extensive research and provided us with the introduction to the story of Fort Congaree II.

The Campbell research gives an excellent background on the development of the first 11 townships of South Carolina. The township plan came from England's King George II in 1730, and it included the Saxe-Gotha township in today's Cayce, SC. A few years later is when the Saxe-Gotha survey (showing a proposed location for a fort) would be created.

By 1746, many problems had developed for the European backcountry settlers and their friendly Indian allies. Supported by the French in their war against the British, tribes like the Cherokee were carrying out attacks and kidnappings against the Catawba people and the settlers. South Carolina's Royal Governor James Glen employed George Haig to negotiate with the Cherokee to persuade them to stop these French-backed attacks. In 1747, conditions in the Congarees worsened when longtime Indian trader Thomas Brown died. British Council records show numerous reports of violence against the settlers.

George Haig with William Brown, the son of Thomas Brown, took on a mission to visit the Catawbas, but they were kidnapped by Nottowegas Indians, who were French allies. Word returned to the Congarees that Haig and Brown had been taken to the area of Ohio. The governor answered the plea of Haig's wife, Elizabeth, and other outraged settlers to help Haig, but the only thing he could do was to pursue having a fort built in the Congarees.

George Haig, exhausted in his ordeal, told his captors he would not cooperate with them and they would have to kill him. Haig was quickly executed. An Indian agent from Pennsylvania would later free William Brown. Haig's death was the last straw for the settlers. Fort Congaree II soon was under construction, and a force was put into motion that would eventually eliminate the hostile Natives and set the colony's course toward independence.

The Campbell research reveals many details of the British in their approval of the plan to build Fort Congaree II. Most of these facts came from the Council Journal of 1747 and 1748.

This old documentation confirmed the completion of a ditch around the fort. Over the period of hundreds of years, this ditch would have filled in and could be detected with a geophysical survey such as resistivity or ground penetrating radar. This was very important, but unfortunately, the Council did not cover design specifications of the fort like the dimensions of any internal buildings. A document that did include those specifications is mentioned, but our research could not find it in the old Council documents.

The 1750 plat gave us the fort's outer dimensions and orientation. Further research by the team, including by Dr. Tortora, focused on a sister fort called Fort Prince George, which was built a few years after Fort Congaree II in the northwest corner of South Carolina. A full excavation of Fort Prince George was completed and documented in 1998. Combining these pieces of information allowed us to develop the visual appearance of Fort Congaree II, and it also gave us measurements to use in the planning for archaeology work.

After all the surveying and digging was done, I used my background as a software developer to recreate the fort in fully immersive Virtual Reality. Fully immersive means you can move about in a 360-degree, 3-D, life-size, and interactive world of the 1750 fort. Standing on the top of one of the fort's bastions will take your breath away, and make you dizzy if you have a fear of heights. The sounds of birds in the trees and water flowing in the nearby Congaree river also fills your sense of hearing. A narrator talks to you about the history of the fort as you move through different areas, including the Catawba Indian camp just outside the fort's palisade walls. A scavenger hunt engages you in more educational discoveries. One of the barracks inside the fort is a museum of 3-D photographs taken during the archaeological dig that located the fort.

Figure 107: Fort Congaree II's main gate on the west side of the fort.

In less than 15 minutes, the Virtual Reality presentation brings Fort Congaree II back to life and leaves you feeling filled with a sense of our forgotten past.

Figure 108: Fort Congaree II looking north.

Figure 109: Fort Congaree II looking south.

Figure 110: Fort Congaree II looking west.

Figure 111: The Catawba camp outside Fort Congaree II.

Now that you know what Fort Congaree II looked like, let's cover what happened in and around this fort.

The construction of the fort began in August of 1748. Local settlers were required to help in the building, and it was in their best interest to have the fort completed as soon as possible for safety reasons. It is estimated there were several hundred settlers in the area at this time, and they were able to complete the fort in February of 1749.

Ensign Peter Ormsby was assigned as the first commander of Fort Congaree II. Supporting him were a sergeant, corporal, drummer, and 30 privates. Given the relatively small dimensions of the fort, these men were probably housed in two barracks.

Early in 1750, the fort's garrison was replaced by Lieutenant Peter Mercier, a new sergeant, and 30 other men. About this time, Indian attacks against the settlers and the Catawbas increased. Fort Congaree II became a refuge for these people.

On May 7, 1751, history records one of these brutal attacks. Mary Gould came to the house of Martin Friday, severely wounded. She was trying to make it to Fort Congaree II but fell a quarter of a mile short. She gave the following narrative to Martin Friday and Captain Daniel Sellider:

> Saturday, the fourth, two Indians came to my house, situated about half way between the Congarees and Savannah Town. They were Savannahs. It was nearly dark when they came in, and sat down quite civilly. My husband being able to speak their language, he conversed a great while with them. I gave them their supper, after which they asked my husband for pipes and tobacco, which he supplied them with, and we all sat up till midnight, and went to sleep. The Indians also laid down, pulling off their moccasins and boots. One of them broke his pipe, and came to the bed of my husband, who handed him his out of his mouth, and laid down again, when he dropped to sleep. When the cocks began to crow, they got up and came to the bed-side and shot my husband through the head; a young man sleeping on the floor was shot dead at the same moment. The Indians, I suppose, thinking the bullet had gone through my husband's head, and mine too, struck me with a tomahawk under my right arm. Believing they had killed me, one of them went to the bed, where they were sleeping, and murdered, in cold blood, both of my children; after which they took the blankets from the beds, and having plundered the house of everything valuable, went off. In this condition, I lay among my dead two days, when one of my horses providentially returning to the house, I was able to mount him and come to this place.

Mary Gould died shortly after her account was recorded.[81]

---

[81]Richland Library: Indian Books, Secretary of State Office

266

In Dr. Dan Tortora's Fort Congaree II paper, Tortora gives the following summary of Fort Congaree II, pointing out the many positive effects the fort had in the area:

> Fort Congaree II played a vital role in the history of the Midlands of South Carolina. It was built at a time of rapid growth and settlement in the area. It commanded a strategic position at an important crossroads: at the intersection of the Congaree River, the Cherokee Path and the northern limits of Saxe-Gotha Town (Saxe-Gotha was the first backcountry settlement of South Carolina up from Charlestown). In peacetime, Fort Congaree II's garrison bustled with activity. Farmers and merchants, African slaves, indentured servants, Catawba Indians, local settlers, and ministers visited often. Soldiers and settlers worshipped together, conducted business, and even married each other. The fort protected upcountry settlers from Indian attacks and gave them peace of mind. It helped South Carolina support the struggling but loyal Catawba Nation. Its soldiers left their wives and children behind and participated in the opening battle of the French and Indian War. The story of Fort Congaree II offers a glimpse into an oft-forgotten chapter in the history of Colonial America.

As Tortora points out, the Catawba people were friendly and loyal to the local European settlers. They would suffer greatly for this in different ways over the next 250 years. In 1751, the alignment with the Europeans made the Catawba Nation an enemy of other tribes, many of whom had sided with the French in their war with Britain in the late 1740s. The settlers and Catawba were the victims of many attacks and kidnappings by these other tribes, and they often sought safety at Fort Congaree II. The Catawba did benefit from trading at the fort, receiving ammunition as well as other supplies. The fort was also at a convenient location in their travels between Charles Town and their home on the banks of the Catawba River in the Piedmont area of North and South Carolina.

The Catawba people were first recorded in 1540 by the Spanish expedition of Hernando de Soto. It is estimated that they lived in the area for, at least, 5,000 years before this first European encounter. The Catawba are believed to have thrived in the area for over 5,000 years before this early recorded history. By 1759, their population had plummeted to less than 1,000 because of smallpox brought by these Europeans.

Despite the declining numbers, the Catawba allied with the Patriots during the American Revolutionary War. Despite their side winning in the war, the Catawba would continue to be victims when they were terminated as a tribe by the federal government in 1959. At the brink of extinction, the Catawba Indian Nation reorganized in 1973 and regained federal recognition in 1993. Today, Catawba live mostly in South Carolina, and their numbers have grown to over 2,500.

Documentation shows us that Peter Mercier went out of his way to please the Catawba, even requesting reimbursements for entertainment expenses related to Catawba visitors. Other Native groups, like the Creek and Cherokee, were only invited to the fort to showcase the fort's abilities to handle a threat.

While commanding Fort Congaree II, Peter Mercier met the widow of George Haig. Elizabeth Haig had worked hard in vain to save the life of her husband, but she was instrumental in having Fort Congaree II built to protect others from a similar fate. A bond developed between Elizabeth Haig and Peter Mercier, and they were married in 1752. By this time, Martin Friday was operating a ferry just north of the fort. Friday's Ferry and a new road from Augusta provided increased traffic to the fort.

By the summer of 1754, a new character came on the horizon. The young George Washington's military career began as a major in the militia of the British Province of Virginia. In 1753, he was sent to Pennsylvania as an ambassador from the British crown to negotiate with French officials and Indians. On an expedition in 1754, Washington and his men attacked a French scouting party, killing the French leader. The act of aggression escalated the French and Indian War and led to the global Seven Years' War. The French immediately started attacking forts Washington was involved with. Under great duress, Washington requested assistance. Mercier and several of his men headed to Virginia to help Washington.

Things were desperate, and Mercier must have been thinking about his wife Elizabeth, who was almost full term with their first child. While en route on June 27, 1754, Mercier wrote his last Will & Testament, leaving everything to Elizabeth.

"WILL OF PETER MERCIER

IN THE NAME OF GOD AMEN

I Peter Mercier of South Carolina Lieutenant of one of His Majesty's three Independent Companys lately in South Carolina aforesaid a Detachment whereof now doing duty is Virginia aforesaid under the Command of Captain James Mckay, being of sound mind memory and disposition but calling to mind the uncertainty of this Transitory Life make and ordain this my last Will & Testament I appoint my dear & Loving Wife Elizabeth Merrier whole & sole Executrix of this my Last Will and Testament that after all my just and Lawful debts are paid I make my said Dear & Loving Wife Elizabeth Heiress of all the Estate Real & Personal. Given under my hand & Seal at the Camp in the Great Meadow this twenty seventh day of June one thousand seven hundred & Fifty Four in the twenty eighth Year of the Reign of our Sovereign Lord George the Second. Signed&Sealed as the Last Will & Testament & declared to be so by the said Testator in presence of us. Joseph Lloyd, James McKay, Maurice Anderson.

PETER MERCIER (L S)"

On July 1, 1754, Mercier arrived to help Washington build Fort Necessity. On July 3, the hastily built fort was attacked with a vengeance by the French and Indians. Mercier and his men from Fort Congaree II fought valiantly and to the death. Mercier continued fighting after being shot on two occasions during the battle. A third shot finally killed him. The battle was lost, but they saved the life of Colonel George Washington, allowing him to fight again for something much bigger.

Benjamin Franklin, Deputy Postmaster General of North America, paid tribute to Peter Mercier later that year with the following publication:

"1754 PETER MERCIER

The following lines, from the Pennsylvania Gazette, of October 31, 1754, published by Benjamin Franklin, were inscribed "to the memory of Lieutenant Peter Mercier, Esq., who fell in the battle near Ohio river, in Virginia, July 3, 1754"—that is, in the engagement, between the British forces, under Washington, and the French forces under the fiery Coulon-Villiers. resulting in the surrender of Washington and the evacuation of Fort Necessity: in what is now Fayette county, Pennsylvania.

Too fond of what the martial harvests yield —
Alas ! too forward in the dangerous field —
Firm and undaunted, resolute and brave,
Careless of life invaluable to save —
As one secure of fame, in battle tried,
The glory of Ohio's sons he died.

Oh, once endowed with every pleasing power
To chase the sad and charm the social hour,
To sweeten life with mild ingenuous arts,
And gain possession of all open hearts.
How have thy friends and comrades cause to mourn!
How wished they for thy peaceable return,
Thy province and thy household to defend,
And happily thy future years to spend!
I hoped the fates far longer would allow
The laurel wreath to flourish on thy brow;
I hoped to greet thee from thy northern toils
Elate with victory, enriched with spoils:
But now, alas! these pleasing dreams are fled!
Sweetly thou sleep'st in glory's dusty bed,
By all esteemed, admired, extolled, approved,
In death lamented as in life beloved.
Georgia, loud-sounding, thy achievements tell,
And sad Virginia marks where Mercier fell.

Ah! lost too soon — too early snatched away
To joys unfading, and immortal day!

The heart of Fort Congaree II was lost at Fort Necessity on July 3, 1754. Peter Mercier would be little remembered over the decades, but his bravery and sacrifice would lead to the birth of a nation. Peter Mercier did, however, leave a living miracle behind when his wife Elizabeth delivered their only child, Margaret, later that year. It did not take much genealogy work to find that Margaret's descendants number in the dozens today. Unfortunately, few of these people are aware of the vital role their sixth great-grandfather played in the making of America. Likewise, Elizabeth's first marriage to George Haig produced three children, which led to numerous living descendants who probably have no idea of the sacrifice made by this generation that set the course for independence. William Brown, who was kidnapped with Haig, suffered mental issues after the ordeal. He would change his name to Jacob Gardner and have six children. Today, there are also dozens of his living descendants.

By 1760, Fort Congaree II had fallen into disrepair. Little is known about the fort during its final years, except that Colonel James Grant chose the fort site as the training ground for a 2,800-man group of British Regulars and South Carolina Provincials in 1761. Among these young men were Francis Marion, William Moultrie, Isaac Huger, and Andrew Pickens. As the group moved out and toward the town of Ninety Six, South Carolina, the Cherokee attempted an ambush. The British and Provincials held their ground, inflicting twice the casualties. The Cherokee expended all their ammunition in the battle. Grant and his men, without resistance, systematically burned 15 Indian towns and 1,500 acres of their crops. With another British army moving in, Cherokee Chief Attakullakulla gave up the fight. By 1763, the French and Indian War was over.

Those young South Carolina men who took part in the final phase of Fort Congaree II (Marion, Moultrie, Huger, and Pickens) would go on to be heroes of the American Revolution. Aided by their former foe, the French, these men would turn the Revolution around in South Carolina and drive the British to their final battle in 1781 at Yorktown. There, the British would fall to none other than General George Washington, who had been saved 17 years earlier by the men of Fort Congaree II.

Figure 112: Fort Congaree II's future heroes of the American Revolution: Marion, Moultrie, Huger, and Pickens.

Figure 113: George Washington (with artifacts) and David Brinkman.

Gone were the hostile Indians, the French, and now the British. In its short and largely forgotten life, Fort Congaree II had played a vital role in the development of the American colony into the independent free nation of the United States of America.

Chapter 16 – A State House and Tavern are Found

In 1786, the South Carolina Assembly voted to move the state capital from Charleston to a more central location. Granby was right in the center of the State, but flooding and health issues there prompted the General Assembly to create the new capital city on the higher ground on the other side of the Congaree River. The new city would be called Columbia. In 1790, a State House was built in the center of the developing city. The legislature held its first session there later that year. The needs of the lawmakers also required a special kind of meeting place near the State House, and Rives Tavern and Inn opened across the street.

This State House is documented reasonably well, with the best snapshot coming from the 1805-1808 diary of Edwin Hooker. A tutor from Connecticut working at South Carolina College, Hooker took a special interest in politics during his stay in Columbia. He described Columbia as a wilderness of pine trees with bushes growing in the streets. There were only a few buildings, and the lone oak trees were around the State House.

He spent many hours in the State House and provided an excellent description, which I used to model it on the computer. Legislative sessions often took days to begin while waiting on a quorum. Goats freely roamed the grounds and were commonly found in the basement of the building because doors were always left open. Hooker often critiqued the House and Senate speakers. Among them, he was most impressed with William Lowndes, who would be the inspiration for the name of my dad's WWII ship.

One bill that caught the attention of Hooker was an 1805 bill to abolish the slave trade. He noted the "thundering and overbearing" speech by Alexander Stark, the man who operated the illegal ferry on the Broad River, suggesting that slavery was okay and an improvement to the lives of the kidnapped Africans. The House approved the bill, and a preliminary Senate vote was 16 votes in favor of the bill and 15 votes against it. A day later, the final vote to abolish the slave trade showed a reversal, with 14 members in favor and 16 members against the bill. There was much celebration, as the Speaker of the House and several members of the House and Senate parading through the streets with a drum and fiddle. Hooker described it as a riotous scene.

273

A few days later, however, the town was in considerable alarm as rumors spoke of retaliation by Negroes. Their purported plan was to attack Granby, then come to Columbia and steal arms and ammunition in the State House, and burn Columbia. The militia came out in full force, and a defense was built around the State House. The leader of the planned rebellion was arrested, and things returned to normal. So much for Alexander Stark's idea that slaves were happy with their situation.

As for Rives Tavern, most of what I knew about it was from research by my fellow Explorers Club member and historian Warner Montgomery. Timothy Rives had no interest in taking part with Wade Hampton and Thomas Taylor in their secret deal to profit from the Columbia land deals of 1786. Instead, all Timothy wanted was to serve people in his own tavern and inn. Thomas Taylor, his brother-in-law, set him up nicely with property for such an establishment at a prime location across from the State House. Historian and tavern expert Roy Vandegrift also pointed out that Timothy took part in many community activities and provided free daily breakfast to all the students of the new South Carolina College.

These bits of information were my collective knowledge of the Old State House and its neighbor, Rives Tavern. I never expected that it would go any further than this.

Things changed, however, while working on the DNA and genealogy of King Richard III. A new feature of AncestryDNA informed me of a DNA Circle match that had grown to include almost 60 people. A DNA Circle is where you and other people have a common ancestor, and each person in the circle has a DNA match to at least one other person in the circle. This implies a possible proof of your genealogy to that common ancestor. The more people you have a DNA match to within the circle, the higher the confidence is of this proof. That DNA Circle match of mine was to a William McGuffy Rives (1767-1839), who was my fourth great-grandfather.

My family tree branch to William McGuffy Rives ended with him, and that was genealogy work I had done many years before my study of the Old State House and Rives Tavern. I never connected the two. William McGuffy Rives was also from Virginia, and none of his descendants came to South Carolina. I had thought I was the first person on either side of my family to have been born in South Carolina. But I started looking in the family trees of the other DNA Circle matches, and a few of them went back

274

further than William McGuffy Rives. In fact, they went all the way back to a Colonel William Rives (1683-1746) of Virginia, my new-found seventh great-grandfather. Still, no South Carolina connection until I looked at his other sons, my seventh great uncles, and there was a Timothy Rives (1710-1772). He was born in Virginia and died in Columbia, South Carolina!

He was a little too old to be the tavern's Timothy Rives, but he had a son named Timothy who would be my first cousin, seven times removed. Further studied proved this was, in fact, the owner of Rives Tavern in Granby and Columbia. I now had a second personal connection to Granby to go along with my King Richard III connection to John Manners, who was the Marquis of Granby. I would soon discover that the descendants of Timothy Rives produced many South Carolina-born relatives hundreds of years before me. I located, right in Columbia, two living eighth cousins through Timothy Rives. It was a little DNA miracle that made this a much smaller world.

I still didn't expect this to turn into a significant project. After all, it was personal and only in my family. But a curiosity began to build about just where Rives Tavern had stood. I wanted to find it and stand on the spot. That's what historians and archaeologists like to do.

Figure 114: Above: 1794 drawing of the State House with Rives Tavern. Below: Today's incorrectly placed marker.

I knew the tavern was across from the Old State House. If I could locate the Old State House site, I could find the tavern's exact location. My previous work on today's South Carolina State House grounds, however, had led to confusion on the location of the old building. One historical marker states, "Here stood the Old State House" while 200 feet away, the corner of the new State House has a marker explaining that the damage on that corner was caused by the burning of the Old State House in 1865. There was no way a fire from 200 feet away could have damaged granite like that. The other marker was clearly wrong. This reminded me of the incorrect Broad River Bridge historical marker that helped hide the location of the Confederate Broad River Bridge and Sherman's crossing sites for over 100 years.

To prove which marker was wrong, I studied all the known illustrations and Civil War era photographs that might shed a clue. A well-known 1865 photograph of the new State House showed the nearby ruins of the burned Old State House. The ruins were close to that damaged corner of the new State House and about 200 feet away from the incorrect marker location. A Harper's Weekly 1865 illustration showed the same thing from a different angle.

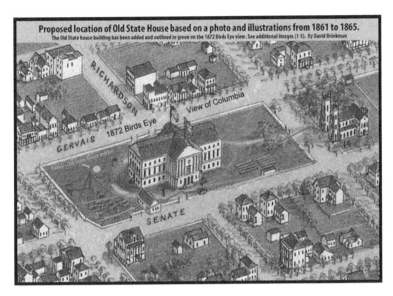

Figure 115: Above: 1870 Bird's Eye view of Columbia showing how period illustrations, and a photo (below) by George Barnard in 1865, pinpoint the position of the Old State House.

The Old State House was built in 1790 at the northwest corner of Richardson (now Main) and Senate streets. A 1938 newspaper article about the unveiling of the Old State House marker, and old postcard illustrations, showed the marker's original placement was aesthetic and not historical. It was aligned to be centered with the west-wing of the new State House and not the historical location of the Old State House. In the late 1960s, the marker was moved even further away from the correct position when the Palmetto (Mexican War) monument took its old spot. It's difficult to believe that people would move a historical marker that says, "Here stood," but it happens. Eight period illustrations, maps, and photographs were studied to nail down the locations of the Old State House. Location turned into locations, as I determined the building was slightly moved in the 1850s to make room for the construction of the new State House building. It really had two locations.

Figure 116: Harper's Weekly: Above: The burned remains of the Old State House (next to the new building) and (below) the Old State House ten years before its destruction.

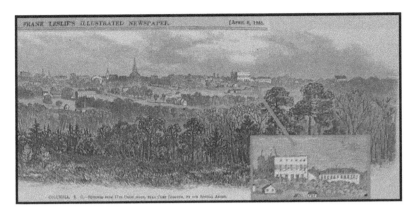

Figure 117: Above: Frank Leslie's Illustrated showing the Old State House just before its destruction in 1865. Below: Today's view of new State House from where the Old State House stood.

The next step in the research was spending several months studying the history of the Old State House and building a computer model of it. It was clear from the documentation that the raised basement of the building was used for the storage of important items.

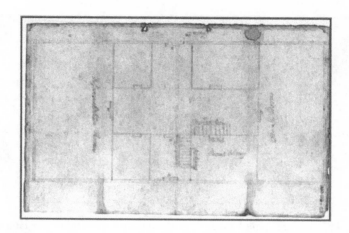

Figure 118: 1839 Floor plan of the Old State House from SCDAH.

Many measurements were taken from drawings of the Old State House and of a floor plan from the 1830s.[82] The floor plan had no dimensions, but I was able to interpolate the size based on carefully drawn steps from the basement to the first floor. The result was a building that was 80 by 37.5 feet. I verified these outer dimensions by measuring the size of the Palmetto (Mexican War) monument on today's State House grounds. This monument stood in front of the Old State House between 1855 and 1861. The illustration in Figure 116 allowed me to make this comparison. The relative sizes matched with the interpolated 80 by 37.5-foot size of the building. Continuing the math, the basement landing would have been two to three feet below ground, which leaves the possibility that fire debris may have covered historically valuable items which went unnoticed after the burning of Columbia.

Some would argue that everything I had discovered so far was just a bunch of circumstantial evidence. To prove the case, I would need to go to the site and find physical evidence. Like I'm just going to walk there and find unique 200-year-old artifacts lying on the ground. That would take a miracle.

South Carolina Governor Nikki Haley would call it the 1,000-year flood of 2015. As we headed into October of 2015, even before radar was showing a storm, the National Weather Service predicted an event that could bring 20

---

[82] South Carolina Department of Archives and History: Item 1939-116-03

inches of rain to South Carolina. Exactly as predicted, the rain started on October 1 and over five days would produce 12 to 27 inches across the state. Over 11 trillion gallons of water fell, causing rivers and streams to overflow and at least 39 dams to breach. Hundreds of businesses and homes were flooded or destroyed, and 19 lives were lost.[83]

With nowhere to go during those flooding rains, I completed the final work to pinpoint the locations of the Old State House and Rives Tavern. They were on a high point in Columbia, so the thought never entered my mind that the heavy rains would have an effect there as it did at the Granby site, where the flooding waters would expose over 600 artifacts.

[83] SC flooding statistics – Dateline Carolina:
http://www.datelinecarolina.org/category/308305/scs-historic-flood

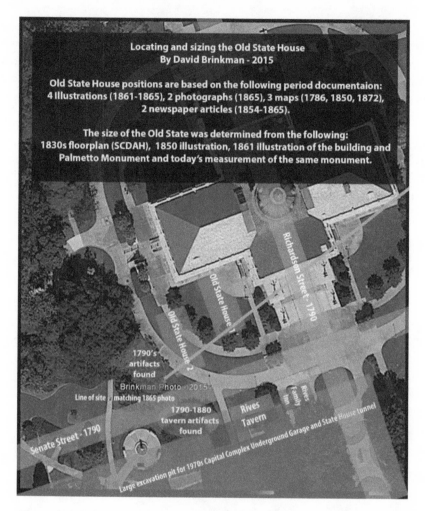

Figure 119: Brinkman's locations of the Old State House and Rives Tavern.

After the weather cleared, I made the trip downtown to the State House grounds and worked my way to the locations. Grass and sidewalks mostly cover the site where the Old State House stood. The southwestern corner, however, is in the shaded area of a large tree. These trees normally have pine straw covering the bare ground of the shaded areas, but recent landscaping work had removed the straw. The heavy rains then had eroded the dirt and clay, and, to my amazement, there were dozens of exposed artifacts. Many of them were very familiar to me.

As luck would have it (I will take a break from the word miracle), the Old State House was built within a few years of when our Granby dig house was built. The two buildings would have been constructed with common local products like bricks and nails. There were exposed brick fragments all over the ground. They looked just like what we find in Granby, but there's no good way to prove the date on something like this. The 1865 photograph of the Old State House ruins showed hundreds of stacked and scattered bricks, so you would expect this to be the most common artifact.

Among other building supplies of that time, there was something else we should expect to find and quickly identify and date. In the 1780s and 1790s of South Carolina, window glass had to be imported from England. After many decades in the ground, this glass takes on a distinct light green color. I found one flat piece exactly like what we find in Granby. More significantly, I found multiple pieces of this melted glass. One blob appeared to have lead in its center. Lead strips were used in that period to hold pieces of window glass together. Unlike the glass of today, this old glass, and lead will melt at the temperature that wood burns. I knew these were artifacts of the burned Old State House. I had scientifically proven the location.

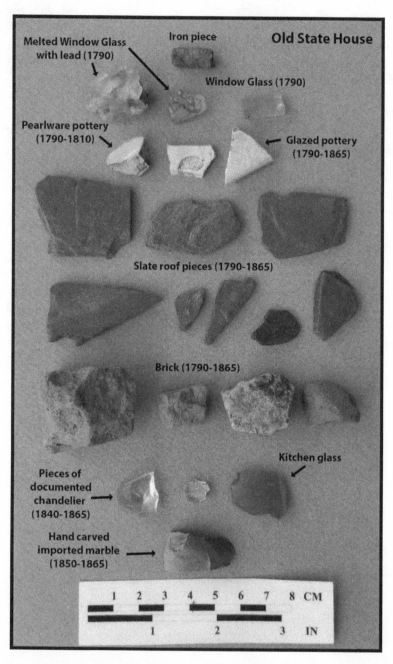

Figure 120: Surface artifacts found at Old State House location.

One more artifact, a piece of hand-cut/polished marble, would send chills down my spine after it was cleaned. Could it be from the construction of the new State House or maybe something else? Could that be another miracle to come? I will cover that in a later chapter.

Figure 121: Surface artifacts found at Rives Tavern location.

As I moved toward my expected location of my cousin's tavern, another shaded area of a large tree provided more exposed ground and more artifacts. This time, however, they were kitchen items ranging from

Colonial period pottery shards and glass to a couple of Civil War ginger bottle fragments, typical artifacts of a tavern site. I had also proven the site of Rives Tavern.

My mission this day had been a personal one. I wanted to stand where my first cousin, seven times removed, had lived over 200 years ago. The surprise artifact finds, and their significance, changed things. I began to think about what could be found and learned from more research and full archaeological excavation of the site.

Thanks to the flood of 2015, and a combination of previous miracles, the Old State House and Rives Tavern were found. Documenting this and educating the public would turn this into another history project, which is spawning more work and discoveries. Part of this new work is a Virtual Reality re-creation of the South Carolina State House grounds in 1865 before the city's burning by General Sherman and crew. This will be a full-blown VR game that includes the real history plus myths and legends like the underground Columbia tunnels that, supposedly, provided secret passageways from the Old State House to other locations in Columbia.

Figure 122: Screenshots from David Brinkman's VR creation of the State House grounds in early 1865. Top left: The view of the Old State House looking west. Top right: A view from the porch of the Old State House looking east at the new State House under construction with Trinity Church in the background. Bottom left: Inside the main hall of the Old State House looking north toward the library. Bottom right: Looking west out of the House Chamber windows.

Chapter 17 – Miracles to Come? Was the Truth and Justice in the Old State House?

While researching the Confederate Broad River Bridge and Sherman's crossing project, I stumbled across an 1858 stereoscopic (3D) photograph of a John C. Calhoun Statue in Charleston's City Hall. Handwriting on the back of the card indicated that the statue was moved to Columbia during the Civil War and that it was lost in the burning of Columbia in 1865. In 2010, I created the smart-phone application "Charleston Tour 3D" which included hundreds of historical markers and 3D stereoscopic images of Charleston. The idea of the app was that, as you moved around historic Charleston, the app would automatically read historical markers to you as you approached them. An option in the app allowed you to view Civil War era stereoscopic views of many of the historical points. Among the stereo-views were several photos of John C. Calhoun's grave and, of course, the statue. As I expanded my research, it did not take long for me to realize the fantastic story behind the statue. I was, once again, dumbfounded at how something like this could have been completely forgotten.

Figure 123: 1858 Stereoview of John C. Calhoun statue.

The above stereoview[84] (made about 1858[85]) is of the magnificent John C. Calhoun marble statue as it stood in Charleston's City Hall. The caption on the back of this early stereoscopic photograph fails to tell the dramatic story behind the toga-covered Calhoun and the amazing journey this piece of Italian marble took as the nation fell into Civil War.

John C. Calhoun was a U.S. Senator from South Carolina and two-time Vice President under Presidents Andrew Jackson and John Quincy Adams. The most prominent political figure in South Carolina history, Calhoun led the South's fight for states' rights and nullification, which would allow states to reject federal laws they deemed unconstitutional. Among the changing tides of the time was the issue of slavery, which was fully allowed and supported by the Constitution.[86] Ten years after his death, Calhoun would be a strong inspiration to the secessionists of 1860. In fact, the

---

[84]John C. Calhoun statue stereoview held at the New York Public Library. Part of the Robert N. Dennis collection of stereoscopic views. An Image is available at: http://commons.wikimedia.org/wiki/File:Sculpture_of_John_C._Calhoun_by_Hiram_Power s_in_city_hall_(later_removed_to_Columbia_and_destroyed_when_Sherman_entered_the _city),_from_Robert_N._Dennis_collection_of_stereoscopic_views.png

[85] The Charleston Mercury reported on 12/24/1857 that the pedestal for the statue was ready and that a new left arm (which had been lost in the wreck of "The Elizabeth") was just received. This means the stereoview must have been taken some time after the date of the article as the photo shows a repaired statue on a pedestal.

[86]Thurgood Marshall speech at the Constitutional Bicentennial Celebration in 1987.

banner of the South Carolina Secession of 1860 shows (top center) the image of this Calhoun statue.[87] Almost 100 years later, a 1957 Senate Committee selected Calhoun as one of the five greatest U.S. Senators of all time. Committee Chairman John F. Kennedy praised Calhoun for being a "forceful logician of state sovereignty" and a "masterful defender of the rights of a political minority against the dangers of an unchecked majority."[88]

Figure 124: Banner of the South Carolina Secession (left)
and drawing of Calhoun Statue (right).

There was little mystery in the political life of Calhoun, but this American-designed and Roman-made sculpture would go through an incredible and tragic journey before being lost in the burning trail of General William T. Sherman's March through the South. After being lost for almost 100 years, did a significant part of Charleston's statue reappear in a North Carolina museum or is it buried in the ruins of the capital city of the state that started the Civil War? It's a forgotten mystery now brought back to life.

---

[87] "The secession banner presided over this state's withdrawal from the Union 150 years ago" by Harlan Greene: https://charlestonmag.com/features/history_unfurled
[88] John C. Calhoun: A Featured Biography: United States Senate Site:
http://www.senate.gov/artandhistory/history/common/generic/Featured_Bio_Calhoun.ht
m

The Statue's unfortunate voyage

The statue's blueprint was based on a portrait bust of Calhoun made between 1835 and 1837. The City of Charleston in 1844 commissioned the life-size (plus a few inches) composition, and a plaster version of it was created later that year by the great American sculptor Hiram Powers. The final massive marble construction was completed in Rome, also by Powers, in 1849.[89]

Powers was born in Woodstock, Vermont and was of Irish descent. He permanently moved in 1837 to Florence, Italy, where he established a studio. His most famous work was the statue *The Greek Slave*, considered the first life-sized nude statue by an American artist. He completed *The Greek Slave* about the time he finished the plaster Calhoun piece. The fame he achieved from *The Greek Slave* would be a distraction, thus explaining a four-year delay in delivering the Calhoun marble statue. Ironically, while the Calhoun statue would become an inspiration for the preservation of the institution of slavery, *The Greek Slave* would become a symbol for abolitionists through Elizabeth Barrett Browning's sonnet "Hiram Powers' Greek Slave."[90]

Charleston's selection of Powers for the job was probably born of the friendship and working relationship Powers had with the Preston family of Columbia. John Preston personally financed the first years of Powers' work in Florence. Preston instructed Powers, "Do not work for money, at least for several years." During this period, Preston had Powers complete busts of Preston family members and several other marble items that can be seen today in the Hampton-Preston Mansion in Columbia.[91]

As the Calhoun statue was going through its final cuts and polishing in Rome, American journalist Margaret Fuller was finishing her book on the short-lived Roman Republic. Fuller was a teacher, writer, and editor from

---

[89] Archives of American Art: Hiram Powers papers, 1819-1953, bulk 1835-1883: Correspondence with H. Gourdin of Charleston.
[90] Elizabeth Barrett Browning's The Greek Slave: https://florencecapital.wordpress.com/2011/04/05/elizabeth-barrett-browning-the-greek-slave/
[91] Archives of American Art: Hiram Powers papers, 1819-1953, bulk 1835-1883: Correspondence with John and William Preston of Columbia, SC.

Cambridgeport, Massachusetts. She also was a strong advocate of equality for women, and she became the New York Tribune's first female editor and later first female foreign correspondent. In 1848, at the age of 38, Fuller married Roman nobleman Marchese Giovanni Angelo Ossoli. A year later, they had a son and settled in the American sector of Florence, Italy. It was there that Fuller worked on her history of the Roman Republic and planned her return to America to have it published. As fate would have it, the Calhoun statue and the Ossoli family would both be transported to America on the merchant ship Elizabeth.

On March 31, 1850, John C. Calhoun died at the age of 68. On May 17, 1850, his great marble image and the Ossoli family, with Margaret Fuller's manuscript in hand, departed Italy. Just days before the departure, Fuller wrote: "I am absurdly fearful and various omens have combined to give me a dark feeling ... It seems to me that my future upon earth will soon close."[92] She also told her dear friend, Elizabeth Barrett Browning: "But our ship is called the Elizabeth, and I accept the omen."[93] Shortly into the two-month journey, smallpox began spreading through the ship, killing the captain. On July 19, as the ship approached land, and into a storm, the new and inexperienced ship's commander thought he had spotted the Cape May Lighthouse off New Jersey. He was wrong. It was the Fire Island, New York lighthouse, and the ship hit an unexpected sandbar causing the Elizabeth to break apart.[94]

Margaret, her family, and manuscript were lost. "Fuller might have saved herself by swimming to shore with the aid of a sailor, but she refused to leave her husband - who couldn't swim - and she refused to be separated from her 2-year-old son, who couldn't be carried in the rough sea."[95] The tragic loss of the Ossolis would be the inspiration of the epic poem "Aurora Leigh," by Elizabeth Barrett Browning.[96] Just before the fateful voyage,

---

[92] Slater, Abby. *In Search of Margaret Fuller*. 2-3: New York: Delacorte Press, 1978. ISBN 0-440-03944-4. Also at http://en.wikipedia.org/wiki/Margaret_Fuller

[93] Margaret Fuller By Margaret Bell, Mrs Franklin D. Roosevelt; pg. 310

[94] McFarland, Philip. *Hawthorne in Concord*. New York: Grove Press, 2004: 170–171. ISBN 0-8021-1776-7 Also at http://en.wikipedia.org/wiki/Margaret_Fuller

[95] American Poetry in the Age of Whitman and Dickinson: http://ampoarchive.wordpress.com/tag/margaret-fuller

[96] Florin.ms's Twelve websites about Florence: TUONI DI BIANCO SILENZIO (THUNDER OF WHITE SILENCE): http://www.florin.ms/tuoni.html : "One vast piece in Carrara marble of his, the John C. Calhoun, which Margaret Fuller had earlier described as 'full of power, simple

Fuller had viewed the Calhoun statue and joked with Powers about his heavy statue traveling with her on the Elizabeth.[97]

The sinking of the Elizabeth also sent the Calhoun statue to the bottom of the sea, but no one knew precisely where. John C. Calhoun was not well-liked by all, and it was easy for many to see the statue as the cause of the great tragedy. Some said the massive tribute to Calhoun shifted its position in the strong storm, causing the ship to capsize. A group of men, believing they knew the location of the sunken sculpture, went out in boats and dropped large stones into the water hoping to destroy Charleston's precious cargo. To save the statue would require something special. Charleston was not about to sit back and let its masterpiece be lost to the sea. The search for "the Calhoun" became a regular item in newspapers around the country.

About six weeks after the sinking of the Elizabeth, the New York Times and Charleston Courier reported that the U.S. Revenue Cutter Morris had located the Calhoun statue in its box. Attempts to raise it, however, failed. James A. Whipple of Boston was employed to take on the recovery of the statue. Whipple was an engineer and inventor who had made significant improvements to submarine armor (diving suits.) Initially, the weather proved to be the biggest problem for Whipple. Many attempts were made to raise Calhoun's statue, but it wasn't until October 31, 1850, that the sea finally settled and Whipple lowered five one-hundred-pound grappling hooks to the bottom. Unable to grab the item from the surface, Whipple put on his submarine armor and took on the dangers of the deep. With the hooks put in place by the engineer himself, the Calhoun statue was pulled to the surface.[98]

---

and majestic in attitude and expression', then caused the shipwreck of the 'Elizabeth' off Fire Island drowning Margaret, her young baby Angelo Ossoli and her consort, the Roman Marchese. Elizabeth Barrett Browning had yearned to write an epic poem with a modern setting, had suffered guilt and anguish at the drowning of her brother, Edward Barrett Moulton Barrett, heir to the family's Jamaican slave estates. Margaret Fuller's surrogate death released Elizabeth to write Aurora Leigh, whose two heroines resemble Margaret Fuller and herself."

[97] Margaret Fuller By Margaret Bell, Mrs Franklin D. Roosevelt; pg. 311
[98] Stryker's American register and magazine, Volume 5; Pg. 160:
edited by James Stryker. Also at:
http://books.google.com/books?id=J2tBAAAAYAAJ&printsec=frontcover&source=gbs_ge_s
ummary_r&cad=0#v=onepage&q&f=false

Initially, it was reported that the only damage to the statue was a fractured right arm, which could soon be repaired.[99] When the statue was finally delivered to City Hall, however, the Charleston Courier reported that the top portion of the scroll (with the words: "Truth and Justice") had been broken off and the left arm from the elbow down was missing.[100] It would be another eight years before Charleston would have all the necessary parts to repair the damage. The statue originally stood at the "westerly end of the hall."[101] After the repairs in 1858, the statue finally took its place "in the recess near the stairs"[102] on a pedestal as can be seen in the 1858 stereoview photograph.

It's not over yet

You might think the story ends there. One problem, though, and that would be a prophecy of John C. Calhoun himself coming true. Over and over in his political career, Calhoun predicted that war between the North and South would be inevitable if the North pursued making slavery illegal in the South.[103] He saw it as a violation of the Constitution and another double standard that had become a means of aggression against the South. Calhoun knew slavery was immoral, but he saw it as a necessary evil that would need to continue until the South developed to the point where it was on a level playing field with the North. On April 12, 1861, Calhoun's prophecy was fulfilled when Southern troops opened fire on Fort Sumter.

With Charleston at the center of the war, many of the city's treasured items were moved to locations outside of the city. One of those items was the Calhoun statue, which was transported to Columbia. Some accounts say it was stored in the courthouse in Columbia, and other reports say the Old State House. No one at the time could foresee the fate the end of the war would bring to the capital city of South Carolina.

---

[99] Steamboats are running everything: Sunk with Margaret Fuller: http://www.steamthing.com/2003/06/sunk_with_marga.html
[100] The Charleston Courier; November 15, 1850.
[101] The Charleston Mercury; Funeral of Hon. Langdon Cheves; June 1857.
[102] The Charleston Mercury; 12/24/1857
[103] The American Journey: Chapter 5, pg. 8: "If Congress admitted California as a free state, Calhoun warned the Southern states had to leave the Union."

Modern historian Theodore Rosengarten described the burning of Columbia, with a mention of the Calhoun statue:

> Bull Street was on fire, five blocks east of Assembly. The old State House burned like a chunk of fat-lighter, and the new granite-walled State House blistered. Marble sculptures of eminent South Carolinians, ... including a statue of John C. Calhoun in a Roman toga, personifying the genius of liberty, dissolved ... in a quicklime puddle.[104]

Years later, the last references from that generation to the great Calhoun statue appeared in the September 1909 issue of the Confederate Veteran Magazine:

> The Charleston News and Courier asks: What has become of the handsome marble statue of John C. Calhoun which was brought to Charleston from Italy in 1854 or 1855 and placed in the City Hall here?

> The statue was very much admired by all who saw it and has been practically forgotten, it appears, by all except a handful of people, none of whom know certainly its fate. The statue was made in Rome by the American sculptor, Powers. It represented Calhoun standing wearing a Roman Senator's toga. In his left hand, which was uplifted, was a scroll representing "Truth, Justice, and the Constitution," the right hand of the figure was pointing toward the scroll. The cost, it is stated, was $10,000.

> The statue was shipped from Rome to New York. In transit the ship foundered. It is said one of the arms was broken just below the shoulder, and was repaired under the direction of Mr. Powers by a stonecutter named Walker.

> One story has it that the statue was placed in the City Hall and remained there until the Civil War, that it was then packed and shipped to Columbia for safe keeping, that upon reaching Columbia

---

[104] New Views on the Burning of Columbia, Theodore Rosengarten: South Caroliniana Library: http://library.sc.edu/socar/uscs/1993/addr93.html Note: Some Marble melts at the temperature at which wood burns.

the boxed statue was placed in the courthouse, but that when Columbia was burned the statue perished in the flames. There are other accounts given as to the fate of the statue, one of which is that it was taken from the Columbia courthouse by Northern soldiers and may still be in existence.

Also, in 1909, was a plea from the Washington Herald for any knowledge of the missing statue:

Printed in The State (8-22-1909):
STATESMAN'S LOST STATUE
Washington Herald Calls Attention to Missing Work Disappearing Years Ago.
Somewhere in this country there is a lost statue of John C. Calhoun. Any person finding himself in its presence may learn of something to his advantage by communicating with the authorities at Charleston. This work of art disappeared during the Civil war. Charleston has just begun to mourn its loss, and will not be comforted. If publicity will aid in the search, it is a pleasure to make that contribution toward the recovery of this work of art and the consequent assuaging of the grief of a bereaved city.

This tale of a wondering figure of a statesman begins in distant Rome where it was wrought into the form of life by the cunning hand of the American sculptor, Powers. The imaginative hand of the artist transformed the South Carolina statesman into a Roman senator, clad in the iconoclastic drapery of a toga. In its voyage across the sea the statue met with misfortune of a broken arm, which was mended with the best skill of a stonecutter in New York City. This ought to aid in its identification. Set up in the City Hall of Charleston, this Ulysses of marble resumed its journeyings upon the approach of Northern troops. Thereafter, its Odyssey is of varied version. One tradition says that it was buried to save it from the invaders; another that it was removed to Columbia, another that it was captured by the Union army and carried north of the Mason and Dixon's line as a trophy of war.

It would seem that the last of these tales would be erased from the list of conjecture. Stalwart as it were, it is not credible that the men of Sherman's army would have been disposed to add an heroic of marble to their impedimenta. Moreover, the possession of a captured statue of a Southern statesman would have been the wonder of camp, and the story of its laborious transportation would surely have become a fretfully enduring reminiscence. Nevertheless, it would have been an act of kindness for the curators of art galleries in the North to pass in review their silent charges, just to make sure that no Calhoun lurks in their midst. In the meantime, Charleston should investigate thoroughly its own recesses. It may be possible that the lost figure reposes placidly in some forgotten nook near its bereaved home.

For the next few decades, the statue remained missing. Most people believed it had been destroyed in the Columbia fire. The statue, and the amazing story behind it were soon forgotten. Years later, a Google search turned up a Hiram Powers marble bust of Calhoun in, of all places, an art museum in North Carolina.

According to the Smithsonian's National Portrait Gallery, the North Carolina Museum of Art once owned a marble statue of Calhoun by Powers, which was only 29 inches tall, but it's currently listed as "unaccessioned."[105]

North Carolina Museum of Art106:

John C. Calhoun (1782-1850) Date: originally modeled 1835, carved 1859

Related People:

Artist: Hiram Powers

American, 1805-1873, active in Italy 1837-1873

Dimensions: H. 29 1/2 in. (74.9 cm)

Medium: Marble

Credit Line: Presented to the State of North Carolina by Wharton Jackson Green, 1861; transferred to the North Carolina Museum of Art, 1956

Object Number: SC.56.3.1

---

[105] Steamboats are running everything: Sunk with Margaret Fuller:
http://www.steamthing.com/2003/06/sunk_with_marga.html
[106] North Carolina Museum of Art catalog:
http://ncartmuseum.org/art/detail/john_c._calhoun_1782-1850

Today, this piece is on display at the North Carolina Museum of Art. The museum presentation includes very limited background information. It falls far short of the history of the original Charleston statue, but it is still from the same era. If you do some basic math, the 29.5-inch museum piece, as a complete human physique, would stand about six feet tall. The Charleston statue was said to be a few inches taller than real size. Calhoun, the man, was slightly taller than average. Six feet seems to be the right size. Looking more closely at the details - the facial features, the curls in the hair, the folds in the toga - it's obvious the statue and the North Carolina bust are almost identical.

Figure 125: The Charleston Calhoun statue on the left and the North Carolina bust on the right. Credit: North Carolina Museum of Art.

Could the North Carolina piece be the salvaged upper portion of the Charleston statue? It seemed possible except for one detail. If you look at the side of the North Carolina bust, where the right arm would be, the North Carolina bust contains marble that could not have possibly been part of the Charleston statue. Could someone have attached extra marble to the North Carolina bust? There's no sign of any repair work.

Further research settled the case. The original plaster bust made by Powers was found in the Smithsonian American Art Museum. It is identical to the North Carolina piece. Did Powers make multiple copies of this plaster bust, possibly using a "pointing machine" (a copying device used since Classical Greek time?)[107]

---

[107] How Marble is carved: http://jasonarkles.com/marble-carving

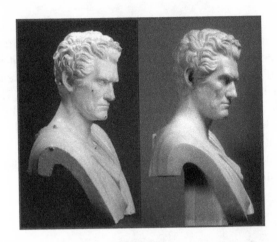

Figure 126: Powers' plaster bust on the left and the North Carolina marble bust on the right. The metal inserts on the plaster bust are probably for attaching the "pointing machine" when Powers made a marble copy of the bust. Credit: North Carolina Museum of Art and Smithsonian American Art Museum - Smithsonian Institution.

More research led to the Hiram Powers Papers (1835-1883) in the Archives of American Art. Powers left a paper trail, including what appears to be an entire set of international correspondence with his customers. Among them: John C. Calhoun, the Prestons, H. Gourdin (the man Charleston put in charge of having the Calhoun statue made), and Wharton Jackson Green (the man who donated the bust to the state of North Carolina). The letters reveal that Calhoun, himself, decided on the scroll text of "Truth, Justice, and The Constitution" as a short description of his life and what he stood for. The Roman toga was also chosen by Calhoun, whose political ideas and work may have been influenced by the study of the fall of the Roman Empire.[108] The letters between H. Gourdin and Powers show Charleston's anxiety and frustration in getting the statue completed in a timely fashion. And finally, the letters between Wharton Green and Powers prove that the North Carolina piece is a copy of the original plaster bust. The bust is a separate work which Powers did not start until 1858, long after the Charleston statue was completed.

---

[108] PBS' History Detectives: Episode 4: 2006: Calhoun Books: http://www-tc.pbs.org/opb/historydetectives/static/media/transcripts/2011-05-11/404_calhoun.pdf

In 2014, historian Tom Elmore joined the research as we focused back on the statue's last known location of Columbia. Tom read through the entire Hiram Powers papers in the Archives of American Art and discovered a post-Civil War letter from Gourdin to Powers stating that the Calhoun statue, just like our "community," "was broken and destroyed & its parts are nowhere now to be found."

Did Gourdin, in Charleston, really have proof of the statue's destruction if no pieces could be found? Tom Elmore's 20 years of research on Sherman's march through South Carolina has not turned up a single reference to the Union Army destroying or coming across the statue. The statue was very well known and would have been a real prize for the Union Army. The research seems to show that the statue was never displayed in Columbia and that very few people knew where it was stored. Tom concluded it might have been moved to Columbia at the last minute and that the lack of men in Columbia might have meant the statue was left in the railroad depot.

The depot was accidentally destroyed by an explosion just days before Sherman's troops invaded the city. Tom believes the statue might have been blown apart with the depot. The few accounts around the burning of Columbia, however, do not make a connection between the statue and the depot, so we need to look at the evidence again. The previously shown 1909 article by the Charleston News and Courier states that the statue was boxed up and stored in the Columbia Courthouse. Other accounts may be more accurate. William Gilmore Simms, the noted 19th century novelist and historian documented the destruction of Columbia in 1865, specifically mentioning the destruction of the Calhoun statue. Modern historian Charles Royster, in his 1991 book "The Destructive War: William Tecumseh Sherman, Stonewall Jackson, and the Americans," stated that this statue melted as he described the burning of the Old State House.

That gives us three possible locations - the depot, courthouse, or the Old State House. Locating a statue, or pieces of it, at the heavily developed areas of the old railroad depot and the old courthouse is not going to be possible. This leaves the Old State House as the only possible place to search. Once again, are my projects miraculously crossing paths?

Could the statue have been hidden in the basement of the Old State House? And could it have survived the burning and collapse of the upper floor and roof? Lying on its back, the statue's box would have had a height of 1.5 to 2 feet. New State House architect John Niernsee gave details of the 1865 destruction of items on the State House grounds. He documented that the only thing remaining of the Old State House was the burned brick walls of the basement. Debris of the collapsing building would have filled the basement. Was the basement deep enough that the boxed statue would have been covered? Research has not provided any evidence that the basement ruins were ever excavated. Immediately following the burning of Columbia, it's doubtful that the residents would have had interest in these ruins. The Reconstruction era after the war was very difficult for the people, and the Old State House and images of John C. Calhoun would have been easy-to-forget symbols of a lost cause.

In my work to locate the Old State House and build a computer model of it, I determined the basement would have been 2-3 feet below ground, which leaves the possibility that the statue could have been covered by debris and gone unnoticed after the burning of Columbia. Since the statue had been secretly moved to Columbia, there is also the possibility it might have been further hidden by burying it deeper in a secured area of the basement of the Old State House. Maybe those few that knew of its location in 1865 just assumed it had been destroyed.

There is, however, an interesting Charleston newspaper article (Figure 127) from 1868 which indicates the possible recovery of a buried Calhoun statue. The article is about Charleston's City Hall. The only statue of Calhoun that appeared in City Hall before 1868 was Powers' Calhoun statue. This article indicates some people had reason to believe the statue survived the burning of Columbia by being buried. If this is our statue, did the railroad depot or courthouse have a basement? We don't know, but we know the Old State House had a basement.

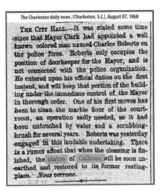

Figure 127: 1868 news about the possible
unearthing of the Calhoun statue.

Royster's report that the toga Calhoun statue melted is unlikely given the maximum burning temperature of a wood building is below the minimum melting point of marble.

So, was the statue's destruction assumed but never confirmed?

Was it buried but never recovered?

Below is the computer model of the Old State House, which was created to help determine the ground depth of the raised basement and theorize on possible hiding spots in the basement.

Figure 128: Old State House and Palmetto monument computer model.

In proving the location of the Old State House, one of the artifacts I found was a hand-cut/polished piece of marble. The first thing that came to mind was the marble Calhoun statue, but more research uncovered other possibilities. One would be the 40 marble Corinthian Caps (the decorative top for the large marble columns) that were destroyed by Sherman's Army. Those, however, would have been in a different area of the grounds. The other possibility has to do with Simms' 1865 mention of marble busts in the Old State House that were destroyed by the Union Army just before they set fire to the building. This possibility would lead to another revelation.

Was another Powers Calhoun piece in the Old State House?

Throughout the research, Tom and I were confused by some conflicting references to a Calhoun statue and a Calhoun bust. When bust was used, did they really mean statue? This began to clear up when we discovered that Powers and his copying mechanism produced at least one other bust like the North Carolina bust. Found in the South Carolina Archives is an 1852 order to pay Powers for a bust and that it be placed in the library of the Old State House. An 1861 Northern newspaper article mentions that the

South Carolina lawmakers moved this bust into the main House Chamber of the Old State House, where it was a "sort of idol" that they worshiped.[109]

We now needed to go back and rethink all the references to a Calhoun bust. It turns out that most of these were to a Calhoun bust that was broken by the Union Army. Some accounts say it was in the Old State House.

Another area of confusion came with John Morrill Bryan's wonderful book "Creating the South Carolina State House." Bryan writes that our toga Calhoun statue was moved into the House Chamber of the Old State House in 1861. His reference for this was art historian Anna Wells Rutledge's newspaper article on the Calhoun statue in 1942.[110] This article had eluded me since the beginning of my research, but I was now able to find it through an online newspaper archive.

Rutledge had discovered many of the same things I found about the early years of the statue, but she never pursued the statue's end, other than to mention that it was destroyed in Columbia, where it had been moved for safe-keeping. Unfortunately, she made no specific mention of the statue being transferred to the Old State House in 1861 as written in Bryan's book. I believe that Bryan also became confused with the multiple bust and statue references, and his 1861 date was really the date that the Powers bust was moved into the House Chamber of the Old State House. It would seem, once again, that the statue's location in Columbia was a well-kept secret.

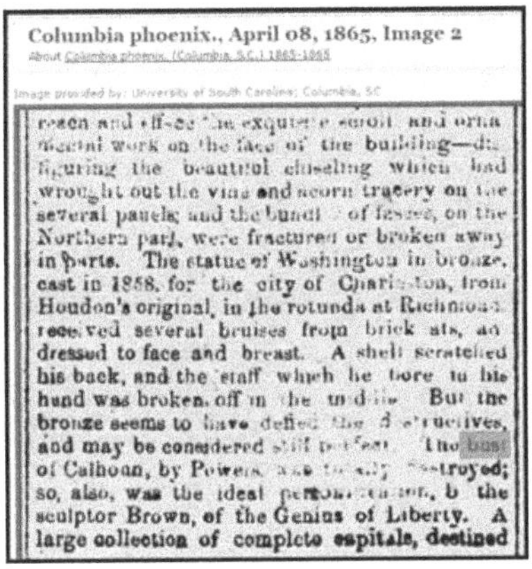
Columbia phoenix., April 08, 1865, Image 2

About Columbia phoenix. (Columbia, S.C.) 1865-1865

Image provided by: University of South Carolina; Columbia, SC

[illegible] and [illegible] the exquisite scroll and ornamental work on the face of the building—disfiguring the beautiful chiseling which had wrought out the vine and acorn tracery on the several panels; and the bunch of fasces, on the Northern part, were fractured or broken away in parts. The statue of Washington in bronze, cast in 1858, for the city of Charleston, from Houdon's original, in the rotunda at Richmond, received several bruises from brick bats, addressed to face and breast. A shell scratched his back, and the staff which he bore in his hand was broken off in the [illegible]. But the bronze seems to have defied the destructives, and may be considered still perfect. The bust of Calhoun, by Powers, was [illegible] destroyed; so, also, was the ideal [illegible], by the sculptor Brown, of the Genius of Liberty. A large collection of complete capitals, destined

Figure 129: Newspaper story stating the destruction of a Powers' bust of Calhoun.

There is little doubt, however, about the Powers bust in the Old State House. A Columbia Phoenix newspaper article from April of 1865 clearly shows it was destroyed by the Union Army.

---

[109] The Dollar Newspaper: Philadelphia: Wednesday Morning, January 16, 1861.

[110] Statue's Curious History by Anna Wells Rutledge: The News and Courier, Charleston, SC: March 1942.

The piece of hand carved/polished marble that I found at the site of the Old State House could be from this bust.

As for the Calhoun statue, it was well hidden and forgotten. And again, those that knew where it was located may have assumed it was destroyed in the burning of Columbia. But maybe a few years after the war, these people were the ones that started the 1868 rumor (Figure 127) about how the statue might hopefully soon be "unearthed."

That takes us back to the theory that the statue was hidden in a basement of a building that burned and collapsed. Of all the identified possible locations, only the Old State House site would be suitable for study. Only that site would be feasible for archaeology that could answer the question. In my opinion, non-invasive archaeology, like ground penetrating radar, could verify the exact location of the basement of the Old State House, in one day's work. You can't lose on that one. That would narrow the search area and make future archaeology work a lot cheaper. Just the study of the Old State House itself is a worthwhile project. Although the odds might be against it, finding a mostly intact Calhoun statue would be the Civil War and art world discovery of the century. It would be another Miracle to Yesterday.

More than 100 years after the last bit of hope was lost in finding Charleston's great Calhoun statue, the new search ends in the same place ... the ashes of Columbia. But this new search leaves us with the possibility that the statue may survive under these ashes. If nothing else, under the water, and sand, off the coast of Fire Island, New York, lies a marble scroll fragment with the words "Truth and Justice."

In October 2010, the 1858 stereoview photograph was taken to Charleston's City Hall, where Lindsay M. Partin (Docent, Council Chamber, City of Charleston)[111] recognized the shutters behind the statue as the shutters that currently cover the windows on the second floor of City Hall. She also pointed out that the walls in the photo were plaster and not wood like today's walls. City Hall, originally, had plaster walls, but they were severely damaged in the 1886 earthquake and replaced with wood paneling. Partin also pulled an inventory of past items held in City Hall and found a

---

[111] Lindsay M. Partin, Docent, Council Chamber City of Charleston (2011)

record and picture of a miniature version of the Calhoun statue. This record mentioned that the miniature was based on a life-size statue of Calhoun that was in City Hall before being moved to Columbia, where it was lost in the 1865 fire.

The miniature Calhoun statue eluded me for several years, but I finally found it in storage at Charleston's Gibbes Museum of Art. The museum's records, however, contained no information on the original life-size Calhoun statue.

Figure 130: The 17-inch tall "Parian ware" version of the Calhoun Statue. Credit Charleston City Hall.

From City Hall Files:
Hiram Powers - John C. Calhoun Parianware statue Parian ware, diameter of base: 15.5 cm, height: 42.8 cm (about 17 inches tall.) The Parian ware statue (left) is modeled after Hiram Powers' life-size statue of Calhoun. These replicas were imported and made available in places like G. & H. Cameron on Meeting Street in Charleston. Parian ware is a hard white unglazed porcelain that resembles Parian marble. Powers was one of the first sculptors to produce Parian ware figures. These little statues could have been mass produced but it appears that the Calhoun Parian was very rare.

Interesting side-note:
From the Hiram Powers Papers (Archives of American Art): In an 1871 response to Mrs. William Sherman about a requested art job, Hiram Powers states: "I am glad to learn that General Sherman is coming here and I assure you I shall have great pleasure in making a personal acquaintance with the man who made the wonderful march through the southern states. I follow him in the spirit with the most intense interest."

Chapter 18 – A Career Cut Short and the Calling

Not all miracles start off well. April 19, 2016, started off as a good day. I was in the 29th year of my engineering career, and on this day, I was exactly two years away from retirement from the Intel Corporation. Things looked good for making that date. Our Intel site in Columbia had opened a little more than 18 years earlier. It was not always a secure job location. The heart of Intel was on the west coast of the United States, and our site several times had been on the chopping block as executives considered the extra expenses involved with our distant location.

How did we stay alive all these years? It goes back to my first engineering job at the NCR (National Cash Register) Corporation. The Columbia NCR site opened in 1971 to build machines that could sort mail for the United States Postal Service. NCR was able to attract engineering talent from all over the Southeast, especially from Clemson University and the University of South Carolina. By 1980, a few of these exceptional engineers had gone beyond their original roles and were working on a computer that would run a spreadsheet application. A year after this achievement, IBM made a similar computer. But instead of being limited to a single application, IBM teamed up with a young Bill Gates and a new company named Microsoft. This gave IBM a computer operating system, DOS, which allowed for multiple software applications, and the IBM PC and the Personal Computer (PC) revolution began.

Our NCR site missed out on all that PC success, but it would turn its focus to a more powerful business computer. By the time I started at NCR in 1987, their Tower computer was very popular, and it would soon put NCR at the top of the world in the design and production of mid-range computer systems. The amazing thing is that this was all done in West Columbia, South Carolina. When I say all, I really mean it. From the initial engineering hardware designs and debug, to the development and support of the world's first multiprocessor UNIX Operating System. From circuit board layout to the state-of-the-art automated manufacturing of the circuit boards and the systems. On top of that, there was a local organization of sales, marketing, and support employees. At the facility's peak, we had 1,600 people.

By 1990, there were only a few locations in the world that could match what we did. But 1990 also marked a change in our product, as NCR moved to a more open-system architecture which would use microprocessors, the brain of a computer, from the Intel Corporation. Our systems would become the size of a refrigerator and would be the heart of the data warehousing industry.

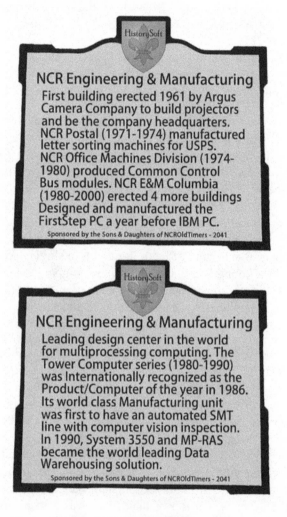

HistorySoft

NCR Engineering & Manufacturing
First building erected 1961 by Argus Camera Company to build projectors and be the company headquarters. NCR Postal (1971-1974) manufactured letter sorting machines for USPS. NCR Office Machines Division (1974-1980) produced Common Control Bus modules. NCR E&M Columbia (1980-2000) erected 4 more buildings Designed and manufactured the FirstStep PC a year before IBM PC.
Sponsored by the Sons & Daughters of NCROldTimers - 2041

HistorySoft

NCR Engineering & Manufacturing
Leading design center in the world for multiprocessing computing. The Tower Computer series (1980-1990) was Internationally recognized as the Product/Computer of the year in 1986. Its world class Manufacturing unit was first to have an automated SMT line with computer vision inspection. In 1990, System 3550 and MP-RAS became the world leading Data Warehousing solution.
Sponsored by the Sons & Daughters of NCROldTimers - 2041

Figure 131: David Brinkman's Proposed Historical
Marker for West Columbia's NCR Site.

Our success and profits, however, gradually declined over the 1990s as the competition stiffened. Even the Intel Corporation started making computers that could match ours but at a lower consumer cost. Unable to match the competition, NCR decided to go back to its traditional bread and butter, which was retail equipment and lots of customer support. In doing that, they stopped making computers and got out of the operating system business. This meant companies like HP and Dell were going to be the ones providing the computers. With NCR looking at shutting down the West Columbia operation, Intel noticed the unusual talent at the site. In places like Silicon Valley, employee attrition rates were high because workers had many places they could go. In West Columbia, there was only one place to do this kind of work. The result was almost no attrition among workers, who had built up many years of experience and many years of working together. Intel looked into picking up the NCR engineers and quickly learned about another reason we had such low attrition. It was the cost of living; people stayed here because it was so much cheaper in comparison to other cities with technical job opportunities. For Intel to get this unique workforce, they would have to open shop in the Columbia area.

NCR worked with Intel, and the local NCR employees, to make sure Intel was committed to creating and maintaining a site in Columbia. NCR would also allow another set of employees to acquire NCR patents to start a new company, KryoTech, which specialized in a new method of cooling a PC. In 1999, KryoTech would team with AMD, the archrival of Intel, to make the world's first 1GHz PC. The achievement was described as "the Holy Grail" of the computer industry and made worldwide news. Many other companies would be spawned or fueled by the local talent that NCR had brought together and nourished here in Columbia.

In 1998, Intel had officially opened the Columbia Design Center with 64 former NCR engineers. By 2002, NCR had shut down their site and Intel had picked up many more NCR workers, including me. By 2016, we had people with 25 to 40 years of experience working together. There was nowhere else in Intel that could come close to that kind of experience.

So that's how we survived. On April 19, 2016, I felt good about our chances to continue at Intel. The company had recently recognized our site as one of their two primary server chip validation sites in the world. We had just signed a five-year lease and were in the middle of a million-dollar upgrade of the site. And on this day, our CEO once again announced record-breaking quarterly results. I honestly never felt more secure in a job.

At 4 p.m. that day, those great financial reports were released with a shocking twist. About 12,000 jobs would be eliminated, over 12% of the company workforce. It didn't make any sense. Logic told me, however, that our site was too important to be affected, and I had already survived many layoffs in the past that were larger than this. Still, something felt very wrong about this one. I slammed my laptop shut and went home. I wanted to think about something else. I gathered Odess and Jeremy, and we went to a movie at our usual theater at the Dutch Square shopping center. After the movie, I took a quick look at the news, and the headline was now about Intel and the impending job losses. I told my family that I was concerned, but it was time to think about something else, and we headed to McDonald's.

The Miracle at McDonald's

While we were eating our fast food and talking about the movie, a roughly dressed man walked in the door. He had long hair and a backpack. As he passed us, a smile came on his face and he said, "God Bless you." Jeremy said, "Wow! Nice guy."

A few minutes later, the stranger started walking in our direction. I shamefully admit that my thought was, "Oh great. Here it comes. He's going to ask for money." He stopped right beside me. There was no smile this time. In fact, there was a dazed and confused look on his face. His words were: "Excuse me sir but, ... God just told me to tell you something. He told me to tell you not to worry about what will happen this week and that everything will be okay." He then walked out the door.

Odess immediately rose in a shiver. Jeremy's response was simply, "What the?" Never in my life, and I have spent much of my life around religious people, has someone said something like that to me. My obvious first thought was that I would be losing my job. Later on, I realized the similarities between this and the story my dad told me about when God spoke to him. I had to wonder just how bad things would get before they would get better.

When I arrived at work the next morning, I opened my email and at the top of the list was what I feared. The subject was Corporate Communication: "All Intel sites with less than 500 employees, no exceptions, will be shut down. Your site is one of those."

Many employees would be released in the next few weeks. Those that qualified could take retirement. Of the remaining, some might be relocated, and the rest would be released when the site closed. Many sites closed by the end of the year. Columbia, being a critical site, would take longer to transition the work. At the most, it would stay open until the end of 2017. That would leave me four months short of retirement. Since there was no backup for my position, I found myself in the group of people who could relocate to Austin, Texas. I considered that, but the significant cost-of-living difference and the extra hours of commute through traffic was concerning. The ability to quickly sell two properties in Columbia could also be a problem. Jeremy would be going to college soon, and we had only saved enough for a school like the University of South Carolina, not the University of Texas.

And of course, close to my heart were all the local history projects still underway. Even a couple of Intel co-workers told me that this history work, although it didn't pay me anything, was more important than anything I would ever do at Intel. One by one, all my friends and colleagues gave the same message. I shouldn't go to Austin. Do a bunch of signs like this add up to a big sign? How I wished a huge stunning sign, or miracle, would happen to make it all clear.

A Calling

In November of 2016, we completed pit #100 in Granby. Joey Holleman had left The State newspaper, but he recommended veteran reporter Lezlie Patterson.[112] After several interviews, which covered a lot more than just the Granby project, Lezlie told me that I should really consider writing a book about all of this. I didn't take it very seriously at the time. I had always thought that would be something good to do when I was too old to explore and do physical things like archaeology.

In the meantime, Odess and I had been taking turns going to two different churches in Columbia. Our main parish was St. Peter's, but the much smaller Good Shepherd had a simple charm to it. We liked getting the two widely different sermon styles between St. Peter's Fr. Linsky and Good Shepherd's Fr. Ladkau.

---

[112] Dig uncovers evidence of 1700s Granby, Columbia's original subdivision By Lezlie Patterson: The State Newspaper: http://historysoft.com/news/newspaper2016.htm

One Sunday, Father Ladkau's sermon went into what I had noticed was a common theme for him. He often stressed that we need to do more than just go to church. He gave ideas on things we could do, and on this day he pointed out the unique experiences we all have and how sharing those could be an inspiration to others. It triggered me to think about all the miracles that kept popping up in my history projects. It was just days earlier that Lezlie (The State newspaper reporter) had suggested that I write a book. At that moment, the two things came together, and the title of the book jumped out. "Miracles to Yesterday."

The idea for an inspirational book that would also be a publication of my historical work was well-planted in my head. It would still take months before it really sprouted into something coherent. How could it all be put together into something that would be easy to follow?

As the year 2017 began, I made a New Year's resolution to learn a new skill. With my job days numbered at Intel, I wanted to add a cutting-edge technology skill to my resume. Jeremy had recently purchased a top-of-the-line Virtual Reality (VR) headset that knocked my socks off. It was evident from the direction of Intel and industry analysts that VR sales would explode. Some estimated growth from a $5 billion industry in 2016 to over $150 billion in 2020. Working a few hours every night, I was able to learn enough to start building several VR applications with content based on my history discoveries. By March, I had created a Fort Congaree II VR educational game based on the project's research and archaeological finds. I also started a much more complicated VR game that was about "Civil War II" and time travel back to Columbia just before it was burned in 1865.

While working on the Fort Congaree II VR project, one Saturday morning in February of 2017, I got a text message from archaeologist Natalie Adams Pope. Natalie had assisted us a number of times in identifying artifacts found in the Granby dig. Natalie had an interest in our finds, since leading archaeological work in 2000 on the Saxe-Gotha site just south of Granby and Fort Congaree II. Natalie, however, was not texting me about these projects. She wanted to know where I was. I had forgotten that the Annual Conference on South Carolina Archaeology was happening that day. Natalie asked me to come now because an award was going to be presented to me.

Since the major upheaval of my career in 2016, my hope was that a significant sign would be given to me to set my course. It was about to happen. To my shock, the professional archaeologists of South Carolina and the Archaeological Society of South Carolina presented me with the Distinguished South Carolina Archaeologist of the Year award. I didn't even know this was possible with me not being a professional archaeologist and not even having a degree in the related fields. It was an incredible honor, and it left no question in my mind. My place was in South Carolina, not Texas. My career with Intel would soon end. The only thing I had to worry about now was how I would support my family. It would be a leap of faith.

As my time ticked down at Intel, things started pointing to an urgency with writing the book. In church one day, I found myself all alone in the right front pews. The Good Shepherd Church was small, and the Sunday service only had an average of 25 people. There seemed to be fewer people this day. Father Ladkau was again talking about people sharing their inspirational experiences. It was a bit different today. He explicitly described this sharing as a calling. As he finished the sermon, he looked over to the corner, where only I was sitting. With direct eye contact, he said: "I hope you find your calling, and I hope you follow it." Father Ladkau knew nothing about my book idea. He probably knew nothing about me, as I had never had a conversation with him. I took it as a sign I needed to get to work.

After church that day, I went home energized and motivated. I first needed to do an outline of the book. I got stuck trying to structure the miracles together with all the history pieces. I decided to take a break with a nap. Just as I was falling asleep, a loud crash occurred outside of our bedroom. I looked all over but could not find any source for the noise. I was no longer tired after that excitement, so I went back to the book outline. I guess the distraction was good because I quickly realized that some of the pieces, I had thought were not related, had strong similarities in the technical ways they were discovered. Everything was related in at least one way but mostly in multiple ways. It now seemed obvious that the outline should go in chronological order of the discoveries and not of the historical events. That seemed like the best way it would fit and the best flow for the reader.

A few days later I discovered the source of that loud crash. A clock with a picture of Jesus on it had fallen off the wall and behind a sofa just outside our bedroom. It had been hanging there for 12 years. I had to wonder if this was more than just something to wake me up. Maybe it was also a sign that time was running out and the book needed to be written now. It was July 2, 2017. I decided to set a goal of the end of the year, also the closure date of the Intel site, to have a rough draft written.

My goal seemed aggressive as I had always thought a project simply to document my historical finds would take twice as long. I was now adding the miracles to this. But things started falling into place quickly. Many mornings I woke up with a significant thought, or an item I had forgotten, that should be in the book. It seemed too good to be true how smoothly things were flowing, as I never hit a moment of "writer's block." Everything I needed was already there or would soon miraculously come to me.

I completed the book's draft, ahead of schedule, during the weekend before Thanksgiving. About halfway into writing the book, I had asked Joey Holleman (who had written seven front-page stories on my projects in The State Newspaper) to read what I had and consider co-authoring it with me. Joey felt it was not a co-authoring project, but he would be glad to copyedit it. So, after less than five months of work on the book, I delivered it to Joey and sat back for a moment to worry about my job situation.

It was then that Father Ladkau, who was already retired, announced that he could not continue working because of health issues. Another sign of spiritual decline in America is the lack of Catholic Priests. Because of this, the Catholic Diocese of Charleston decided to shut down Good Shepherd Church. On November 24, 2017, the little church, where I had just received my calling to write this book, had its final service.

The Intel Columbia Design Center, right on schedule, shut down at the end of the year just a few days before what would have been its 20th anniversary. Local management had warned me that, if I were not in Austin, TX at the start of 2018, I would be terminated. I decided to use a four-week sabbatical which I had been holding on to. So, during January of 2018, I spent that time making the final edits and formatting of Miracles to Yesterday.

At the completion of my sabbatical, I gave a two-week notice just three months before reaching my Intel retirement. My immediate manager at Intel was disappointed and genuinely sad at the fact that I would fall short of retirement. He would propose a three-month extension which would get me to retirement and give Intel more time to train a replacement. The temptation of the financial benefits of retirement was too much for me, even though so many signs had been given to me to walk away from the job immediately. My manager's manager, however, would insist on me providing an address where I lived in Austin. I was confused at first. I'm not living in Austin. Why would I have an address there? I would later realize that he was trying to cover himself. All his employees should have moved to Austin by now. This would look bad on him. Once again, I use the "shame" word. I shamefully requested, from an online service, a virtual Austin mailing address to meet the improper address request. By the end of the week, however, the service had surpassed their guaranteed two-day approval process. With only one day left for my manager to request the extension, I discovered the service had tagged my request as "rejected" but no explanation was given. I left several voicemails to customer service but never a reply. Frustrated that Intel had pushed me to do this, and disappointed in myself for attempting it, I told my manager that if my job extension was dependent on such a meaningless technicality, then I feel I should not continue with Intel. In about an hour, the reply was simply: "We accept your resignation." My reply was: "Thank You". A few hours later, that "virtual address" company informed me that there was a mistake and that my application had just been approved. I informed them that they were too late and asked for a refund. I realized another miracle (the "rejection" glitch) had occurred to push me back on the path.

My goal of retiring early was now gone. Fortunately, connections with former local NCR employees produced another job opportunity. After 30 years, it's a reset, but I'm excited about the journey to come.

When you receive and accept a calling, you don't know where it's going to take you. The only thing you know is that the road may be rougher, and it will be lined with uncertainty. But, with faith, you look for the signs, and you stay the course that is laid out before you.

Chapter 19 – Miracles or not?

Miracles or not? Those who believe in God will have a much easier time seeing the miracles. Those who don't believe might instead see just a bunch of unusual cases of luck and coincidences. There is also the observation and experience level of a person. Like the 1796 bridge abutment in my backyard - an archaeologist recognized it from 50 feet away, while the average person would see it as just a pile of rocks. As you have read, my belief in God goes back as far as I can remember. The miracles go back almost as far. Some may say I'm seeing what I want to see, but I have always been wary of unusual happenings. Most are nothing and forgotten. Some hang around and are not understood for years. I don't take any of these lightly.

I had a great mentor, my father, who had a strong faith but was always rational, practical, skeptical, and never one to exaggerate. At about the age of 11, I was so excited to show him a list of surprising similarities between Presidents Abraham Lincoln and John Kennedy. Some were silly meaningless things, but others would really catch your attention, like Lincoln's secretary (who was named Kennedy) warning Lincoln not to go to the theater the night he was assassinated and Kennedy's secretary (who was named Lincoln) warning Kennedy not to go to Dallas, where he would be assassinated. My father quickly discounted these so-called facts and explained that amazing coincidences like this could be found in the lives of any two people studied as thoroughly as Kennedy and Lincoln.

A few years later, I would become interested in Bible prophecy. Although my father was happy to see me reading the Bible, he quickly discounted the modern-day interpretations of Armageddon, pointing out that the New Testament's Book of Revelation could be interpreted into just about anything.

I always remember the example my father set, but in the case of my historical discoveries, I believe much weight must be placed on the discoveries themselves. Every one of them had a fantastic miracle or happening that made them possible. If just one of these had not happened, all the remaining possible finds would have never happened. In the middle of it all, a pivotal point in my accepting these occurrences as miracles was my near-death experience, which I absolutely know was a full-blown miracle.

As an engineer, I can apply numbers to a few of the so-called miracles. Regarding the first lot we purchased on the Broad River, the real estate agent described my getting the lot as the strangest sale of her career. At about eight sales a year over 15 years, that would have been a one in 120 chance this would happen to me. The discovery the next day of that old bridge abutment on the property would also be a long shot. A month later Joey Holleman, in a story in The State newspaper, would show that only 125 home sites existed on the three rivers of Columbia. My research over the years would identify 12 possible historic sites on these riverbanks. But just one would fall on a home site, making the secondary odds of my first discovery at 1/120 multiplied by 1/125, or a one in 15,000 chance.

In Granby, research indicates the density of home sites would have made the odds of us finding one of the sites a one in five chance. The chances of also finding the home site of Indian trader Thomas Brown would be a one in 5,445 chance, thus making the combined find a chance of one in 27,255. As far as the exact mitochondrial DNA match to King Richard III, the odds would prove to be one in 757,333. And what were the odds that every history project in this book, from King Richard III to the D-Day invasions of WWII, would all be connected in multiple ways? I can't calculate that one.

After all the amazing events that led to these finds, the happenings and miracles continued and then shifted to multiple miracles that led me to document my experience.

If you think that a miracle has never happened to you, you might want to think again. Scientists have determined the following[113]:

1. On the average, the chance that your parents would meet was only one in 20,000. The chance this meeting would turn into a relationship and produce you was only one in 2000. That brings us to a combined probability of one in 40 million.

2. The unique genetics created by one egg and one sperm would come from a staggering set of possible combinations of eggs (100,000 eggs over your mother's productive years) and sperm (12 trillion sperms over your father's

[113] Are You a Miracle? On the Probability of Your Being Born by By Dr. Ali Binazir: https://www.huffingtonpost.com/dr-ali-binazir/probability-being-born_b_877853.html

productive years). The probability now goes to one chance in 400 quadrillion.

3. There is still more genetics to consider. All those eggs and sperm were crafted by the 150,000 generations of your human ancestors and their fantastic ability to survive and reproduce. The probability of your existence now becomes one chance in 10 to the power of 2,640,000. Printing this number (with all the zeros) would require another 1,174 pages in this book.

Our brains can't process numbers like this. How about statistically comparing this number with the odds of winning the lottery? We can all understand this. Winning the Powerball Lottery is one chance in 292,201,338. I asked my friend, Edsel A. Pena (a Professor in the Department of Statistics at the University of South Carolina) to put the odds of life into perspective with the odds of winning the lottery. Dr. Pena's analysis would show that you would have to win the Powerball Lottery 317,163 consecutive times (which would take 6,100 years) to match the probability that each of us faces at coming into existence. Our lives are miracles. It's probably the most apparent scientific fact in the Universe, and yet most of us don't see it.

Unfortunately, the conflict people feel between science and religion is taking a toll on all of us. For example, religious homeschooling parents who hide the teachings of evolution from their children are fueling a disaster. Once these kids get into the real world, they will be immediately exposed to the overwhelming evidence and acceptance of evolution. They will view their parents and their parents' religious beliefs as blinded ignorance. They will abandon religion. We can already see this in the declining numbers in churches.

While writing this book, a new entry to American pop culture popped-up. In the television series "The Orville," about an exploratory spaceship of the 25th century, many of the problems of the 21st century have been solved by science. No more poverty. No more disease. Major injuries repaired in seconds. Of hundreds of intelligent alien civilizations in the universe, there is one that stands out as the really bad guys, the reptilian Krill. This is also the only intelligent species that still practice religion. Is it comedy, or is this a statement on the direction of the human species?

On the other side of the religion/science spectrum, you have the so-called scientists who arrogantly proclaim that God does not exist, even though there is not a single piece of evidence to support that. In the case of proving God does exist, these scientists need to also be reminded that absence of evidence is not evidence of absence.

But religion and science can live together. After all, isn't science just really an understanding of the universe and what created it? A search for God?

One of the religious organizations leading the way is the Catholic Church and how it has adapted to science. Pope John Paul II said, "There can never be a true divergence between faith and reason, since the same God who reveals the mysteries and bestows the gift of faith has also placed in the human spirit the light of reason."

The Catholic Church through the centuries has had its share of embarrassing encounters with science. In the 20th century, however, the Church employed a body of scientists for consulting purposes. In 1950, these scientists informed the Church that the evidence supporting the theory of evolution was overwhelming. At that time, the Church instructed Catholics to be open to the idea of evolution. In 1996, after DNA discoveries left no doubt that humans and primates share a common ancestor, Pope John Paul II made it official. The Church's position was refined to state that God created all life through evolution. Adam and Eve were not the first humans, but they were the first humans to have a soul.

On the science side, we now have a few people that are once again talking about how God created and may control the universe. They have raised the possibility that new theorized dimensions could be the domain of the creator. Maybe these new dimensions could show a pattern of intelligence. But the bottom line today is that science is still young and very simple. It is all about taking measurements. Anything immeasurable cannot be proven or disproven.

But what about measurements that could be taken today? Is a miracle measurable? To the many who have experienced one, there is no question that miracles exist. But is the human body, the most complex creation we know of in the universe, a device for scientific measurement? With the correct skill set, measurement devices, and timing, is it possible to measure a miracle? Many believe it has already been done, in a dramatic way.

Neurologist Dr. Ramon M. Sanchez was a skeptic when he was asked to be involved in a project to scientifically prove or disprove the claims of so-called visionaries. These were people who claimed to be seeing frequent apparitions of Jesus or mother Mary. The first case involved Nancy Fowler, "the Visionary of Conyers." Starting in 1990, Fowler had been having monthly apparitions of Jesus and mother Mary, and they continued for eight years. By 1993, people by the tens of thousands were making pilgrimages to Conyers, Georgia to see miracles and hear the messages given to Fowler.

Bolivian Professor of Neuropsychology Ricardo Castanon had approached Dr. Sanchez. In 1992, Castanon (a hardened atheist) heard about Fowler and her visions. He visited Fowler in Atlanta and concluded that she was not crazy and not lying about the visions. He invited her to South America where he assembled a team of seven scientists (all atheists) to study her brain. In March of 1993, his team captured data while Fowler was experiencing apparitions. They were all baffled at the results which showed Fowler instantly going into deep sleep when the apparitions appeared. Dr. Castanon decided it would be best to complete more extensive tests in the United States using a new team of scientists. That's when he contacted Dr. Sanchez.

Many discounted Fowler because most of her received warning messages were very vague. One recurring message about the communist threats of Russia, China, and Korea, did not make sense in the early 1990s. They described Russia and China as being on American soil. During the time of these messages, however, the recent breakup of the Soviet Union left Russia as a friend to the United States, and Korea would have seemed harmless during this period. The fear of communism was at a low. And why did Fowler's messages state "Korea" when there was such a clear division between a North Korea and a South Korea? Certainly, South Korea would not be a threat. Many years before the recognition of climate change, Fowler's warnings in 1993 of increased natural disasters in the United States and places being colder and hotter than ever also seemed vague or did not make sense.

Look at things today. Climate change is now a scientific fact. You could say that Russia is already on American soil, with the potential influence it had in the 2016 presidential election. In China, the underground Catholic Church has been targeted, and those caught taking part in it are imprisoned.

Chinese people are being forced to replace their pictures of Jesus with images of President Xi Jinping because "Jesus cannot help you. Only the Communist party can help you."[114] And fed by China and Russia, North Korea has nuclear weapons on rockets. Imagine what would happen if Kim Jong-un carried out his threat and nuked a major American city like Los Angeles, California. Millions of lives would be lost, and the American economy would crash. Fowler's prediction of America being brought to her knees would be fulfilled in an instant. With Americans now so desensitized to violence, her military response, as quoted by our leaders and the President, could be to "wipe out the people of North Korea." That would be 25 million people. What about Fowler's use of "Korea" as opposed to "North Korea?" As I was finishing this book, news headlines were about diplomatic breakthroughs and a "Korean unification".

The Catholic Church does not rush into things when it comes to accepting miracles and apparitions. It can take many years. In the case of Fowler's visions and messages, many Catholics are disappointed that the case has not received an official investigation by the Church. Instead, Catholics were initially advised to avoid pilgrimages to the site. A future Bishop would back off of that statement and simply ask people to "Leave them alone, for if this plan and work of theirs is a man-made thing, it will disappear; but if it comes from God, you cannot possibly defeat them."[115]

The warnings given to Fowler had much to do with people in the United States, particularly the young, who are turning their backs on religion.

"There is too little faith here... I am sad."[116]

The visions and messages at Conyers are similar to Our Lady of Fatima, where in 1917, visions and warning messages were given about Russia just six months before the Bolshevik Revolution, which marked the beginning of communism in that country. In this case, the warnings proved valid, and the Church officially declared Fatima a miracle 13 years later in 1930. Fortunately, like Fatima, the messages given through Fowler were warnings

---

[114] China Tells Christians to Replace Images of Jesus with Communist President https://www.christianitytoday.com/news/2017/november/china-christians-jesus-communist-president-xi-jinping-yugan.html
[115] James Lyke, Archbishpo of Atlanta, 1991.
[116] In His Living Presence 333 by Ramon M. Sanchez: pg.127.

that should be heeded through specific changes. In other words, bad things don't have to happen. The choice is ours.

For the scientific tests in 1993, Fowler's case was ideal because the visions/apparitions always occurred on the 13th day of the month. This would allow a team of scientists to set up and complete the testing in one day.

In the initial 1993 tests by Dr. Sanchez, he first eliminated the theory that Fowler was experiencing hallucinations. Dr. Sanchez's next step was to work with a team of technicians and doctors to perform brain activity tests on the visionary. Among the group were several atheists and a Jewish doctor. Extended neurological and baseline tests were performed, and the results were synchronized to video footage of Fowler.

After hours of testing with no visions appearing and no unusual readings recorded, Fowler was sarcastically asked to pray by one of the atheists. Suddenly, the visionary became excited, and the people involved in the testing had a profound feeling of peace come over them. Fowler stated that Jesus was in the room and she could see him. After one minute, the vision went away. Later on, the experience repeated with everyone feeling the same effect. It happened a third time. At the instant of all these visions, Fowler's brain waves showed she had moved directly into a deep sleep state even though she was fully awake and talking. Deep sleep is something that naturally occurs after a move through two previous states of drowsy and early light sleep. Moving directly to deep sleep was something the investigators had never seen before without the use of special drugs. Furthermore, being fully awake with eyes open and carrying on a conversation is not something that naturally occurs when in a deep sleep.

The jump from normal to deep sleep was recorded by an electroencephalogram (EEG) and cameras to have occurred within milliseconds of when the visionary said "Jesus" as the apparition occurred. There were also two other events when the visionary received a message. In all five occurrences, the EEG recorded the same unique pattern of brain activity.

Dr. Sanchez stated that in his career of doing this type of testing, he had never witnessed anything like this nor could he find where other neurologists had documented something similar. Even people trained and experienced in advanced forms of meditation cannot achieve a deep sleep transition like this.[117]

Another device was used to measure muscle tension in the body, which can reveal stress in the patient. At the instant the apparition appeared, Fowler's muscle tension dropped to zero - a completely unnatural result, as it takes many minutes for muscles to relax. In fact, the Jewish doctor stated that the only time she had ever seen a zero reading was in the case of death. Dr. Sanchez documented the apparition test results, saying Fowler was alert, active, and in a deep sleep, all at the same instant in time.

Dr. Sanchez would repeat the tests in his own laboratory on Fowler and a member of a religious order who claimed to be having similar visions. Both Fowler and the other person had similar visions in parallel with the same unique brain activity. Further instrument tests by Umberto Velasquez, a radiation scientist from the Florida State Department of Health, showed low ionized radiation in the room when the apparition of Jesus appeared (but not Mary).

The visions were not limited to just Fowler and the young man. Dr. Sanchez would later interview the Jewish doctor who gave her stunning experience:[118]

> "Yes. I saw a tremendous bright white light... followed by a chorus of angels, all in a bright light. Then, I saw the most beautiful and magnificent Lady. I presume... the Virgin Mary. She was holding and caressing her baby. Then, the light got even brighter and a man holding a staff appeared next to Mary with her baby. I heard Nancy say this was St. Joseph. Then, many more people appeared all in light and fast almost like -flash cards- or fast flashing pictures - similar to what Nancy was saying.- Then, the light really turned super-bright and I saw... the shape of a man appear who Nancy called Jesus - in the form of a bright white, white dazzling, brilliant light ... in three dimensions. "

---

[117] Science Confirms Faith: Interview of Ramon M. Sanchez, M.D. by Mary Our Mother Foundation (segment 4): Zen Masters are only capable of a transition to Alpha and the best can achieve Theta. They have never been observed to achieve Delta (deep sleep).
[118] [118] In His Living Presence 333 by Ramon M. Sanchez: pg.127.

The team of testers also reported seeing flashes of light during these periods, and Velasquez used photo-spectroscopy to detect this light. Physicist Dr. Philip Callahan, a former research scientist and professor with the University of Florida, measured atmospheric Schumman waves that passed through the body of Fowler. During the apparitions, the normal 14Hz frequency of the waves dropped to 4Hz. A range of 4Hz to 7Hz is consistent with a person who is sleeping, so this test went along with the results of the Dr. Sanchez's EEG test. The results of the Conyers tests are well documented by Australian attorney Ron Tesoriero, who was present during the testing, in his book and video documentary both entitled "Why do you test Me?" Dr. Sanchez documented the results in his book "In His Living Presence 333: Journey Science to Faith."

The test results provided a wide range of scientific measurements that defy medical and scientific explanation. The fact these measurements coincided with the apparitions shows the two are related.

After the tests were done, the scientists would also reveal their first impression of Nancy Fowler. As it turned out, Fowler had received and documented the following messages just months before she was approached about taking part in the scientific measurements. She informed the scientific team of this just before the testing began:

> "Nancy, scientists are coming. You will outwit all of them because I will do this. Watch what I will do. The result of the scientific team will be astonishing."

> "I will give a message for the United States: Who are men who think they know My ways? Who are you to question Me? I have set Conyers apart. I tell you scientists, doctors, theologians will be confused because they cannot figure Me out. My way is not man's way."[119]

There was a specific message for the scientists:

> "You are here not because you wanted it. I called you."

For almost 25 years now, the scientific community has not challenged the test results. The medical doctors and scientists that took part in the testing

---

[119] Why do you test me? By Ron Tesoriero: Chapter 11.

have proven to be respectable people of sound integrity.[120] The experiment has passed the test of time. Unfortunately, time-predictable miracles and apparitions (always occurring on the 13th day of the month in this case) are extremely rare, so the opportunities to capture them are few and far between.

While investigating the Fowler visions and testing, it became clear that I needed to go to Conyers and experience this place. Odess and I would spend several days there. My first impression was the size of the site. Simply called "The Farm" it covers over 100 acres and includes dozens of statues and grottos of Jesus, mother Mary, and the Saints. It is operated entirely by volunteers and a non-profit organization (Our Loving Mother's Children). Obviously, the simple on-site donation boxes could not possibly cover the expenses of a place like this. After we talked with the man who oversees the daily operation, I began to see the magnitude of belief in the people who have kept this alive.

Nancy Fowler was a simple woman and had no business experience. During her visions, as the numbers of pilgrims grew from the dozens to the thousands, Nancy needed help and believers stepped up and purchased adjacent land properties and formed the non-profit that would take care of things Nancy could not handle. When her visions ended in 1998, Fowler decided, under the advice of her Bishop (Eastern Rite), to separate herself from the non-profit which was now transitioning the site to a place of inspiration. You will not find the name of Nancy Fowler anywhere on The Farm. It seems this was her choice. As we interviewed other people, we learned that, for the most part, Nancy was not appreciated by the people of Conyers. She left her farmhouse (which included the Apparition room) to the non-profit company and moved to Texas. After a battle with cancer, Nancy died there in 2012 at the age of 63.

---

[120] The group was led by Ricardo Castanon, a professor of neuropsychophysiology. The other members of the team were Neurologists Ramon Sanchez and Norma Augosto Maur; Electroencephalogram technicians Scott Prandy and Ted Blume; New York Psychiatrist George Hogben; Radiation specialist Umberto Velasquez; Biophysicist Philip Callahan; Cameraman William Stellar; Lawyer Ron Tesoriero.

During our time at The Farm, I engaged in my hobby of taking 3D photographs of the many religious monuments.[121] I did not experience any unusual feeling of peace or any form of apparitions, even when standing on the exact spot where Nancy Fowler had her visions. What I was searching for was not in the place itself. It was in the people that came here and worked here. While in the Apparition room, Odess and I prayed the Rosary with a Spanish couple. They recited the Rosary in Spanish while we did it in English. The passion of this couple was so evident that I had to ask them about their experience here. They knew very little about Nancy Fowler and nothing about the scientific work that had been performed here. Instead, they were drawn to the site by others who had extraordinary experiences here. They said they could feel the Holy Spirit here and that they were filled with it.

Our final day at Conyers was spent at the nearby Roman Catholic Monastery of the Holy Spirit. I was not expecting any positive information here about Nancy Fowler. After all, the Church initially discouraged Catholics and the Monks from visiting The Farm. Once again, however, we were guided to a special person. Odess posed the question to the first Monk we came across; What do you think of Nancy Fowler and her apparitions? The Monk knew a lot about Fowler and said he believed her and he thought the apparitions were real. A feeling of peace came over Odess and me as this sank in. The old Monk said it would be just like God to choose a simple person like Fowler for this purpose. The Monk then expressed great sorrow for the terrible way Conyers had treated Fowler and how they drove her away.

Nancy Fowler suffered much during her last few years while battling cancer. She "offered all her sufferings for the conversion of sinners." Just a few days before she died, in 2012, her Spiritual Director was present when Nancy saw mother Mary one more time. He said the experience filled her with serenity. She was then given the last sacraments. Her final words were a prayer: "Lord, I want what you want. Your will and not mine be done always."[122]

---

[121] 3D pictures around The Farm at Conyers: http://www.miraclestoyesterday.com/farm3D/
[122] Luisa Piccarreta: Little Daughter of the Divine Will: http://luisapiccarreta.co/wp-content/uploads/2013/08/pNewsletter-No.-128.pdf

The effect of Conyers now lives beyond her visionary. The scientific results at Conyers will also live on. And what about those atheist scientists that took part in the testing? They became believers.

The Australian lawyer, Ron Tesoriero, who documented the test results at Conyers has gone on to lead more "Science Tests Faith" projects.[123] One of them may be even more astounding than Conyers. During the early tests of Fowler in Bolivia, another visionary woman (Catalina Rivas) was tested and shown to exhibit the same EEG deep sleep pattern while having a vision. Rivas would travel to Conyers to see Fowler where she claimed to experience her first Stigmata (an unexplained condition where open wounds, like those from a crucifixion, appear on a person). The Stigmata would reoccur with Rivas (on a date that Rivas predicted) and was captured on video by Tesoriero and a team of investigators. Many people believed that Rivas was self-inflicting the wounds, but this was not apparent to the scientists and medical professionals that were present. One thing no one could explain was the fact that the injuries were completely healed in less than 24 hours. The Rivas case, however, has something even more astounding. Messages from God are received, and Rivas writes them as they come. Rivas, who did not even complete high school, routinely changes her writing between Spanish and languages she does not know (Latin, Polish, Italian, and Greek.) Theologians say the content of her writing is consistent with Christianity but beyond what a person of her background could produce. When being filmed, she wrote for an hour without a pause and without ever lifting the pen off the paper.

The writings of Rivas are being studied all over the world. Unlike the case of Nancy Fowler and Conyers, the Catholic Church has recognized her case as authentic when her bishop, René Fernández Apaza, give his imprimatur to her "messages."

---

[123] Science Tests Faith: DVD: Ron Tesoriero, Michael Willesee

328

Figure 132: The Apparition Room in Conyers, now and in 1993. The corner of the room where Nancy Fowler had her visions from 1991 to 1998 has changed little since the scientific testing on her in 1993. The upper right corner inset is Nancy having a vision while scientific measurements are recorded. During the monthly apparitions of Nancy Fowler, thousands of people gathered on her farm in Conyers, GA. At the same time as the apparitions of Nancy, many people witnessed signs in the cloud formations[124], the scent of roses, Rosaries turning gold in color, and the "miracle of the sun"[125] which was captured on video.[126] Also witnessed by many and caught on video was rose petals falling from the sky in the dead of winter.[127] During the apparitions, testimonies of healings, conversions, and blessings were documented. In all, these documents filled seven file boxes and were delivered to the Archdiocese of Atlanta.[128]

So maybe miracles can be measured, but the few impressive recorded cases do not represent an overwhelming set of evidence. We will just have to wait, as Carl Sagan stated, for the evidence to build.

Maybe the creator instilled in us a desire to search for the truth; a need to search for him. There are more ways than science to do this. In the

[124] Conyers photos: (l) by Ferdinando in 1990, (r) Why do you test Me? by Ron Tesoriero on May 13, 1992.

[125] https://en.wikipedia.org/wiki/Miracle_of_the_Sun

[126] Stunning video of the sun spinning: FOX Television: Miracles and Visions: Fact or Fiction: https://www.youtube.com/watch?v=4K6Nw63hUIU

[127] Paranormal TV: The Georgian Visionary & Her Contact with the Virgin Mary: https://www.youtube.com/watch?v=-w60oroc_40

[128] Welcome To "THE FARM": Place of Pilgrimage: http://conyers.org

meantime, what do we have to lose in believing in both science and religion? Is believing in God and miracles bad in some way? Scaring our children away from science or religion would be detrimental. No one can argue against the power of positive thinking, but the most powerful form requires belief in a supernatural power science cannot provide. A religious faith frees us from fear and can lead us on incredible journeys into the unknown. Faith can give us an unbreakable direction in life and provide hope in the darkest of times.

Powerful examples of faith are everywhere. One etched into my mind forever involved a very active family in my parents' church. After school one day back in the 1980s, the family's three teenage children were making a half-mile drive home from school. The car, driven by the middle son, approached a double railroad crossing. A train had stopped on one of the tracks, and it obscured the driver's view. Maybe because the windows were up, and/or the radio was on, the driver did not hear a second approaching train. He decided to cross the tracks and was hit by the oncoming train. The driver walked away without a scratch. His brother was instantly killed. His younger sister would fight through multiple surgeries for a week before dying.

Days later at the funeral, the parents and surviving son presented a celebration of the lives of their lost family members. The mother sang with a perfect pitch a stunning and beautiful set of songs during the service. The family remained active in church, and they focused on the remaining son to help him heal and grow. The most powerful side to all of this, however, is the example that was set to the other families in this church. An example which can never be forgotten.

Now, let's think about a life without a religious belief or the hope that goes along with it. A few years back, I was talking to a co-worker outside my cubicle about one of my history miracles. Another co-worker passing by stopped for a minute and stated that he did not believe in miracles and proudly proclaimed that he was an atheist. A few years later, he lost his job. He then lost his house and his marriage. With our job-site closing and seemingly no hope of finding a good job, he committed suicide.

Science may seem to be an exciting and noble cause in the search for truth, but what can it do for you when life floors you? What harm can it do to believe beyond science? What harm could it do accepting a set of moral values that have developed from thousands of years of passed-down wisdom?

I wrote this book with the intention of it being inspirational as well as a publication of historical discoveries. Going back to the beginning of the book and those great physicists of the past, I wanted to challenge people on the extreme sides of both science and religion to return to the middle ground of nature. The word science first came into use during the 18th century. During this time, there was little conflict between faith and reason, as it was all a part of nature. The word science came from the Latin word scientia, which means knowledge. By the end of the 19th century, the meaning of science became more associated with the discipline and procedure called the scientific method.[129] In our time, our obsession with the exponential growth of knowledge and technology has left faith behind.

We all need to be open-minded and try to believe.

Matthew 13:58: And He did not do many miracles there because of their unbelief.[130]

---

[129] Superstition and Science, 1450-1750: Mystics, sceptics, truth-seekers and charlatans by Derek Wilson
[130] The New American Standard Bible

Chapter 20 – A Final Tribute and Miracle

After my father's initial cancer diagnosis, he told us that it may be God's will that his life ends now, and that we all needed to accept this. In his last week, his doctor performed a blood transfusion in an attempt to give him enough energy to travel to Myrtle Beach to receive an honorary doctorate in public service from Coastal Carolina University. The transfusion backfired and likely triggered the spread of cancer through his body. At the last minute, my dad asked me to take his place at the graduation ceremony and accept the award for him. The speech he gave me was too simple and only two sentences. My dad did not like to impose on people. Given that I had never spoken in front of a large group of people (it would be thousands in this case), he merely gave me what he thought I could handle with limited stress.

During the two-hour drive to Myrtle Beach, I expanded the speech in my head. Many of my dad's colleagues and friends were greatly distressed that he was not there. My dad was as dependable as a person could be, and I'm sure they realized that for him to miss something like this meant he was near death. I guess I also began to realize this, and the speech became even more difficult. Somehow, I got through it, and we traveled home to take some of the last pictures of my dad holding his doctorate degree. A few months later, the president of Coastal Carolina University sent me a video of the graduation. It would be 19 years later before I had the courage to watch it and cry.

During his last few weeks, my father's cancer treatment was failing, but he made it clear he had selected his medical team. He would not deviate from that. After all, my father had been a diehard Atlanta Braves baseball fan for almost 30 years before they won their only World Series championship in 1995. The Braves were miserably bad most of those years, and I was forced to watch their games on our only TV set. But my dad was not a fair-weather fan. He was a man of strong and life-long loyalties.

I am happy to say that it was I who introduced him to the University of South Carolina Gamecock baseball team. I was a teenager in 1975 when the Gamecocks became a national power. My dad loved baseball, and he jumped at the rare opportunity to tag along with his teenage son to the regional playoff games in Columbia. The Gamecocks fell short of a national title in the championship game of the 1977 College Baseball World

Series. My dad and mom, however, over the next 20 years would become one of the top power couples of Gamecock baseball.

Figure 133: Fred and Roberta Brinkman, married in 1947.

The team, under Coach Ray Tanner, gave the Fred Brinkman award to the most inspirational player each year. The two following stories by me appeared in The State newspaper on Father's Day 1997, shortly after my dad's death, and in 2010, shortly after the team captured its first national championship. It's no surprise to me that Coach Ray Tanner, a believer, is the one who finally made the University of South Carolina a champion, and that he did it in more ways than one.

> Many people knew Fred Brinkman as a leader in South Carolina tourism. Fewer people knew him as the avid Gamecock baseball fan that he was. As such, it was much to my dad's delight that his final moments included not only his family and South Carolina (posters of the Grand Strand, the mountains and Charleston taped to the walls around his hospital bed), but also his Gamecocks.

> My dad's last week with us included 16-hour work days to complete his last scrapbook for the Gamecock players and the Dugout Club. My dad knew, more than us, that his time was near and that his last projects had to be completed. He finished compiling the book as the Gamecocks entered their final weekend series.

A couple of days later, Coach Ray Tanner, former Coach June Raines, their wives and the Gamecock team captains visited Dad during his final hours. I will never forget the excitement in my father's eyes as the team captains presented him with a baseball signed by the entire team.

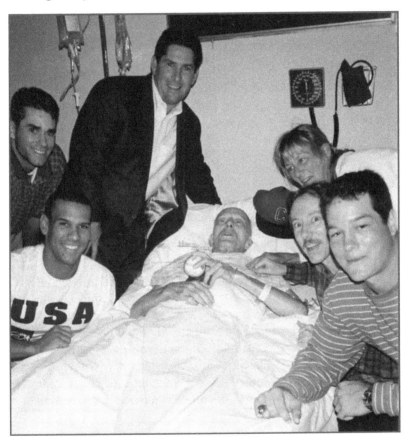

Figure 134: Fred Brinkman's last moments. Cancer took his body, but not his Spirit. (clockwise) Etienne Hightower, Ryan Szwejbka, coach Ray Tanner, Fred (holding the Gamecock autographed baseball), Terri Stevens (Fred's daughter), David Brinkman and Rob Streicher.

Later, my father's oncologist, (an outspoken and enthusiastic Clemson grad) entered the room and was not too happy to see my father's Gamecock baseball cap on the pillow. He laughed in disbelief when we told him of the team visit. I then handed him the autographed baseball (which Dad had held tightly for the last hour.) Expecting a witty Tiger comeback, I was surprised when the doctor paused as emotion seemed to take him for a moment. Changing looks between the baseball and my dad's cap, he replied, "Class act."

Early the next morning, our beautiful, loving father passed away — all projects complete. The Gamecocks' season ended later that day in the SEC baseball tourney.

Just in the positive way my dad had lived his life, he headlined his last Gamecock book: 1997 Baseball Gamecocks Well Surpass All Pre-Season Forecasts.

In 2010, after the school's first national championship, the following was reported in The State newspaper:

David Brinkman shared this moment: "I'm a USC grad and Tuesday was my 50th birthday. My wife prayed throughout the day that the spirits of my mom and dad would shine down on the Gamecocks and give me a birthday to remember. At 11:57 p.m., it happened with Merrifield's hit (in the bottom of the 11th inning). The first National Championship in a major sport for the over 200-year old University of South Carolina. My wife (Odess), son (Jeremy), and I, went wild. An hour later (sorry neighbors), we used fireworks for the 4th of July to continue the celebration.

Figure 135: (l) Coach Ray Tanner and Jeremy Brinkman after the first National Championship. (r) Fred Brinkman's punched Gamecock season ticket.

Figure 136: Fred Brinkman's retirement party with Coach June Raines and longtime secretaries, Dottie Fisher and Pat Lake.

Coming Full Circle

You may have noticed that a part of the story is incomplete.

Where did the virtues of my father come from? Although reinforced in the sands of Iwo Jima and the many challenges of life, all his special qualities were well in place long before he landed on Iwo Jima's Yellow Beach. But there's one more miracle that brought me back to my father's first miracle. It confirms what I had suspected all along. It all started with Alice, the grandmother I never knew.

My dad did not like to talk about the losses and painful experiences of his past. My mother and my father's baby book gave me the little bit of information that I have on my grandmother Alice. Maybe my dad's sister or brother could have told me more, but we lost them before I had sense enough to search for the answers. What I knew about Alice Potter was that she developed, just like my mother, rheumatic fever at a young age. As Alice became a teenager, the typical complications of rheumatic fever started showing.

By her early 20s, Alice's health temporarily improved, and she would meet and marry a young Harry Brinkman, my grandfather. They lost their first child, but then came Freddy, followed by sister Alice Jean and brother William. To my knowledge, only my grandmother Alice called my father Freddy. This was seen in the baby book she kept for my dad. The first entry in the book was the christening of Freddy just days after he was born. She also noted Freddy's first recited prayer was "Now I lay me down to sleep." Soon, every night, he would be saying "Five Little Angels at My Bed" followed by "The Lord's Prayer." For many years, this is all I knew about Alice.

What about my dad's father? Although I know my dad loved his father, they were opposites in many ways. My grandfather had several marriages after Alice died. He died all alone, on my father's birthday, with not even enough money in the bank to pay for the funeral. Every Christmas and summer holiday, we always visited my mother's family, not my dad's father. My father's life was all about setting good examples, and maybe the stable marriages and family on my mother's side were the better environment for us to grow up in.

About a year after my dad died, Uncle William (Harry) died of the same cancer. A few years later, Aunt Alice Jean followed. My mother was too ill to make Aunt Alice Jean's funeral, but I made the trip to St. Louis. Driving to the funeral service, we picked up the last member of my father's previous generation, Aunt Harriet who was 91. For as far back as maybe 15 years, Aunt Harriet had been having dementia-like issues. She wrote to us every Christmas, but each year the letters were more difficult to understand. The letters had stopped about five years earlier.

When we picked her up, as expected, there was no conversation. On the drive to the funeral service, Aunt Harriet was silent until I pointed out a bowling alley. Suddenly she responded with "I used to love to go bowling." She then looked at me and asked, "Who are you?" I told her: "I am David, the son of your nephew Fred Brinkman." There was a pause and then aunt Harriet said: "You mean Freddy? Freddy is the son of my sister Alice."

I realized Aunt Harriet had come alive, but it was her memories from over 50 years in the past. And what happened next was the completion of the miracle. It would be the last thing Aunt Harriet would say that day. The last thing I would ever hear her say: "I miss my sister Alice. She was an angel." Aunt Harriet's flashback was a first-hand account and confirmation of what I had thought for many years.

So, there you have it. I know where the qualities of my father came from, and I also have come full circle to the first miracle he told me about in 1969, when that day in 1936 when my grandmother Alice was fetching water for the farm animals. Her damaged heart gave way, and she fell unconscious into the pond and drowned. In that first miracle, God spoke to my father as it happened and led him to his mother's body. God promised my father then that everything would be all right and he would be taken care of.

Just like in archaeology and other sciences, you take the limited data you have and make the best conclusion you can. Some would call it a theory. It seems to me, this is where all our miracles began.

Figure 137: The Potter sisters (1915). Left to right: Harriet, Grace, Ruth, and Alice. Right: Alice's 19-year-old son, Fred Brinkman and his buddy Norman Richards (1944). Norman would be killed just a few months after this photo while trying to save the life of a wounded Marine during the invasion of Iwo Jima.

In closing, this book was not just about finding lost places. Had it been a purely scientific endeavor, that's all it would have been. Miracles to Yesterday, however, was also about bringing back to life the forgotten good of special people - people who set the right examples and gave much to their family, community, and country. And, most importantly, it was about how our unclear path to the truth can be paved with belief.

APPENDIX A: The History Timeline of Miracles to Yesterday

Date	Event	Discovery
8000 B.C.	A Native American drops a unique arrowhead near the Congaree River.	Chapter 11
October 2, 1452	Cecily Neville passes her extremely rare mitochondrial (maternal line) DNA to her new son, Richard of Gloucester.	Chapters 12 and 13
August 22, 1485	King Richard III is killed in the Battle of Bosworth. A hastily dug grave will preserve his bones and DNA for centuries.	Chapters 12 and 13
1490	Anne St. Leger (maternal line grandniece of Cecily Neville) marries George Manners (the Marquis of Granby).	Chapter 13
1520	The Hernando de Soto expedition brings the first Europeans to the banks of the Congaree River.	Chapter 11
1620 - 1650	A Plantagenet woman in the maternal line of Cecily Neville moves from England to the new Jamestown, VA settlement.	Chapter 13
1680 - 1710	Charles Town, South Carolina is founded, and the first Indian Traders move into the back-country of South Carolina.	Chapter 11
1718	Fort Congaree I is created on the Congaree River and turns into a trading post.	Chapter 11
1725	Indian Trader Thomas Brown arrives from Ireland and acquires land near the fort on the Congaree River.	Chapter 11
1740	The Saxe-Gotha settlement is formed between where the old Fort Congaree stood and Brown's property.	Chapter 11
1747	Thomas Brown dies and problems with French supported Indian attacks	Chapter 11

	begin to rise.	
1747	Indian Representative George Haig and Thomas Brown's son are kidnapped by Indians. Haig is executed.	Chapter 15
1748	British Fort Congaree II is created and manned to provide protection for the local settlers.	Chapter 15
1750	Saxe Gotha resident Martin Friday buys the old Brown property just north of the new fort and starts Friday's Ferry.	Chapter 11
1750	Lieutenant Peter Mercier becomes the Commander of Fort Congaree II and he builds strong ties with the Catawba Indians.	Chapter 15
1751	Mercier meets the widow of George Haig and the two marry in 1752.	Chapter 15
1753	War builds with the French and Indians.	Chapter 15
1754	Peter Mercier, and men from Fort Congaree II, are sent to help Lieutenant Colonel George Washington in Virginia.	Chapter 15
July 3, 1754	Mercier and his men fight to the death against the French and Indians at Fort Necessity. They save the life of George Washington.	Chapter 15
1758	A village has formed north of Fort Congaree II around Friday's Ferry.	Chapter 11
1760	Led by John Manners (the Marquis of Granby) the British defeat the French in the Battle of Warburg.	Chapter 11
1761	The village is named Granby after John Manners who was the 7th great-grandson of the DNA maternal line niece of King Richard III.	Chapter 11
1761	Fort Congaree II becomes the training ground and launch site of a decisive war against the Cherokee.	Chapter 15
1763	The French and Indian war ends and the French leave America.	Chapter 15

1770	Granby has developed into a major trade center with goods being moved daily with Charles Town.	Chapter 11
1776	South Carolina forms a new Constitution and prepares for war with the British.	Chapter 11
1780	Charles Town falls to the British. The British convert the main store in Granby to a Fort and call it Fort Granby.	Chapter 11
1780 - 1781	South Carolina Patriots overwhelm the British at Kings Mountain and Cowpens.	Chapter 11
1781	Led by men who trained at Fort Congaree II, South Carolina turns the tables on the British by taking Fort Granby. The British soon abandon South Carolina and head to Virginia.	Chapter 11
1781	Cornwallis and the British meet General George Washington (who was saved by the heroes of Fort Congaree II) at Yorktown.	Chapter 11
1781	Washington, with help from the French, end the Revolutionary War at the Battle of Yorktown.	Chapter 11
1786	Granby becomes the county seat of Lexington and is considered for the new Capital of South Carolina.	Chapter 11
1787	Health issues in Granby lead to it being rejected as the Capital and the new city of Columbia is created across the river.	Chapter 11
1790	A State House is built in Columbia and Wade Hampton builds the first bridge on the Congaree River at Friday's Ferry in Granby.	Chapter 11 and 16
1791	George Washington visits Granby and Columbia and stays at Timothy Rives Tavern next to the State House.	Chapter 11 and 16
1791	Frenchman John Compty builds the first bridge on the Broad River just north of the new city of Columbia.	Chapter 7

1799	Epidemics take their toll on Granby as the population moves to Columbia.	Chapter 11
1800	Wade Hampton gives up on bridges after losing his 3rd bridge to a flood. John Compty dies and his final bridge collapses.	Chapter 7
1801	River crossings into Columbia are now handled with ferries.	Chapter 7
1802	John Compty's widow marries Henry McGowan and the old Compty crossing becomes McGowans ferry.	Chapter 7
1812	Many conflicts arise with McGowans ferry and a nearby illegal ferry of Alexander Stark.	Chapter 7
1818	The County seat is moved from Granby to the new town of Lexington.	Chapter 11
1829	Bridge companies have now been formed and bridges, once again, cross the Broad and Congaree rivers.	Chapter 7
1832	South Carolina, led by Vice President John C. Calhoun, writes the Ordinance of Nullification in the SC State House in Columbia.	Chapter 17
1840	John C. Calhoun predicts the American Civil War.	Chapter 17
1848	The city of Charleston commissions a statue of John C. Calhoun.	Chapter 17
1849	Obsessed with the fall of the Roman empire, John C. Calhoun specifies that his statue be in a Roman toga and carved in Rome.	Chapter 17
1849	Calhoun's statue is completed in Rome by Hiram Powers.	Chapter 17
1849	Hiram Power's completes The Greek Slave which is considered the finest sculpture of 19th century.	Chapter 17
1850	John C. Calhoun dies and his statue is lost at sea with Margaret Fuller.	Chapter 17
1850	The Calhoun statue is later found, recovered, repaired, and is placed in Charleston's City Hall.	Chapter 17
1854	Margaret Fuller's loss is the	Chapter 17

	inspiration of Elizabeth Barrett Browning's epic poem "Aurora Leigh".	
1855	Granby has gradually faded away and is erased by 1855.	Chapter 11
1860	John C. Calhoun becomes an inspiration to the Secessionists and his statue becomes the symbol of Secession.	Chapter 17
1860	The Ordinance of Secession is drafted in Columbia, SC.	Chapter 17
1861	Calhoun's prediction comes true and the Civil War begins in Charleston at Fort Sumter.	Chapter 17
1862	The Calhoun statue is hidden in Columbia (possibly in the Old State House basement).	Chapter 16 and 17
1864	Many view the Calhoun statue as a symbol of Slavery and Hiram Power's Greek Slave statue as a symbol of Abolition.	Chapter 17
1864	General Willian T. Sherman's March through the South begins.	Chapter 17
February 15, 1865	Sherman's troops camp in old Granby.	Chapter 11 and 17
February 16, 1865	30 Confederates, led by General Joseph Wheeler, stop Sherman's 30,000 men at the Broad River bridge.	Chapter 9
February 17, 1865	Sherman and troops cross the river on a pontoon bridge at the old site of Alexander Stark's ferry.	Chapter 9
February 17, 1865	Sherman's men burn Columbia with one of the primary targets being the Old State House.	Chapter 16 and 17
February 18, 1865	Unable to find the prized statue of their arch enemy (John C. Calhoun), the Union Army leaves Columbia in ruins.	Chapter 17
February 18, 1865	For all practical purposes, the American Civil War is over. The Calhoun statue is forgotten in a Lost Cause.	Chapter 9

April 1944	WWII: Operation Tiger, Slapton Sands in Devon, England.	Chapter 5
June 1944	WWII: Invasion of Normandy	Chapter 5
February 1945	WWII: The Battle of Iwo Jima	Chapter 4 and 5
August 5, 2012	The bones of King Richard III are found under a parking lot in Leicester, England.	Chapter 12
February 2014	David Brinkman's unique full sequence mitochondrial DNA test leads to the documentation of a new haplogroup: J1c2c3.	Chapter 13
December 2014	The full sequence mitochondrial DNA test is completed on King Richard III's bones and he is also a J1c2c3. An exact match to Brinkman.	Chapter 13

APPENDIX B: History Corrected in Miracles to Yesterday

Item	Corrected
Iwo Jima photo date	Chapter 5
The fate of Seaman Ellis Morton	Chapter 5
Broad River Historical Marker	Chapters 6 and 7
1825 Mills' Atlas	Chapters 6 and 7
King Richard III's reputation	Chapters 12 and 13
State House location marker	Chapter 16

APPENDIX C: The USS Lowndes
Ship and Beach Party

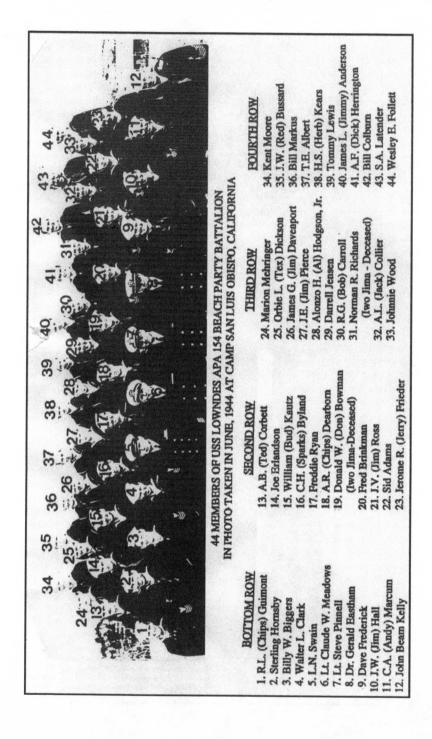

44 MEMBERS OF USS LOWNDES APA 154 BEACH PARTY BATTALION
IN PHOTO TAKEN IN JUNE, 1944 AT CAMP SAN LUIS OBISPO, CALIFORNIA

BOTTOM ROW

1. R.L. (Chips) Guimont
2. Sterling Hornsby
3. Billy W. Biggers
4. Walter L. Clark
5. LN. Swain
6. Lt. Claude W. Meadows
7. Lt. Steve Pinnell
8. Dr. Gerald Eastham
9. Dave Frederick
10. I.W. (Jim) Hall
11. C.A. (Andy) Marcum
12. John Beam Kelly

SECOND ROW

13. A.B. (Ted) Corbett
14. Joe Erlandson
15. William (Bud) Kautz
16. C.H. (Sparks) Byland
17. Freddie Ryan
18. A.R. (Chips) Dearborn
19. Donald W. (Don) Bowman
    (Two Jima-Deceased)
20. Fred Brinkman
21. J.V. (Jim) Ross
22. Sid Adams
23. Jerome R. (Jerry) Frieder

THIRD ROW

24. Marion Mehringer
25. Orbie L. (Tex) Dickson
26. James G. (Jim) Daveaport
27. J.E. (Jim) Pierce
28. Alonzo H. (Al) Hodgson, Jr.
29. Darrell Jensen
30. R.G. (Bob) Carroll
31. Norman R. Richards
    (Two Jima – Deceased)
32. A.L. (Jack) Collier
33. Johnnie Wood

FOURTH ROW

34. Kent Moore
35. J.W. (Red) Bussard
36. Bill Markus
37. T.E. Albert
38. H.S. (Herb) Kears
39. Tommy Lewis
40. James L. (Jimmy) Anderson
41. A.F. (Dick) Herrington
42. Bill Colburn
43. S.A. Latender
44. Wesley E. Follett

APPENDIX D: The people of Sarah Friday's 1810 Granby

With Sarah Friday's 1810 snapshot of Granby, we will now look at the people and businesses she identified, starting with our Granby dig site and Samuel Johnston. Many of these sites have been destroyed by the mining of granite or have been buried under a huge slag pile from the quarry pit. What created Granby has, ironically, swallowed her up. Granby came into existence because of the fall line. It was the farthest point that could be traveled on the rivers before hitting the rocky and unnavigable water. Today, this fall line at the river is the ideal place to quarry granite.

We will now move south to north through Sarah Friday's drawing.

Note: By law, you cannot dig on a property without the owner's permission. You should follow the education and permission process we did at the Confederate bridge site and the Fort Congaree II site before you enter and dig on a site. The quarry owner, Martin Marietta, has supported previous history and archaeology work on their property and may be open to future work.

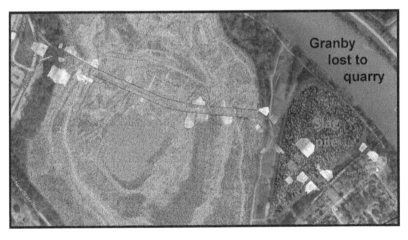

Figure 138: Quarry takes Granby.

Samuel Johnston home site:
Status: The Finding Granby dig has completed about 60% of the possible archaeology that can be done on the site. Location: 33.965782°, -81.039405°

 Samuel Johnston was the son of David Johnston (b. 1727) and Sarah Meek. He was born September 29, 1769, in the County of Londonderry, Ireland. With his mother and several brothers, he immigrated to South Carolina, arriving in Charleston on September 4, 1787. He settled in Fairfield County, where he became a planter. At one time, Johnston's property included two tracts totaling 708 acres near Winnsboro, two houses and four lots in Winnsboro, another 100 acres in Fairfield District, seven lots and 368 acres in or near the town of Chester, and one house and lot in the village of Granby.

The 1800 Census shows Samuel living in Granby next to his brother, Henry Johnston. At that time, it appears Samuel had a son between 10 and 15 and another son younger than 10. Another male in the house was between 26 and 44. This could not have been a son of Samuel since Samuel was only 31 years old in 1800. This may have been a brother. Also, in 1800, Samuel had three daughters between 10 and 15, and his wife was also between 26 and 44. Records on "Find A Grave" show Samuel's first wife Catherine Harrison Johnston and daughter Carolina both died on August 28, 1799, in childbirth or maybe from Yellow Fever. The graves are "unknown" and could be in the area of the Granby dig. The "Find A Grave" records show Samuel and Catherine had one other child born in 1796, Sarah Dargan "Sally" Johnston Randell, but the 1800 census does not show her in Samuel's Granby home. Maybe she is the child under ten shown in Henry's household. In addition to the eight family members in Samuel's Granby home, there were also ten slaves listed in the census. There were eight people in Henry Johnston's 1800 Granby household but no slaves.

Writing his will on June 5, 1852, Samuel mentioned a Wateree plantation and 850 acres on Connells Creek in Richland District. According to inventories of his estate, he owned 55 slaves at Wateree plantation, 39 slaves at Lower plantation, and bank and railroad stock.

Public service for Johnston began with his election to the House. Fairfield chose him for the 18th General Assembly (1808-1809), but the house declared him ineligible, as he allegedly did not meet citizenship and residency requirements. However, he was re-elected and qualified November 28, 1809. Subsequently, he represented Fairfield in the 19th General Assembly (1810-1812). While in the House, he was a member of the committees on schools (1810-1812) and pensions (1810-1812). Johnston was elected to the state Senate by Fairfield and served in the 20th (1812-1813), 21st (1811-1815), 24th (1820-1821), and 25th (1822-1823) General Assemblies.

Johnston married three times. His first wife was Catherine Harrison, daughter of Burr Harrison and Eliza Dargan. Six children were born to them: David, Burr, Eliza Meek, Sarah Dargan (m. Theodore Randall), Harriett (m. Birt Harrington), and Carolina (B.&D. 1799). Catherine Harrison Johnston died August 28, 1799. He then wed Rebecca Surginer, who bore him eight children before she died July 16, 1823. These children were John Surginer, Charlotte A. (m. John David Means), Caroline (m. Sylvanus Chambers), Juliet C. (m. John Caldwell Johnston), Samuel E., J. Madison, William David, and Rebecca Surginer (m. Harry Walker Adams). His third wife was Elizabeth Crawford, daughter of Andrew Crawford and Jane Bones. They were the parents of five children: Andrew, Jane S. (m. Rufus Kirkpatrick Porter), Margaret Crawford (m. James Pickett Adams), Robert Crawford, and David. Survived by his wife and, at least 14 children, Samuel Johnson died May 13, 1853, in Winnsboro.

Samuel Johnston is buried at the Sion Presbyterian Cemetery in Winnsboro, South Carolina.

Burr Johnston (the Granby Gamecock) was born in Granby in 1791. He attended Newberry Academy in 1807 and 1808 and started college in 1809 at the new South Carolina College (USC). He and Granby friend William Arthur became the first Granbyans to graduate from South Carolina College in 1811. No doubt, Burr knew Sarah Friday and may have observed her, as she included the Samuel Johnston house in her drawing of Granby.

After Burr's graduation from South Carolina College, he studied medicine in Newberry for two years. He then opened a practice in Newberry. In 1840, he moved to Macon, Alabama, and continued to practice medicine there until his death in 1855. Burr's son, John Foote Johnston (born in 1821), would also become a medical doctor.

The Cake Shop site:
Status: Archaeology is possible in the Riverland Park neighborhood at: 33.964876°, -81.040990°

Figure 139: Cake shop in Colonial Williamsburg

Nothing is known about the Granby Cake shop, but like in other Colonial villages of the time, it would have been a place to go to meet and socialize. It might have been more popular with women, while men might have frequented a nearby tavern to do the same. Of course, the sweet products of the shop would have been enjoyable to all.

In "Random Recollections of a Long Life, 1806 to 1876," Edwin J. Scott gives us a period description of the popular role cakes played in Granby.

At weddings, which were nearly always in the forenoon, all neighbors attended with or without invitations, cards being unknown, and were welcomed with whisky to drink and a plentiful dinner, set out, when the weather permitted, on a long table of boards laid on benches under trees in the yard. Then the young folks and some of the old ones walked for the cake, a ceremony confined, so far as I know, to the German settlers. For this purpose, those proposing to engage in the game contributed small sums of money, which were given to the bride, in payment for a large pound cake, that became the prize, depending upon the following chance:
Each young man selected his partner of the other sex, and they, headed by the bride and groom, marched in double file around the house, where at the front door one stood with a long rod, which he handed to the first couple, and when they reached the door again it was taken from them and delivered to the next pair, who in turn surrendered it to their immediate followers. Meantime a party of three or four took a loaded gun into the woods, out of sight from the house, and after waiting a quarter or half hour fired it off, the couple having the rod in hand when the gun was fired winning the cake, which was usually cut up and divided among the players,

the girls saving a small bit to put under their pillows at night, on which to dream of their future lovers. I have seen, and sometimes joined in, the parade with as many as thirty or forty pairs.

The Tobacco Inspection and storage facility:

Status: Metal detector scans show a high density of iron hits, probably nails from the old building. Archaeology is possible in the Riverland Park neighborhood at: 33.966355°, -81.039404°

Figure 140: David Brinkman's Granby computer model looking over the Samuel Johnston house (Granby dig site) and the Tobacco Inspection warehouse. Wade Hampton's bridge is also shown crossing the Congaree River. The documented cornfield and church are also shown.

In 1786, Wade Hampton, Thomas Taylor, and Urich Goodwin were made commissioners of the State Tobacco Inspection station at Granby. A tobacco warehouse there was washed away by the 1796 flood. This happened in January, and 150 hogsheads of tobacco were also swept away. The warehouse was not near capacity in January, so it probably could have handled two or three times as much. Given the size of a hogshead, each weighing 1,000 pounds, you would need 2,700 to 4,000 square feet to store that much tobacco and have extra room to move around. The warehouse may have been nearly 5,000 square feet in size.

The fact that all this was washed away in the flood also confirms that the warehouse was near the river. They would have built it as close as possible to the river because water moved most of the area's tobacco.

The Town Well site:

Status: Archaeology is possible in the Riverland Park neighborhood at: 33.965385°, -81.041020°

Figure 141: Colonial Williamsburg Wells.

Figure 142: Today's William Pou's Grave

Wells are exciting opportunities for archaeologists because they tend to have interesting items at their bottom. Our Granby dig team didn't have the resources to excavate a deep well, but we were always on the lookout for one. The 1790 newspaper ad, for what we believe was Samuel Johnston's future property, stated that the town well was on that property. Wells don't last forever, and the well that Sarah Friday has in her drawing was nearer to the town square, in a vacant lot of today's Riverland Park neighborhood. The most efficient way to locate a well like this would be with ground penetrating radar (GPR). Unfortunately, without any funding for our dig project, that was not something we could afford. So, there are two Granby wells still waiting to be found.

Lewis Pou home site:
Status: Resident has reported Colonial-period pipe stems and pottery found during garden work near this location. Archaeology is possible in the Riverland Park neighborhood at: 33.965716°, -81.040820°

Revolutionary War veteran William Lewis Pou's grave is at Hebron Southern Methodist Church in Lexington, SC. Pou was active in the Granby community, as can be seen in a letter in which Pou and his neighbor Henry Seibels served as commissioners for the county. Other records in the

South Carolina Archives show Pou taking civic responsibilities in many issues of the time, including overseeing repairs on the Granby courthouse and jail.

Figure 143: Mills' Atlas 1825, showing Geiger's Platt Spring Academy and Granby.

Abraham Geiger site:
Status: Archaeology is possible in the quarry property at: 33.966496°, -81.039557°

Major Abraham Geiger was a very educated man and was described as a "remarkable personality."[131] He was a soldier in the War of 1812-14 and then an author and agriculturist. He owned a store in Granby, which probably also served as his home for a number of years. He was a son of John Geiger and Ann Murff, grandson of Herman Geiger and Elizabeth (Lisabet) Habluzel, and great-grandson of Gov. Hs. Jacob Geiger and Margrit Fehr of Switzerland and SC.

From "The Geigers of South Carolina," compiled by Percy L. Geiger: Abraham Geiger was prominent in politics when Granby flourished, and later he became interested in educational matters, moved to Platt Springs and established the Platt Springs Academy.

From Mill's Statistics, 1826:

"The Platt Springs Academy has long been known to the public as a first-rate institution for the education of Youth preparatory to entering college. It owes its foundation and present eminence to the liberality and indefatigable care of Abraham Geiger, Esq., who for several years supported it from his private purse. The Academy is now one of the most flourishing in the state. The institution has a small but well selected library attached to it. The average number of students is from sixty to seventy. The price of tuition is

---

[131]The State Newspaper: A Ghost for Lexington County: January 6, 1963.

very moderate, also boarding (there being several respectable private homes for this purpose) which is at the rate of $8.00 per month."

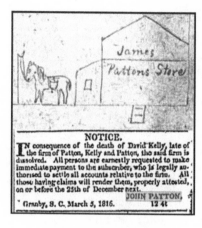

NOTICE.

IN consequence of the death of David Kelly, late of the firm of Patton, Kelly and Patton, tho said firm is dissolved. All persons are earnestly requested to make immediate payment to the subscriber, who is legally authorised to settle all accounts relative to the firm. All those having claims will render them, properly attested, on or before the 25th of December next.

JOHN PATTON,

Granby, S. C., March 5, 1816.   12 4t

Figure 144: Columbia Telescope newspaper article.

James/John Patton's store site:
Status: Archaeology is possible in the quarry property at: 33.966027°, -81.040960°

Very little is known about James/John Patton. A Columbia Telescope newspaper article, dated March 1816, indicates that John Patton was a Granby lawyer as well as a store owner. There is also a recorded marriage in Granby between the Bell and Patton families. Sarah Friday's addition (to her drawing) of a horse at Patton's store may indicate the store was a favorite place for travelers to stop.

About the last of August last, from the subscriber, living in Spartanburgh District, S. C., a Negro Man, named JACK, but will probably change his name; about 24 or 25 years of age, 5 feet 7 or 8 inches high, two of his under fore teeth out, a scar or tumor over each eye near the edge of his hair, stutters or stammers in his speech, reads and writes tolerably well, and likely he will write himself a pass. Any person who will give information where he can be had, will be rewarded for his trouble and expense by the subscriber.

John Means.

September 30   3

Figure 145: John Means' lost slave

Means store site:
Status: Archaeology is possible in the quarry property at: 33.966088°, -81.041577°

John Means, like his neighbor Lewis Pou, took part in civic duties of the Granby community. He was an election/voting manager with Alexander Bell and Jacob Geiger in Granby between 1810 and 1812. He also was on a committee to nominate South Carolina College trustees in the first years of the college. Means left Granby in 1812, and he became an election/voting manager in Spartanburg County after moving. The 1800 census showed

Means had nine slaves. An 1813 newspaper ad shows one of these as a "Run-away."

Bell's store site:
Status: Under a slag pile. Archaeology is not feasible at this location on the quarry property at: 33.966388°, -81.041743°

Figure 146: The Granby Cemetery's Alexander Bells' (left to right) 1752-1816, 1794-1835, 1829-1852.

Alexander Bell was a Lexington County Tax Collector and an Election Commissioner, according to documents at the South Carolina Archives. The Bells' home also served as a store in the town square of Granby. Three generations of Alexander Bell in Granby have headstones in the old Granby Cemetery, but a Riverland Park resident says she remembers a Bell family cemetery just inside the quarry, near where Bell's Store was located according to Sarah's drawing. The last Alexander Bell died at the age of 22, and his gravestone includes a Freemason triangle of Hope, Faith, and Charity. Between the years 1733 and 1737, the Freemason Grand Lodge in England sanctioned Provincial Grand Lodges in Massachusetts, New York, Pennsylvania, and South Carolina. It is possible this once-secret society had a strong presence among the wealthy men of Granby.

The following excerpt is from "Random recollections of a long life 1806 to 1876," by Edwin J. Scott. He gives a view of Granby very similar to Sarah's drawing but about ten years later. Edwin also tells a story centered around the Bells' daughter, Harriet Bell, who would have been 20 years old at the time.[132]

OLD GRANBY

At Granby the British had a fort in the war of the Revolution, and Mr. Cayce's house, that stands on the hill just North of the place, shows a hole in its Northern end made by a small cannon ball when the fort was besieged, and I believe captured by the Americans, towards the close of the war.

The town being at the head of navigation on the Congaree, with a ferry on the road leading to the up country, and broad, fertile river swamp lands extending many miles below, was a place of considerable business, and some of its merchants made fortunes and lived in good style.

Their families were well educated and formed a circle of refined society, that was at once moral and elevated. Among them were the Bells, Hanes, Arthurs, Fridays, Seibels and others, whose representatives go to make up the present population of Columbia and its vicinity. But when the State capital, the South Carolina College and the sessions of the Supreme Court were established at Columbia, Granby began to decline. It had always been unhealthy, the superior capital and enterprise of the merchants in Columbia in time drew trade from the place, and after the removal of the County seat to Lexington it became a deserted village; so that in 1822 but two or three stores remained, those of Muller & Senn and Pou & Seibels (Lewis Pou and Henry Seibels) being all that I recollect.

When I first collected taxes there in 1825, General Henry Arthur, Wolf Hane, son of Nicholas Hane, a rosy old gentleman, owner of the ferry, Mrs. Elizabeth Bell, Friday Arthur and James Cayce, who kept a public house, a mill and blacksmith and coach-making shops, were the most prominent reliques of Granby's former prosperity. And here I will repeat an anecdote related by John Caldwell, which may be called:

---

[132]Random recollections of a long life, 1806 to 1876 by Scott, Edwin J., b. 1803. Not in Copyright.

A TALE OF A SHIRT

On a fine sunny morning in May, 1806, a gay party of young folks, both male and female, assembled at the residence of Alexander Bell, Sr., in Granby, to take an excursion on horseback some ten miles up the river to the ferry on Saluda, then known as Kennerly's, just above which James Kennedy, Esq., resided; his dwelling, a roomy, rambling country house, being on the East bank of the river, so close to it that a heavy body dropped from one of the windows would fall into the water.

Among the gentlemen present were John Caldwell of Newberry, and John Mayrant of Sumter, both then in College, and it was arranged that they, with two of the girls, should pass the night and part of the next day at Kennerly's, while the rest of the cavalcade, after all had enjoyed themselves boating and fishing in the river, were to return to Granby at the close of the day. The two collegians were rivals for the favor of one of the young ladies who remained behind when the others had gone back. They were dressed in the tip of the prevailing fashion, but Mayrant rejoiced in the display of a magnificent ruffled shirt, got up in better style and of finer material than usual, so that it attracted the attention and excited the applause and admiration of the fair sex, and, as Caldwell thought, gave its owner an advantage that he was not otherwise entitled to.

At bed time they were put into the same room with several other young men who had called to see the belles from Granby, and Mayrant, to save his shirt from being rumpled, pulled if off and hung it upon a chair. This was observed by Caldwell, who, instigated by the demon of mischief and jealousy, and counting all means fair in love and war, resolved to put the offending garment out of the way. Accordingly, at the dead of night, while all the others were asleep, he rose stealthily, and, wrapping the object of his hate around a brick, threw it from one of the windows as far as he could into the river.

Next morning when Mayrant arose his shirt was missing, and, after a thorough and fruitless search, he was forced to button up his vest and coat, and, leaving an apology to the ladies and family for his sudden departure, to order his horse and take the road to Columbia, leaving Caldwell in full possession of the field. Whether he suspected his rival of any agency in the mysterious disappearance of the garment was not known; but Caldwell said twenty years afterwards that he could never muster up the courage to tell Mayrant what had become of his shirt.

Neither of them succeeded in gaining the young lady, a Miss Bell, who was first married to a Mr. Heron and afterwards to Major Benjamin Hart.

As already stated, the old court house, after being used as a Presbyterian church, in Columbia, became the residence of Mr. Kinard.

James G. Gibbes, whilst manager of the Saluda Factory, bought the rest of the old houses in Granby from Captain Alexander R. Taylor, for three hundred dollars, and moved them to the Factory, where he converted them into dwellings and outhouses for the operatives, but he found great difficulty in drawing out the wrought nails with which they had been built. These had been made before the introduction of cut nails, and were hammered out separately on the anvil by the blacksmith, and, owing to their roughness, they adhered to the wood so as to split the boards and leave Gibbes less profit than he had expected from the purchase.

Granby Courthouse site:
Status: Under a slag pile. Archaeology is not feasible at this location on the quarry property at: 33.967277°, -81.041707°

From 1785 until 1818, Granby was the Lexington District judicial seat, and there was a courthouse and jail in Granby. The court was in session eight days a year. The courthouse and jail were built on a one-acre piece of land owned by Nicholas Hane. Hane filed a petition in 1806 stating that he was never paid for the land. There were several petitions signed by the "merchants" of Granby and one by 62 citizens of Granby fighting efforts to move the courthouse from Granby to the new town of Lexington. Unhealthiness in the jail was the main reason for moving the judicial center. The old Granby courthouse was dismantled and rebuilt in Columbia at the northeast corner of Lady and Marion streets. Despite being recognized as the oldest building in Columbia, it was torn down in 1944 to make room for an electric company building.

Seibels Burying ground site:

Status: Under a slag pile. Archaeology is not allowed on graves. Location in the Quarry property is at: 33.966270°, -81.042645°.

In 1957, the headstones of the Seibels burying ground were moved to another location to avoid being covered by a quarry slag pile. The old stones, and a new monument, surrounded by a stone wall, are now at the location: 33.968677°, -81.042882°

Figure 147: 1957 Seibels' Granby Monument.

Seibels store site:

Status: Under a slag pile. Archaeology is not feasible at this location in the Quarry property at: 33.966994°, -81.042219°

The Seibels store was also the family house. John Jacob Seibels was born in Germany in 1752 and died in Granby in 1816. He married Sarah Sally Temple (1765-1838) in Charleston in 1785. Their son John Temple Seibels (1791-1853) was surveyor-general of South Carolina. John Temple Seibels appears to have purchased the Samuel Johnston house (our Granby dig site) sometime between 1815 and 1820.

In 1806, a Jacob Seibels served as an election manager in Granby. In 1826, Henry Seibels served as an election manager in Sandy Run, while John Hane was doing it for Granby. The Seibels had their own family cemetery in Granby that included several generations.

Hane home site:
Status: Partially buried under a slag pile. Archaeology may be feasible at this location on the Quarry property at: 33.967546°, -81.042626°

Figure 148: Nicholas Hane.

With maybe the exception of the Friday family, the Hanes were probably the greatest longtime residents of Granby. The 1970 Hane Memorial in the Granby Cemetery states that Nicholas Hane was one of the founders of Granby around 1771, but this does not agree with Nicholas' paper trail from his German home to England in the early 1780s and then to Charleston in 1784. Nicholas owned the land on which the Granby courthouse and jail were built in 1785. Nicholas, despite the downfall of Granby after the creation of Columbia and the move of the district seat to Lexington, remained in Granby until his death in 1829. The Nicholas Hane story is an excellent story of immigration and persistence through multiple failures to success. Our story of Nicholas Hane begins with the following public recording of a London bankruptcy on December 20, 1783. Nicholas and Gerard Berck owned this failed store in London.

The next thing we find, in 1784, is the first of dozens of Charleston newspaper ads (SC Gaz - 6/5/1784) for the store: "Hane and Berck" at 100 Broad Street.

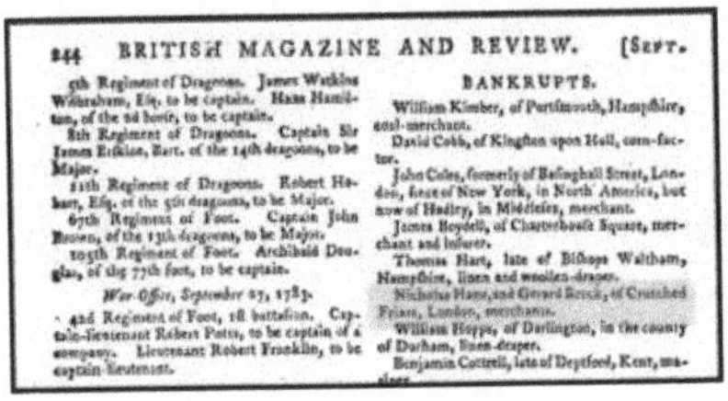
244 BRITISH MAGAZINE AND REVIEW. [Sept.

5th Regiment of Dragoons. James Watkins Wilbraham, Esq. to be captain. Hans Hamilton, of the 2d horse, to be captain.
8th Regiment of Dragoons. Captain Sir James Erskine, Bart. of the 14th dragoons, to be Major.
11th Regiment of Dragoons. Robert Hobart, Esq. of the 5th dragoons, to be Major.
67th Regiment of Foot. Captain John Brown, of the 13th dragoons, to be Major.
105th Regiment of Foot. Archibald Douglas, of the 77th foot, to be captain.

War-Office, September 27, 1783.

42d Regiment of Foot, 1st battalion. Captain-lieutenant Robert Potts, to be captain of a company. Lieutenant Robert Franklin, to be captain-lieutenant.

BANKRUPTS.

William Kimber, of Portsmouth, Hampshire, coal-merchant.
David Cobb, of Kingston upon Hull, corn-factor.
John Coles, formerly of Basinghall Street, London, since of New York, in North America, but now of Hadley, in Middlesex, merchant.
James Boydell, of Charterhouse Square, merchant and insurer.
Thomas Hart, late of Bishops Waltham, Hampshire, linen and woollen-draper.
Nicholas Hane, and Gerard Berck, of Crutched Friars, London, merchants.
William Hopps, of Darlington, in the county of Durham, linen-draper.
Benjamin Cottrell, late of Deptford, Kent, ma-

Figure 149:
London Bankruptcy

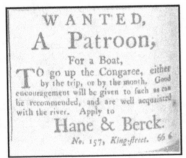

Two years later, Hane and Berck have moved to 207 King Street, and there is a change in the business (Charleston Gaz 2/3 and 2/24 1786).

Figure 150: Hane and Berck working their way to Granby.

A year later, there's another address change to 157 King Street, and now there is a significant change. Hane and Berck are looking for someone to take them up the Congaree River (Columbian Herald 3/26/1787). Three years later, we see the final Charleston newspaper reference to Hane & Berck. The Charleston store is closed and sold (SC Gaz 10/21/1790).

Nicholas would spend the rest of his life, 40 years, in Granby, where he and Gerald would successfully raise large families and operate stores next door to each other.

According to the 1800 Census of Granby, a little over half of the people in Granby were slaves -- 170 black slaves and 162 whites. The Census of 1810 shows the Hane household with a similar ratio, with seven family members and seven slaves. Sarah Friday's drawing shows the Hanes had a salt house, and documentation shows the Granby Ferry was owned by Nicholas Hane after Wade Hampton gave up on building bridges at Granby around 1800.

Hane Burying ground site:
Status: Archaeology is not allowed on graves. Location on the quarry property is at: 33.967288°, -81.043379°

Figure 151: Modern-day Hane memorial

The most famous of all the graves in Granby is probably that of Nicholas Hane. During our Granby dig project, we spoke to multiple witnesses to this grave. It seems the grave's marker has now disappeared, but these were the words on the stone:

"Stranger, what is this to Thee, Ask not my name, but as I am, So shall you be."

Just 10 months after Nicholas died, his son Deidrick married Henrietta Kaigler. One year later, another Nicholas Hane was born to Deidrick and Henrietta, but he died after only three weeks. The little boy was buried in the flower garden in front of the home at the "old place." Henrietta and Deidrick were living with her parents at the time. One year later, Henrietta was near term with another child when Deidrick came in from the plantation with a very large rattlesnake he had killed. Henrietta was sitting in a low chair on the piazza sewing when he thoughtlessly dropped the dead snake in her lap, "just playing." She began to convulse and had seizures until she died. Dr. Muller said she was frightened to death. A practical joke gone horribly wrong. Henrietta was 22 years old and was buried with her unborn child next to her infant son, Nicholas. Deidrick would remarry five years later to Margaret Keitt. They had two sons and a daughter, whom they named Henrietta Margaret.

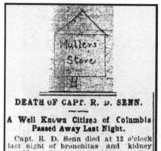

Figure 152: Muller partner Senn dies.

As in the case of the Seibels family cemetery, the Hane family was notified when the quarry slag pile would soon cover their family cemetery. In 1970, the family built a new monument in the main Granby cemetery. This new memorial is located at: 33.970016°, -81.042504°

Muller's store site:
Status: Archaeology is possible on the quarry property at: 33.968428°, -81.042611°

Muller's store in Granby was started by Ernest Henry David Muller shortly after he arrived from Germany in 1805. The store was passed on through several generations and was a thriving early 20th century business in Columbia. Early on, documentation shows a business relationship to a couple of generations of Senn (the firm of Muller & Senn). This partnership seemed to end with Captain R.D. Senn.

Henry Muller home site:
Status: Archaeology is possible on the quarry property at: 33.968626°, -81.042924°

Ernest Henry David Muller was born in 1774 in Saxony, Germany. He was orphaned at the age of six and grew up in Bremen, Germany. On December 16, 1805, he moved to America. He first lived in Granby, where he married Ann Elizabeth Geiger. He and Ann had four sons and five daughters. After Granby's decline, the Muller family moved to Sandy Run, South Carolina. Ernest died there in 1850.

Hane Salt house site:
Status: Destroyed by quarry hole. Archaeology is not possible at this location on the quarry property at: 33.968029°, -81.043274°

 Pork was a popular meat in Granby. Without refrigeration, other methods had to be used to preserve the meat. This was the purpose of a salt house. There were many different stores in Granby, and the fact the Hanes had a salt house probably means the Hanes store was mostly a meat store. In the salt house, salt and brown sugar were rubbed onto the hams. They were left sitting in salt for weeks and then washed off and covered in pepper or ashes. Many of the hams were then placed in a smokehouse, where they could hang for very long periods of time, sometimes years. [133]

Burk's store site:
Status: Destroyed by quarry hole. Archaeology is not possible at this location on the quarry property at: 33.968187°, -81.044454°

We know very little about Burk, also known as Gerard Berck, except for his business relationship with Nicholas Hane and that he followed Hane from Germany to England, to Charleston, and to Granby. They were next door neighbors in Sarah Friday's 1810 drawing of Granby.

---

[133]Making Virginia hams at Colonial Williamsburg and Edwards Ham.

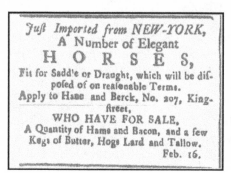

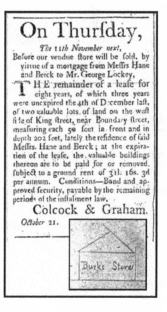

Figure 153: Newspaper ads showing the Burk (Berck) and Hane business in Charleston prior to their move to Granby in 1787.

Toy store site:
Status: Destroyed by quarry hole. Archaeology is not possible at this location on the quarry property at: 33.968749°, -81.044385°

The only thing we know about the Granby toy store is the simple drawing of it in Sarah Friday's image of Granby. Re-creations of Colonial period toy stores can be seen in the Cayce Historical Museum and at Colonial Williamsburg in Virginia.

Figure 154: The Granby Toy Store exhibit at the Cayce Historical Museum, SC and the William Pitt Toy store in Colonial Williamsburg, VA.

Mill site:

Status: Destroyed by quarry hole. Archaeology is not possible at this location on the quarry property at: 33.969334°, -81.045227°

Martin Friday started the first mill at Granby on Mill Creek, just off State Road. By the time the mill had been passed to his grandson, John Jacob

Friday (Sarah Friday's father), the Mill Creek had been dammed, and there was now a mill pond, which acted as a reservoir to guarantee the mill wheel always had water to drive it. A distillery was built next to the mill, which probably means the mill was designed to grind wheat for the ultimate production of beer, whiskey, or rum.

Figure 155: Left: Period mill (Pope, Rudolph, and Ethridge) in Lexington, SC). Below: 1820 map showing Friday's mill.

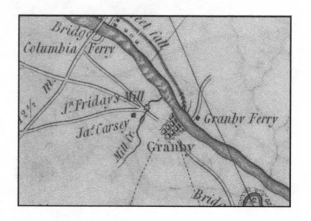

The fact that John Jacob Friday also owned Friday's Entertainments, a pub just two doors down, also points to the priority production of alcohol through the mill and distillery. It is also possible the mill was grinding wheat into flour, as a grist mill.

The mill, shown in Sarah's 1810 drawing, was probably built by Granby resident Captain John Hart, who built various mills in Lexington District during this period.

Distillery site:

Status: Destroyed by quarry hole. Archaeology is not possible at this location on the quarry property at: 33.968559°, -81.045169°

Distilleries and mills often developed next to each other in Colonial times for the production of alcohol. It's very likely that Sarah Friday's father, John Jacob Friday, used the products of this distillery for his pub, Friday's Entertainments.

Peter the Barber site:

Status: Destroyed by quarry hole. Archaeology is not possible at this location on the quarry property at: 33.971025°, -81.048902°

It's possible that Peter the barber is the Peter A. Pluet in the Granby census of 1800. Pluet lived by himself, with no slaves. A Revolutionary War claim by a Pierre Antoine Pluet is found on microfilm at the South Carolina Archives. Could this apparent Frenchman be Granby's Peter the Barber?

Jesse Sharp site:

Status: Archaeology is possible on the quarry property at: 33.971379°, -81.049615°

Not much is known about Jesse Sharp, but a Richard Sharp was the second most frequent customer of the Congarees store in the 1780s. William Sharp and Christopher Sharp were also customers during that time. We know much more about Christopher, as he was one of the ferry owners on the Broad River starting about the time Sarah made her drawing. Jesse was, likely, a brother of Christopher or maybe a son. It is interesting to note that these German Sharps had basically one purchase item at the Congarees store; they were the biggest consumers of alcohol.

Friday's Entertainments site:

Status: Destroyed by quarry hole. Archaeology is not possible at this location on the quarry property at: 33.970765°, -81.049465°

Figure 156: The grave of Sarah Friday Bryce and John Bryce in
Columbia's First Presbyterian Church Cemetery.

Sarah Friday's drawing is the only known image we have of Granby. It was not dated, but Sarah shows the home of Captain Hart, who died in 1814, and the home of Abraham Geiger, who we believe left Granby before 1812. Based on this, we think Sarah made her drawing in about 1810 when she was 15 years old. Sarah was the daughter of John Jacob Friday, who owned Fridieg's (Friday's) Entertainments. John was a private in the South Carolina 2nd Regiment during the American Revolution. His father, also John Jacob Friday, probably owned this land during the Revolution and maintained a store at the site. Sarah's 1810 drawing shows what looks like a house attached to Friday's Entertainment, which was a tavern and inn. The 1800 Census shows John Jacob and his wife Barbara Booker as having 12 children in their home. Genealogy work shows John Jacob as having only five children, so he may have been housing the children of other family members. By the 1810 Census, the number of children had dropped to three, but the number of slaves has grown from six in 1800 to 15. This is probably a sign of his tavern and inn operation. Of all the buildings in Sarah's drawing, Friday's Entertainment is the only one shown to have three chimneys. Even the large Cayce house (Fort Granby) only shows two chimneys. This may be another indication of the multi-function use (home, tavern, and inn) of Friday's Entertainment.

Sarah grew up in the Friday's Entertainments house and probably spent much of her time in the Fort Granby House, where her sister Ann lived with husband James Cayce. That house would later become known as the Cayce House.

Just a few years after making her drawing, Sarah blossomed into what people of the time described as the most beautiful woman in Granby and Columbia. She caught the eye of the young and wealthy John Bryce, and they married in 1814 and moved to Columbia. John Bryce later became the mayor of Columbia in 1836. Sarah's beauty continued in her offspring. Two of her granddaughters were described as the most beautiful women of their time. Sadly, Sarah died in 1870, heartbroken after losing her husband and both of her sons.

Mr. Cayce (Fort Granby) site:
Status: Destroyed by quarry hole. Archaeology is not possible at this location on the quarry property at: 33.970919°, -81.049991°

377

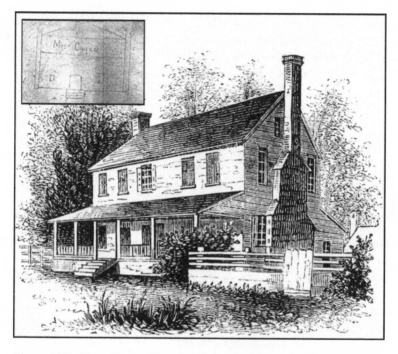

Figure 157: Cayce House (Fort Granby): The Pictorial Field-book of the
Revolution: Or, Illustrations, by Benson John Lossing, Volume 2.

There is little argument that the Chesnut and Kershaw Company about
1766 built a Granby store that would later be known as the Cayce House.
The role of this store as a British fort in the Revolution is well documented.

A newspaper story from 1935 states that, due to neglect, the house is
beyond repair and will soon collapse. The quarry owned the house, and
with attention focused on the Great Depression and WWII, there was little
interest in saving the building and few resources available. Today, the
Cayce House is long gone. The quarry has expanded its hole and
completely destroyed the site. Most of the Granby shown in Sarah Friday's
drawing is now in the quarry hole or under quarry slag piles. Only the
southernmost portion of the town can be walked on today, and that is in the
Riverland Park neighborhood where we are doing the Granby archaeology
work.

Today's Cayce Historical Museum is a replica of Cayce House, the old
trading post, and fort. You can go there and learn much more about what

may be the most historic three miles in South Carolina and maybe the United States.

Mr. Cayce's store site:
Status: Archaeology is possible on the quarry property at: 33.971691°, -81.049745°

 Nothing is known about Mr. Cayce's store, which was just off the State Road on the property of the Cayce House (Fort Granby).

Black Smith site #1:
Status: Archaeology is possible on the quarry property at: 33.971869°, -81.049857°

Black Smith site #2:
Status: Destroyed by quarry hole. Archaeology is not possible at this location on the quarry property at: 33.969771°, -81.047311°

In his 1884 book "Random Recollections of a Long Life, 1806 to 1876," Edwin J. Scott gives us the only real information we have on the Granby Blacksmith shops.

> When I first collected taxes there (Granby) in 1825, General Henry Arthur, Wolf Hane, son of Nicholas Hane, a rosy old gentleman, owner of the ferry, Mrs. Elizabeth Bell, Friday Arthur and James Cayce, who kept a public house, a mill and blacksmith and coach-making shops, were the most prominent reliques of Granby's former prosperity.

From this description, we can see that in 1825 James Cayce took over the mill operation from the Friday family. It's very likely the blacksmith, and coach-making shops are the two blacksmith shops Sarah Friday identified in her 1810 drawing. It's likely the rough wrought nails Scott mentioned were produced at these blacksmith shops and may be the nails we find in the Granby dig.

Captain John Hart home:
Status: Archaeology is possible on the quarry property at: 33.971969°, -81.050595°

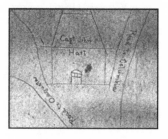

In 2016, James G. Boogle, Jr. of Columbia discovered a letter in an old family desk that contained information about a former Granby resident. The letter, dated 1982, was from Mrs. A. Waldo Jones of Atlanta, Georgia. Mrs. Jones provided us with the following biography on Granby's John Hart. Mrs. Jones also gave the Granby team just the information we needed to find Hart's damaged and worn gravestone.

Captain John Hart was born in Charleston, S.C., March 6, 1758; he died March 17, 1814 at Granby, S.C., and was buried there. He was the son of the Reverend Oliver Hart and his first wife, Sarah Breese. The Reverend Oliver Hart was the minister of the Baptist Church at Charleston from 1750 until the British captured Charleston during the Revolution, at which time it was recognized that because of his patriotic activities, he would fare badly if he should fall into the hands of the British. He removed to Pennsylvania and from there to Hopewell, New Jersey, where he died in 1795.

Concerning Oliver Hart's patriotic services: in 1775 the Provincial Congress of South Carolina sent William Drayton, the Reverend William Tennent and the Reverend Oliver Hart to the western counties "to explain to the people at large the nature of the unhappy dispute between Great Britain and the American colonies; to endeavor to settle all political disputes between the people; to quiet their minds and to enforce the necessity of a general union in order to preserve themselves and their children from slavery." This six weeks mission was one of great hardship and personal danger for Oliver Hart.

In 1773 the Reverend Oliver Hart sent his fifteen-year-old son, John Hart, to
Rhode Island College (now Brown University), a Baptist institution. The records state that John "was a wild youth and gave sore displeasure to his father." Oliver wrote to the college president (Dr. Manning) on November 5, 1773:

"I am sorry John has conducted so as to give you so much trouble, and to forfeit the place he had under the management of Mrs. Manning. Had I been apprised of his unworthy conduct sooner, perhaps I should have remanded him back to Carolina, for I am not in such affluent circumstances as to throw away money in the education of one who has no view to his own advantage. I thank you, however, for all the pains you have taken with him, and that you have made trial of the discipline of the rod. I should be sorry he should return a worthless blockhead."

Reverend Hart went on to say that he hoped Dr. Manning could prevail on John to write, as he had written only once in twelve months! The father had more cause for anguish when, in the midst of his college career, John, being an enthusiastic patriot too, took up arms. He fought as a private at Bunker Hill and probably was in the group of students who marched to the defense of Boston. Some delay prevented his presence at Lexington. However, John did return to college and was graduated in 1777 at age 19. He was commissioned a lieutenant in a South Carolina regiment and in January 1778, his father wrote:

"John is still in the army, and seems to long for an opportunity of improving his valor, I doubt not his courage, but wish he may have equal conduct, and not be too rash."

John rose to the rank of Captain in the Revolutionary forces in the 2nd South Carolina regiment, and served till the close of the war. He was taken prisoner when the British captured Charleston on May 12, 1780.

Captain John Hart married on June 17, 1784, in St. Thomas's Parish, South Carolina, Mary Esther Screven, daughter of Brigadier General James Screven who had been killed in the war by the British at Midway, Georgia.

One record says that after the war, since he had not finished his course in medicine at college, he entered trade and opened a store at Monck's Corner, SC, which failed, after which he tried teaching school. Then he was elected Sheriff of Charleston District. Sometime during 1801 to 1803, he moved to Lexington District, SC and erected mills. The records show that he had a son born on Dec. 9, 1803 at "Pine Grove Mills, Lexington County, Orangeburgh District, SC." Then he moved to Granby, SC, his home being three miles from town, where he was Clerk of Court, Ordinary, Judge of Inferior Court, etc.

Captain John Hart died in Granby, SC on March 17, 1814, and in December of 1815, his widow and children removed to Sunbury, Georgia, to be near her people, no doubt. She lived to be nearly 80 years old, dying in 1845. Late in her life, she received a government pension for her husband's Revolutionary services.

Captain John Hart was an Original Member of the Society of the Cincinnati, whose first president was General George Washington.

The grave of Captain John Hart in what was the Baptist churchyard at Granby and what is now the Martin-Marietta Company's gravel quarry, is in deplorable condition in April 1975. The top half of his tombstone, which gave his name and dates, has been broken off and disappeared. There is a footstone which has the letters J. H., but it would be impossible to identify the grave unless one knew the inscription by heart and happened to recognize the remaining words as belonging to his stone.

In 1967, Mr. Joseph E. Hart, Jr., of York, South Carolina wrote, as follows:

Captain John Hart was buried in the Baptist Churchyard, at old Granby, SC. I copied his tombstone:

> "Sacred to the Memory of
> CAPT. JOHN HART
> who departed this life
> March 17th 1814
> Aged 56 Years 11 days
> His country
> has lost a zealous Patriot
> The Church
> an active member
> His family
> an affectionate and indulgent
> Head."

In April 1975, Mr. & Mrs. Waldo Jones finally found the grave at the Martin Marietta Quarry. The stone was close to the fence & could be read from outside; a large Colonial Dames marker was to the right, outside the fence & around the stone was broken off in a jagged line from the upper right corner. These were the only words left on the stone:

> "country
> Patriot
> The Church
> an active member
> His family
> an affectionate
> and indulgent
> Head."

The stone had sunk & the last two lines were located by digging. There was a footstone marked "J. H.". Probably the broken-off part of the stone is still there and could be repaired.

By the time our Granby team made it to the Granby Cemetery, Hart's marker was down to even fewer words, but the miracle 1982 letter from Mrs. A. Waldo Jones provided us with that handful of unique words to identify Captain Hart's grave.

Figure 158: Captain John Hart's "almost lost" Grave in Granby. Photo by DC Locke.

APPENDIX E: Those that Dig History

A special thanks to all these people who helped on the history and archaeology of these miracle projects.

Jim Alexander	Tom Elmore	Elyse Luray	Chris Rodenkirchen
Linda Alexander	Helena Ferguson	Canute Magalhaes	Steven Rougeau
James Allen	Sam Finklea	Liam Magalhaes	Catherine Sawyer
John Allen	John Fisher*	Luke Magalhaes	Carrie Schelling
Kristy Allen	Adriana Fouste	Laura Marini	David Schelling
Peter Allen	Jeff Fouste	David Massie	Katie Schelling
Tony Allen	Sean Fouste	Lexus Maurer	Todd Schelling
John Allison	Terry Funderburk	Patrick McCawley	John Scialdo
Jimmy Armstrong	Ann Fur	Jim Merrill	Randy Scialdo
Alicia Ballagh	Meg Gaillard	Sarah G. Messer	Richard Scialdo
Cooper Banks*	Elaine C. Gherardi	Azuna Mitchell	Tim Scialdo
Emma Kate Banks	IC Go	Joe Mitchell	Miles Sexton
Ken Banks*	Wayne Grooms	Teresa Mitchell*	Steve Shaffer
Martin Banks*	Shannon Herin	Cristian Monaco	Erika Shofner
Sean Blackmer	Walter Hill	David Moore	Michael Shriver
Debbie Bloom*	John Hodge	Tonya Morris	Woodrow St. Pierre
Sarah Bobertz	Carolyn Hudson	Fred Morrison**	Lynn Jordan Stidom
Jack Boggs	Dean Hunt**	Baron Moye	Richard Sylvester
Jacob Borchardt*	Alexis Jodie	Rob Murray	Gloria Talens
Katherine Boyle	Faith Jodie	Al Nooft	Lance Tijing
Tim Bradshaw	Stacey Jodie	Kay Oliver	Lara Tijing
Jerry Bright*	Kathy Keenan	Dan Ostergaard	Neil Tijing
David Brinkman**	Charles Krawczyk	Jack Ostergaard	Daniel Tortora
Jeremy Brinkman*	Elizabeth Krawczyk	Katie Ostergaard	Sally Turner
Odess Brinkman**	Meg Krawczyk	William Ostergaard	Ron Vaughn
Joe Burch	Ken Kyte	Steve Pigott	David Villa
Dylan Cambre	Steve Lambert	Joseph Ready	Alex Wallace
Eric Cambre	Jon Leader*	Kandi Cochran Ready	Julie Wallace
Debra Carlsen*	Grayson Lewis	David Reuwer	Kate Wardlaw

385

Don Chenoweth	Taylor Lewis	Nena Rice	Jim Welch
Zuzanna Chruszcz	DC Locke**	Tim Ritter	Kevin Whaley
Jan Ciegler*	Jocelyn Locke	Alma Robichaud	Adam Whitaker
Noah Cochran	Tehya-lani Locke	Andrea Robichaud*	Tina Whitaker
Art Coogler*	Ian Logan	Clover Robichaud*	Cody Wyatt
Pat Coogler	Joe Long	David Robichaud	Stacey Young
Krys Wood-Elmore	Shane Long	Michael Robichaud	Tim Ritter
Martin Phipps	James Strong-Oak		

** Top 5 digger, *Top 20 digger

INDEX

Family Research Society of
  Northeastern North Carolina, 234
Faraday, Michael, 5
Fatima, 322
Ferguson, Helena, 249, 385
Ferguson, Patrick, 188
Fire Island, 291, 292, 304
Fisher, John, 249, 250, 251, 252, 255,
  257, 385
flood of 2015, 136
Flood of 2015, 136
Follett, Wesley, 39, 41, 45, 56, 57,
  70, 71, 75
Fort Congaree II, vii, 174, 175, 180,
  196, 242, 245, 246, 247, 248, 249,
  250, 252, 255, 257, 258, 261, 262,
  263, 264, 265, 266, 267, 268, 269,
  271, 272, 312, 342, 343, 353
Fort Granby, 175, 177, 179, 180, 182,
  183, 184, 185, 187, 206, 214, 343,
  377, 378, 379
Fort Necessity, 269, 270, 271, 342
Fort Prince George, 263
Fort Sumter, 293, 345
Fowler, Nancy, 321, 325, 326, 327,
  328, 329
Franklin, Benjamin, 104, 269, 270
Frederick, Dave, 45
Freider, Jerome, 45, 52, 56, 57
French and Indian War, 103, 175,
  176, 246, 267, 268, 271
Friday, Ann, 177
Friday, David, 176, 177, 179
Friday, Martin, 175, 176, 177, 206,
  266, 268, 342, 373
Friday, Sarah, 206, 207, 208, 209,
  210, 353, 355, 358, 360, 368, 371,
  372, 374, 375, 376, 377, 378, 380
Fridig, Martin, 172
Fryml, Father, viii
FTDNA, 231, 233
Fuller, Margaret, 290, 291, 292, 293,
  296, 344

Gahan, Father, viii
Gaillard, Meg, 249, 254, 385
Galilei, Galileo, 5
Gamecock, 20, 188, 333, 334, 335,
  336, 355
Gates, Bill, 307
Geiger, Abraham, 185, 359, 377
Geiger, Ann, 178, 185
Geiger, Emily, 185, 187
Geiger, Jacob, 191, 192, 359, 360
Genbank, 232
Genealogy, 172, 175, 261, 377
General Assembly, 101, 102, 106,
  108, 113, 115, 116, 118, 119, 127,
  154, 179, 193, 273, 354
Gervais, John Lewis, 195
Gherardi, Elaine Campton, 235
Gherardi, Greg, 235
Glen, James, 262
Gould, Mary, 266
Gourdin, H., 290, 298, 299
Gradiometer, 142
Granby, vii, 105, 106, 107, 108, 111,
  113, 126, 155, 156, 159, 162, 163,
  165, 166, 167, 168, 169, 170, 171,
  172, 173, 174, 175, 176, 177, 178,
  179, 180, 181, 182, 183, 184, 185,
  187, 188, 191, 192, 193, 195, 196,
  197, 198, 199, 200, 201, 202, 203,
  204, 205, 206,207, 208, 209, 210,
  211, 212, 213, 214, 215, 216, 217,
  218, 221, 222, 231, 242, 245, 246,
  247, 248, 254, 273, 274, 275, 281,
  283, 311, 312, 318, 341, 342, 343,
  344, 345, 353, 354, 355, 356, 357,
  358, 359, 360, 361, 362, 363, 364,
  366, 367, 368, 369, 370, 371, 372,
  373, 374, 375, 377, 378, 379, 380,
  382, 383, 384
Granby courthouse, 193, 213, 359,
  364, 367
Granbyans, 205, 211, 355
Grant, James, 271

Niernsee, John, 300
Ninety Six, 185, 271
Normandy, 84, 85, 86, 88, 89, 91, 92, 168, 346
North Carolina Museum of Art, 296, 297, 298
Old Granby, 165, 207, 214
Old State House, 274, 276, 277, 278, 279, 280, 281, 282, 283, 286, 287, 293, 299, 300, 301, 302, 303, 304, 345
Old State Road, 206
Operation Tiger, 90, 91, 92, 346
Oregon Shipbuilding Company, 34
Ormsby, Peter, 265
Our Loving Mother's Children, 326
Palmetto monument, 302
Partin, Elise, vii, 168
Partin, Lindsay M., 304
Parton, Elise, vii
Patton, John, 360
PBS, 139, 141, 143, 144, 254, 298
Peale, Norman Vincent, 27
Perrett, Marvin, 88, 89, 90
Philippines, 22, 23, 24, 154
Plantagenet, 238, 240, 242, 243, 341
Pope John Paul II, 1, 20, 320
Pope, Natalie Adams, vii, 312
Porr, Greg, iv
Potter, Alice, 338
Pou, Lewis, 358, 360, 362
Powers, Hiram, 290, 296, 298, 299, 344
Preston, John, 290
Raines, June, 335
Rawdon, Francis, 185, 186, 187
Rea, Elizabeth, 178, 181
Redmond, Leo, vii, 105, 156, 188
Revenue Cutter Morris, 292
Ricardian, 218, 225, 243, 244
Rice, Nena, 249, 251, 386
Richard III, v, 217, 218, 219, 220, 221, 222, 223, 224, 225, 226, 227,

230, 231, 232, 234, 235, 238, 239, 240, 241, 242, 243, 244, 248, 249, 255, 256, 274, 275, 318, 341, 342, 346, 347
Richard III Society, 218, 219, 220, 224
Richards, Norman, 38, 41, 45, 55, 61, 70, 77, 79, 340
Richland County Conservation Commission, 154
Rivas, Catalina, 328
River Alliance, vii, 168
Riverland Park, 181, 209, 247, 356, 357, 358, 361, 378
Rives Tavern, 108, 199, 273, 274, 275, 281, 286, 343
Rives, Timothy, 106, 274, 275, 343
Rives, William McGuffy, 274
Roberson, Allen, vii, 39, 125, 137
Robichaud, Andrea, 162, 386
Robichaud, Clover, 162, 386
Robichaud, David, vii, 386
Robichaud. Alma, 162, 386
Rosenthal, Joe, 69, 73
Roy Vandegrift, 274
Rugborck, Elizabeth, 105, 111
Rutledge, Anna, 179, 303
Sagan, Carl, 4, 329
Sawyer, Polly, 233, 234, 236
SCANA, 168
SCDAH, 280
Schaffer, Clifford, 83
Schumpert, William, 155, 156, 175
Schurer, Kevin, 226, 235
Scoliosis, 224, 227
Sea, Andrew, 152
Seibels, 189, 204, 358, 362, 365, 366, 367, 370
Seven Years' War, 268
Shakespeare, William, 218, 224, 244
Sharp, Jesse, 375
Shelby, Isaac, 188

Sherman, William, 98, 101, 120, 123, 127, 128, 132, 133, 138, 142, 144, 145, 146, 147, 148, 151, 152, 153, 165, 214, 220, 242, 246, 276, 286, 287, 288, 289, 296, 299, 302, 345
Shofner, Erika, 249, 385
Simms, William Gilmore, 180, 299
Simson, Alfred, 184, 198
Slapton Sands, 90, 346
Slave, 290, 344, 345
Smithsonian, 296, 297, 298
South Carolina College, 273, 274, 355, 360, 362
South Carolina Confederate Relic Room and Military Museum, 39, 125
South Carolina Department of Archives and History, 101, 128, 129, 130, 131, 132, 134, 138, 140, 144, 154, 155, 280
South Carolina Institute of Archaeology and Anthropology, 101, 175
South Carolina Secession, 289
South Carolina State Museum, 66, 134, 136
South Caroliniana Library, 180, 206, 207, 208, 209, 294
Southern Tour, 198
Sprague, William, 134, 135
St Leger, Anne, 231, 341
St. George's Chapel, 231, 232
St. Peter's, 95, 160
Stanley, Elizabeth, 112
Stark, Alexander, 113, 114, 115, 116, 117, 118, 119, 120, 127, 128, 143, 144, 205, 273, 274, 344, 345
Stark, Sarah, 119, 120
State House, 106, 108, 112, 140, 198, 199, 273, 274, 275, 276, 277, 278, 279, 280, 281, 282, 283, 285, 286, 287, 293, 294, 299, 300, 301, 302, 303, 304, 343, 344, 345, 347

Stevens, Dean, 138, 141
Stevens, Terri, 11, 65, 335
Stewart, Colonel, 185
Sumter, Thomas, 179, 180, 184, 185, 186, 187, 188, 293, 345, 363
Tanner, Ray, 334, 335
Tarleton, Barnastre, 188
Taylor, Thomas, 106, 165, 184, 198, 274, 357
Tesoriero, Ron, 325, 326, 328, 329
The Church of Jesus Christ of Latter-day Saints, 261
The Elizabeth, 291, 292
The Greek Slave, 290, 344
The State, vii, 91, 98, 108, 123, 125, 136, 156, 180, 207, 295, 311, 312, 314, 318, 334, 336, 359
Thurman, Strom, 25
Tingley, George, 128, 135
Tortora, Dan, 247, 248, 255, 263, 267, 385
Tower computer, 307
Tudor, Henry, 218, 224, 243
Union Army, 98, 101, 123, 140, 145, 153, 154, 165, 299, 302, 303, 345
University of Leicester, 220, 223, 226
University of South Carolina, 3, 18, 19, 20, 21, 31, 101, 106, 139, 140, 188, 247, 307, 311, 319, 333, 334, 336
USC, 20, 336, 355
USS Bayfield, vii, 84, 85
USS Gage, 84
USS Lowndes, vii, 31, 34, 38, 39, 45, 46, 48, 55, 66, 67, 71, 77, 84, 87, 98, 99, 242, 349
Vandegrift, Roy, 274
Vanport, 37, 38
Virtual Reality, 14, 263, 264, 286, 312
Waites, Robin, vii
Wallace, Alex, 385